T0368781

The Scandal of the Century

The Scandal of the Century

LISA HILTON

MICHAEL  JOSEPH

PENGUIN MICHAEL JOSEPH

UK | USA | Canada | Ireland | Australia
India | New Zealand | South Africa

Penguin Michael Joseph is part of the Penguin Random House group of companies
whose addresses can be found at global.penguinrandomhouse.com

First published by Michael Joseph, 2024

002

Copyright © Lisa Hilton, 2024

The moral right of the author has been asserted

Set in 13.5/16pt Garamond MT Std
Typeset by Jouve (UK), Milton Keynes
Printed and bound in Great Britain by Clays Ltd, Elcograf S.p.A.

The authorized representative in the EEA is Penguin Random House Ireland,
Morrison Chambers, 32 Nassau Street, Dublin D02 YH68

A CIP catalogue record for this book is available from the British Library

HARDBACK ISBN: 978-1-405-95332-0
TRADE PAPERBACK: 978-1-405-95333-7

www.greenpenguin.co.uk

Penguin Random House is committed to a
sustainable future for our business, our readers
and our planet. This book is made from Forest
Stewardship Council® certified paper.

For Camilla and for Erik

Alas! A woman that attempts the pen,
Such an intruder on the rights of men.
Such a presumptuous creature is esteemed
The fault can by no virtue be redeemed.
They tell us we mistake our sex and way,
Good breeding, fashion, dancing, dressing, play
Are the accomplishments we should desire.
To write, to read, to think or to inquire
Would cloud our beauty and exhaust our time,
Whilst the dull manage of a servile house
Is held by some our utmost art, and use.

The Introduction, Anne Finch

Introduction

*The psychographer is apt to be hampered in his
study of women by lack of material . . . Those who
have public careers, historical figures, artists,
writers, are approachable enough . . . Yet they
are not fairly representative. It is the quiet lives that
count, the humble lives, the simple lives,
lives perhaps of great achievement and
great influence.*
Gamaliel Bradford, *Mrs Pepys* (1914)

Aphra Behn is a person in whom one is supposed to
be interested. Amongst the most successful writers of
her day, celebrated for her plays and poems, she was
also a spy, an outspoken political polemicist, a some-
time jailbird and the friend of several of the most
important figures of her age. A defiant champion of
women, her enemies naturally accused her of being a
whore.

One of the best-known observations on England's
first professional female playwright comes from Virginia Woolf:

> All women together ought to let flowers fall on the
> tomb of Aphra Behn . . . for it was she who earned
> them the right to speak their minds.*

Women writers were by no means unknown to seventeenth-century England, but neither medieval mystics nor aristocratic poets made their living from it. It is Aphra's profession that Woolf is praising, the fact that her works were endorsed by a market which had hitherto belonged to men. The works themselves she tactfully glosses over.

It's awkward that, frankly, seventeenth-century drama is a snore. Woolf suggests that Aphra Behn deserves to be venerated as a pioneer, but when was the last time you excitedly booked tickets for *The Rover* or *The Man of Mode*? Reading the drama written for London's two theatrical companies, the Duke's and the King's, in the Restoration period (1660–88), it's easy to conclude that they basically had just the one play. Characters' names transpose from plot to plot; the stage business of cross-dressing and audibly whispered secret conversations is laboured and unconvincing; the endless bawdy jokes really aren't funny any more. In her lifetime, the carping cabal of critics who resented Behn's gender even more than her success were eager to point out that her physical charms weren't ageing well; cheap misogyny when it comes to

---

* Woolf, Virginia, *A Room of One's Own* (1929)

the playwright but spot on when it comes to the plays themselves.

Aphra Behn's life, moreover, is in many ways an inconvenient, even impossible topic. Biographically she is more subjunct than subject. Generations of devoted and brilliant scholars have gradually weaselled out a few established facts, but her opinions, as expressed in her stories, poems and plays, don't necessarily make for smooth reading. The mindset of the Restoration feels in many ways impossibly remote. Dominated on the one hand by religious dissent with which few modern readers can identify with in anything but the abstract, and on the other by the prerogatives and limitations of a royal power which has long since dwindled into symbolic celebrity, the concerns and thought patterns of the late seventeenth century often appear repellently alien.

And yet, walking through London now, however scarred and altered, the Restoration is everywhere present. Not only in its architecture, which delineated much of the city in its modern form after the Great Fire of 1666, or in the scientific, economic and cultural legacies it left, nor even in the horror of the Transatlantic slave trade, which funded many of those legacies and with which we are still attempting to come to terms today, but in the pushy, greedy, jostling spirit of the city itself, that scintillating and squalid 'Town' which shaped Aphra's life and her writing.

Aphra arrived in the capital at a revolutionary

moment. England had recently abandoned the most radical political experiment ever attempted in Europe, the deposition and execution of its anointed King, Charles I, and the replacement of the monarchy with a short-lived republic. The ensuing upheaval impacted public and private life across the island nation of Britain but equally on the other side of the world, in the new colonies of North America and the West Indies, where Aphra most likely lived before emigrating to London.

The Civil Wars claimed over 100,000 lives and reduced many to destitution and starvation, but they also produced 'an era of social mobility which England had never seen before'.* The quantity of printed material – books, newspapers and pamphlets – positively exploded, providing an increasingly literate and curious population with ideas and information on an unprecedented scale. The dearth of manpower had shown women, willingly or not, that they could manage businesses and estates and even lead troops; in small but increasingly influential numbers women's voices began to be heard and acknowledged. The return of King Charles II from exile in 1660 was met (largely) with joy and optimism, a sense of urgency and possibility within which traditional ways of thinking and living could be investigated, examined and, thrillingly, rejected.

* Larman, Alexander, *Blazing Star: The Life and Times of John Wilmot, Earl of Rochester* (2014)

Restoration London was also a *young* world. To a modern eye, seventeenth-century demographics would surprise not by the scarcity of elderly people but by the huge gap in the healthy middle aged. King Charles was thirty years old at his coronation, already the father of four illegitimate children, a seasoned diplomat and soldier in an age when teenage boys commanded armies and teenage girls became the wives and mistresses of great men. The early years of the Restoration were thus characterized by youthful energy and exuberance, the desire to refashion the world on a fresh generation's terms. For Aphra, a young woman from the colonies, London offered the chance to invent herself as she chose, and she succeeded.

Aphra Behn's London lives still in the sharp young people with ribboned shoes (though these days they might be Gucci), alert and on the make. Fresh to the excitements and challenges of the capital, they're hungry and ambitious, eager to get on, to make something of themselves, but also to experience the culture and nightlife of the big city. They strive to get ahead, make improvements to their properties to increase their value, they love shopping and theatre and gossip, socialize with friends and colleagues, keep up with current affairs and the latest trends in the capital. They spend too much on fashion and beauty treatments, put in long hours at the office, experiment with the newest health fads. Alert to all the temptations and distractions of the metropolis, they want to *be* someone.

Then as now, love and glamour and fame were the lures of Aphra's London. Another young woman, Harriet Berkeley, wanted to be there, at the centre of it all, making her own life away from the strictures of her parents' home in the Surrey countryside. In 1682, at the age of eighteen, she escaped to the city with her boyfriend in nothing but the clothes she stood up in. But Harriet wasn't just another teenage runaway. She was Lady Henrietta Berkeley, daughter to one of England's most powerful men, and her lover was her own brother-in-law, Ford, Lord Grey. Her flight, capture and the lawsuit that followed were the scandal of the year.

In Aphra Behn's hands, Harriet's story became what is arguably the first novel in English literature, *Love Letters Between a Nobleman and His Sister*. The original 'true life' fiction, it tells the story of a passionate clandestine affair and concludes in an outrageous elopement. Complete with stolen letters and scheming servants, sex, sensation and celebrity: suddenly Aphra's work feels accessible, contemporary, alive. On the stage, Aphra had already created daring, independent-minded heroines who shocked audiences not only with their saucy wit but their insistence on sexual freedom. They condemn the hypocritical financial transactions which lay behind seventeenth-century marriage and dare to laugh at men's erotic inadequacy. Behn's heroines are sharp, clever and determined to resist the stunted existence their fathers and brothers attempt to impose upon them.

In many ways, Henrietta Berkeley was a living example of such a woman, rebellious, tough and even ruthless in her insistence on choosing her own destiny. The conflicts Aphra presents between love and duty or the limits to women's right to resolve their own choices remain as passionately engaging today as when she set down Harriet's notorious drama on the page.

Behn's novel was an immediate bestseller and continued so well into the eighteenth century, long after her plays fell out of performance. Henrietta Berkeley's fame was short and disgraceful. As daughter to one earl and eloping mistress of another, she was briefly the most talked-about woman in London. Today, even less is known of her life than of Aphra's. Did her courage and defiance prove more fulfilling than the conventions Aphra Behn also explored and defied?

For Aphra, the intervening centuries have seen her loathed, proscribed, ignored, rehabilitated and ignored all over again. Yet *Love Letters* still confronts today's readers with issues that modern feminism struggles to resolve. It parodies the novelistic convention of love as definitive to a woman's identity in a manner which still disarms, whilst undercutting moralistic views of 'cheating' and monogamy. In death as in life, Aphra is a slippery character, not quite the feminist heroine many critics would have her be.

Behn was an outsider, the child of nonentities who had fashioned herself in the tumultuous society of the Restoration as a professional, mixing with the greatest in the land as an intellectual equal. Harriet Berkeley was an insider, a child of the tiny aristocratic elite, whose father had entertained the King at the family seat the year his fifth daughter was born. Harriet's choices and the realities of women's lives which they exposed were precisely the subject of Behn's plays. From *The Forc'd Marriage* to her smash hit *The Rover*, Behn gave voice to female characters who were resourceful, witty, independent and determined to use the masculine prejudices of their society against the constrictions it imposed. In play after play, Behn's work insisted on the legitimacy of women's voices, and of her own as an author.

Both Aphra and Harriet were extraordinary because of what they were not. They both refused to 'know their place', to occupy the position which society had assigned them, and in doing so they had to content themselves with the realities of their compromised positions after the curtain fell on their public existence. Assessing the extent of their respectively rebellious trajectories requires considerable detective work. Neither woman left a great deal of biographical material outside the novel which connects them, but we do know that neither enjoyed the kind of happy ending

Aphra gave to the zesty, dashing leading ladies of her comedies. Harriet Berkeley was quite literally written out of history. Deciphering the mysteries of Aphra's existence, as well as looking at their lives together, reinstates something of the courage and daring of one of the greatest Restoration characters who never set foot upon the stage.

PART ONE

Beware of Master Maybe and Mistress Must-Have.

Antonia Fraser

I

We know what Harriet looked like. In September 1682, her desperate parents the Earl and Countess of Berkeley posted a missing persons appeal in the *London Gazette*:

> Whereas the Lady Henrietta Berkeley has been absent from her Father's house since the 20th August last past, and is not yet known where she is, nor whether she is alive or dead; These are to give notice That whoever shall find her, so that she may be brought back to her Father, the Earl of Berkeley, they shall have 200 Pounds Reward. She is a young Lady of a Fair Complexion, fair Haired, full Breasted and indifferent tall.

Later editions removed the reference to Lady Henrietta's bosom.

Harriet, as she was known to her family, was about eighteen years old when she absconded from Durdans, the Berkeleys' country house in Surrey, between midnight and one in the morning in nothing but a striped petticoat. She had travelled by coach to London to join the man with whom she had been having an affair for the past year. Her lover was the twenty-seven-year-old

Ford, Lord Grey of Werk. As the hero of a romantic elopement, Grey ticked all the boxes – handsome, rich, dashing, aristocratic, a brave cavalry officer, a writer of passionate love letters. He was also the husband of Harriet's older sister Mary.

The Berkeley family's opinion of themselves is captured in their motto 'Dieu Avec Nous' – *God is with us*. King Charles had raised Harriet's father from the rank of Baron to Earl (the third in the English peerage after Duke and Marquis) in 1679, but the Berkeleys had been grand for centuries before anyone had heard the name Stuart. As her ancestors had been for 500 years, Harriet was born at the principal family seat, Berkeley Castle in Gloucestershire, a Norman fortress which had been occupied almost as long as the Tower of London. Secure in their lands, their wealth and their ancient status, the Berkeleys had seen out three successive royal dynasties and had always been loyal servants to the crown. During the Civil Wars, Berkeley Castle had been a Royalist stronghold, only surrendering to the forces of Parliament in 1645 after its walls were breached by cannon fired at point-blank range from the roof of the parish church. Nonetheless, the family had retained their property and their titles, and when Charles II was restored in 1660 Harriet's father was a member of the commission of grandees appointed to travel to The Hague to welcome him home. Public exposure of any kind was anathema to such a family, yet after the revelation of their daughter's disgrace in the press failed to produce a result, the Berkeleys went even further in their attempts to recover her.

In November 1682, the Earl of Berkeley brought suit against Lord Grey at the court of the King's Bench for:

> inveigling the lady Henrietta Berkeley away, and causing her to live an ungodly and profligate life, carrying her about from place to place and obscuring her in secret places, to the displeasure of Almighty God, the utter ruin of the young lady, the evil example to others, offending against the King's peace, his Crown and Dignity.

For the wits of Charles II's court, the elopement of an aristocratic teenager with her own brother-in-law was an irresistible draw. For the pamphlet hawkers, the ale-sellers, the orange girls and the pickpockets who haunted every public gathering, the trial promised an excellent day's business. For Aphra Behn, one of London's leading playwrights, it was an opportunity.

After a disappearance lasting nearly three months, Harriet had been discovered and her seducer brought to trial in a plot as complex and scandalous as anything the famous Mrs Behn had contrived in the plays she had written for the Duke's Company at the Dorset Garden Theatre. A scheming lord who banished his wife to the country in order to pursue her sister, erotic correspondence discovered by the family, the hero locked up for two days in a closet while the heroine broke out of her father's home in nothing but her underclothes – the crowd in Westminster Hall slavered over every salacious detail.

One by one, the prosecution called their witnesses. They included Harriet's mother, the Countess of Berkeley, and her sisters Lady Arabella and Lady Lucy, all three sheltering their faces under heavy hoods from the impertinent stares of the crowd. These grand ladies shared the witness box with other women – a midwife, a lodging-house keeper – who would usually have been far beneath their social attention. Harriet had betrayed not only her own honour and that of her sister, but her class. No shameful detail went unexamined, from the pages of the lovers' secret letters to the grubby under-garment in which Harriet had made her escape. The court heard how Grey had 'abducted' Harriet with the help of a team of servants, how she had been moved in secret from lodging to lodging in some of the seamiest districts of London, how the couple had managed to conceal their whereabouts even as the whole city searched for them. What Lady Harriet couldn't conceal, as she sat listening to some of the most eminent legal minds in the country argue over who had the right to her body, was that she was heavily pregnant.

Eventually, Sir Francis Pemberton, the Lord Chief Justice, began his summing up. And Harriet, a woman and a minor, forbidden to speak in court, rose to her indifferent height and denounced her father's charges. She refused to go with her father, she said, for she had left his house of her own free will and she had no intention of going back. This was breath-taking. For all her animation, Henrietta was a property whose ownership was being contested, a possession to be restored to its rightful owner. For a long moment, the girl's audacity brought the hall to silence. Her father and her lover drew their swords. Mrs Behn picked up her pen.

Of course, we don't know that it happened like that. We don't know if the most notorious adulteress of a notoriously adulterous age locked eyes across the highest court in the land with London's most celebrated writer. What we do know is that in 1682 Aphra Behn was famous, revered and broke. Now in her forties, Aphra's work had dominated the London stage for a decade, but that year she had been charged with libel. Her plays could not be produced and she was in debt. Behn had no husband to support her, no family to call on, and whilst Charles II knew and admired her, her success as a writer, not to mention her claim to loyal service as a spy for his government, meant nothing to the cash-strapped King.

We also don't know exactly what Aphra Behn looked like. We don't really know very much about her at all. In life, she was none of the things she claimed to be – certainly not a lady, possibly not a wife, perhaps not really a spy. Nor was she, as has been suggested centuries after her death, a feminist in the contemporary sense, a political progressive or an anti-slavery campaigner. What she definitely was, was England's first professional woman writer.

Aphra has famously been described as 'not so much a woman to be unmasked as an unending combination of masks and intrigue'.* The historical sources for her life include her own writing, particularly her late novel *Oroonoko*, two largely fictionalized contemporary biographies, two marginal notes by people who claimed (not necessarily accurately), to have known her, various notes to her publisher, Jacob Tonson, a set of official instructions issued by the secret service and a few samples of what is believed to be her handwriting.

Nonetheless, this scant material has furnished several biographies and a huge corpus of academic papers. An accepted version of Aphra's early biography has now existed for nearly fifty years, painstakingly teased by scholars from the further meagre evidence provided by parish registers, a posthumous record by a man who claimed to have known her and a marginal note to a poem by a snobbish Countess. Further, and much-debated 'facts' have been construed from the several versions of her life-story rushed into print after her death and extrapolations from Aphra's own works. Much of this theorizing is plausible, some fanciful and some downright absurd, but from it Aphra has acquired a birth date and a backstory, a family and a first home. However, regardless of how frequently the narrative of

* Todd, Janet, *Aphra Behn: A Secret Life* (2017)

her early life is repeated, regardless of the reliability it has apparently attained, it remains, at base, pure speculation.

Any attempt to recover Aphra's life beyond its barest bones must inevitably involve the hopeful conjuring of possibilities, yet where she came from matters, not just in adding to the context of her plays and stories but in appreciating the tremendous extent of her achievements. This book offers an alternative theory of her early years, one which may serve to widen the scope of enquiry into her intriguingly mysterious origins.

Harriet's life outside Aphra's writing is similarly obscure. After the detailed proceedings of the 1682 trial she seems to disappear. No mention of her is made in the lengthy and sensational confessional memoir written by her lover Lord Grey in 1685. Yet she does sporadically emerge – in Chancery documents and parish records, in newsletters written by foreign agents and in the 'lampoons' or 'libels' which reported the shameless doings of the court to a public which consumed them with equal measures of shock and relish.

Social media might seem like an entirely twenty-first-century phenomenon, but Aphra Behn's age had its own, highly effective version. It could have been called 'Rustle'. Rustle for the sound of a paper being hastily slipped into a sleeve, rustle for sheaves of the latest gossip passed around in coffee houses, rustle for the manuscripts of scurrilous poems passed hand to hand, hidden, added to, stolen and sold. The rustling of letters accompanied the commotion and clamour of London in a minor but potent key, whispering into private closets, fluttering through the antechambers of the court and the most squalid taverns, susurrating through maidservants' pockets and duchesses' drawing rooms.

In the trial of Lord Grey for abduction and seduction, letters are as much protagonists in the case as the witnesses themselves. They are copied and hidden, passed between the principals, produced as evidence, sent in pursuit. From the first evidence, where Lady Berkeley testified to her discovery of her daughter Harriet writing in her closet, a new type of English fiction was born, a multi-layered narrative told in 'real time' by its imitated protagonists. In the case of *Love Letters*, readers were encouraged to believe that the letters described so abundantly in the Berkeley trial were the very same they were now reading in adapted form.

Letters were flammable objects, likely to explode in scandal if they went astray. Before Aphra had the idea of combining them to recount a novel, fictionalized letters, like the 'open letters' published in the news today, were a means of scoring political points or delving into the latest celebrity rumour. Poetry was likewise a weapon for the wits at court, where quips were brandished as speedily as swords; it could make and break reputations, create scandals, topple ministers. The satires or lampoons which poured from multiple, anonymous pens were everybody's guilty pleasure – no one wanted to admit to reading them but everybody did. As Lady Frances Brudenell wrote to her doubtless disappointed friend Lady Hallam in 1680:

> The lampoons that are made of most of the Town are so nasty that no woman will read them, or I would have got them for you.

The satires were spiteful and explicit in a way that would make even the most vicious of present-day Twitter trolls gasp. Here are two of Charles II's mistresses, Nell Gwynn and the Duchess of Portsmouth, bitching about one another and their mutual rival Hortense Mazarin:

NELL: When to the King I bid good morrow
    With tongue in mouth and hand on tarse
    Portsmouth may rend her cunt for sorrow
    And Mazarin may kiss mine arse.

PORTSMOUTH: When Englan'd monarch's on my belly.
    With prick in cunt though double cramm'd
    Fart of mine arse for small whore Nelly
    And great whore Mazarin be damned.

One of the most irritating words used to describe Aphra's writing is 'naughty'. Restoration libels weren't timorous or arch, they were scabrously pornographic, and as a known writer, hence both an author and a target of lampoons, Aphra knew the risks of the market. Showing oneself to be in the know, alert to every rustle of scandal, was currency, a means of publicizing more formal productions. The most brilliant (and spectacularly filthy), poet of the Restoration, the Earl of Rochester, dressed one of his footmen as a royal guard and had him patrol the corridors of Whitehall every evening for a whole winter, listening at the doors of women he suspected of conducting affairs. Captain Robert Julian was a professional supplier of tips to lampoon writers, nicknamed the 'Secretary to the Muses'. Trotting from bordello to boudoir with his satchel full of sauce, Julian sold the latest racy news and picked up the stories from the street for the writers. Thousands of satires were written during the Restoration, their numbers reaching a peak about 1680. Copied into private correspondence, newsletters and gazettes, they were sent all over the country to be devoured at breakfast tables or in private closets, serving up outrage and titillation to the same recipe as modern tabloids.

When Lady Henrietta Berkeley made her first appearance at his court aged sixteen in 1680, Charles II had been on the throne for twenty years. From the moment he had swaggered into Whitehall Palace with his ravishing twenty-year-old mistress Barbara Palmer on his arm, Charles's circle had been seen as a roiling cauldron of vice, scandal and corruption. Adultery and even incest, the defining transgressions of Harriet's life, were common currency to the aristocratic satirists who drank, swore and fought their way through the corridors of power. The Duke of Buckingham's poem on Barbara set the tone of the time:

> She was so exquisite a whore
> That in the belly of her mother
> Her cunt she placed so right before
> Her father fucked them both together.
> Had she been male as female without doubt
> She'd acted incest at her coming out,
> And least her Daddy should not fuck it home
> She frigged his pintle in her mother's womb.

On the Duchess of Cleveland

Arrogant, crude and entirely unrestrained, the words conjure a vicious world whose surface of exquisite clothes and fine manners concealed a debauched life-style enacted in absolute contempt of majority values and morals. Conditioned by arrant masculine and class privilege, the strutting wits of the Restoration saw women as little more than disposable title deeds, whilst their social inferiors of either sex counted only as collateral damage in their revels. The diarist Samuel Pepys recorded an incident at the aptly named Cock Inn in the summer of 1663 when the Duke of Monmouth (the King's illegitimate son), Lord Buckhurst and Sir Charles Sedley drunkenly disported themselves for the entertainment of a furious, jeering crowd:

23

acting all the postures of lust and buggery . . . saying that he (Sedley) hath to sell such a powder as should make all the cunts in town run after him . . . and that being done he took a glass of wine and washed his prick in it and then drank it off and then took another and drank the King's health.

The outrage culminated with the performers urinating on the indignant bystanders. No one got into any particular trouble. Charles's courtiers could be boors and buffoons, but these were also the men who were steering England towards modernity. The Restoration is often thought of as one long party, presided over by that weary old cliché, the 'Merry Monarch', but by its end England had changed immeasurably. The constitution, the economy, the arts, science, the military, the physical geography of its capital were all touched by its influence. This was the world of which Aphra wrote and in which Harriet lived, a cruel and ugly world still in many ways, but also one of the most vivid and dynamic periods of English history.

The rustling lampoons which issued from the circles of the court sometimes combined a measure of genius with their bawdy doggerel. Poetry was not yet written in private for print publication but circulated informally and frequently anonymously in manuscript, the verses altered and sharpened as they whispered from author to author. Collections or 'Miscellanies' from the period have proved a nightmare for later editors, as poems are cheerfully misattributed, muddled, retitled and stolen, but they retain the vivacity of lived rhythms, lines scribbled extempore on tavern tables or during dreary Sunday sermons, the conversation of an inner circle throwing a paper bridge across time.

A popular framework for comparing and savaging public figures was the 'Session' poem, conceived as a competition for places, beauty or wit. For writers, the session device was often a contest before Apollo, the classical god of music and poetry, to determine which of them best deserved the laureate's crown of bay leaves. In the mid-1670s, Aphra was mentioned in flattering if tactless terms in *A Session of the Poets*, attributed to Rochester and his boon companion the Duke of Buckingham. Whilst downright rude about her physical appearance, it is professionally complimentary about her work:

> The poetess Aphra next showed her sweet face
> And swore by her poetry and her black ace
> The laurel by double right was her own
> For the plays she had writ and the conquests
>   she'd won.
> Apollo acknowledg'd was hard to deny her,
> But to deal frankly and ingenuously by her,
> He told her were conquests and charms her
>   pretence,
> She ought to have pleaded a dozen years since.

Relative to the other poets named, Aphra got off lightly with the slight on her ageing looks. Thomas Shadwell is mocked for his paunch and his unfaithful wife, Nathaniel Lee for drunkenness, Thomas Otway for venereal disease, whilst 'Starcht-Johnny' Crowne boasts 'his right to the Bays / For writing Romances and Shiting of Plays'. It's a fairly back-handed compliment, but unlike many of the other characters in the session, Aphra's prowess as a writer goes unquestioned. She is the only woman in the poem, which features her alongside all the best-known authors of the day, including Dryden, Wycherley and Etherege.

A Session also makes the distinction between gentlemen authors and professional men of letters. With reference to William Wycherley, author of *The Country Wife*, the poem claims:

> Apollo e'ene thought him too good for the
>   Place,
> No Gentleman-Writer that office should bear,
> 'Twas a Trader in Wit, the Laurel should wear.

(This is in turn a snark on the then-impecunious Wycherley's social pretensions, the real gentlemen of the poem being its absent aristocratic authors.) Since Aphra then is grouped with the professionals rather than the amateur dabblers, the physical insult to which she is subjected can be read as a sign of her equality amongst them, since they are all treated similarly. On the page, Aphra could more than compete, overcoming the traditional limitations of her sex – based on physical attractiveness – with her brain, just as men could.

Aphra was always open about the fact that she wrote for money – indeed she was proud of her capacity to earn an independent living – but she also claimed the right to literary fame on masculine terms. In the preface to *The Luckey Chance*, performed in 1686, she rebuffed the hypocrisy and prejudice her work had faced:

> All I ask is the Privilege for my Masculine Part the poet in me . . . to tread in those Successful Paths my predecessors have so long thriv'd in, to take those measures that both the Ancient and Modern Writers have set me, and by which they have pleas'd the World so well. If I must not, because of my Sex, have this Freedom, but that you will usurp all to yourselves; I lay down my Quill, and you shall hear no more of me, no not so much as to make Comparisons, because I will be kinder to my Brothers of the Pen than they have been to a defenceless Woman; for I am not content to write for a Third day only. I value Fame as much as if I had been born a Hero and if you rob me of that I can retire from the ungrateful World and scorn its Fickle Favours.

Aphra's points here are the absurdity of gendering literary talent and seeing work for pay as inevitably second-rate. She was no gentleman dabbler, but nor was she a lady, cosseted and praised for the least of her efforts. She had won the right to her laurels in the toughest arena of them all, the marketplace of the London theatre, but she refused to be reduced to a jobbing artisan. There is pride here, and defiance and scorn. She utterly rejects the dismissive image of women expressed in lampoons such as *Woman's Wisdom*:

> Nature does strangely female gifts dispense
> Lavish in lust and niggardly in sense

Much of Aphra's writing explored the conflict between desire and convention, between libertine adherence to 'natural' law and the duty owed to society, investigating and caricaturing the paradoxes produced by the tension between them. She is not endorsing the attribution of talent to the 'masculine' so much as exposing it as ridiculous, the product of a code which permits women to be slandered whilst protesting they need the protection of the superior sex. Since that code can be broken, the 'heroism' of male literary ability is exposed as a similarly dysfunctional category – it is talent alone which matters, and talent is not confined to gender or (even more radically), to class.

For the majority of women, though, such a robust self-defence on the page was impossible. Women were particularly vulnerable to the smears of the lampoons, as unlike men they could not defend their honour in combat. 'Smugly secure in their masculine ethos, Court satirists felt justified in firing their

blunderbusses, however innocent their targets.'*
Appearing in the satires was part of the price paid for
life at the centre of high society and Henrietta Berkeley and her sister Mary, the wife of Lord Grey, duly
received their share of abuse. In *The Ladies' March* of
1681, the pair appear in an imagined procession of
women courtiers across a stage, a vision of berib-
boned burlesque where each subject displays her vices
to the 'audience'.

Mary, Lady Grey is referenced in terms of a ghostly
visit she had supposedly received from her lover, the
Duke of Monmouth:

> Next fair Lady Grey appears,
> Her charming eyes all bathed in tears,
> In such a pitiful condition,
> That most men thought it was her Vision.

Harriet does even worse:

> Next Berkeley's Harriet greets the eye,
> The females of which family,
> By nature or by education,
> All love the act of generation

The next verse suggests that Harriet's affair with
Grey was already sounding on the tongues of the town,
and in light of what was to follow the next year, is
remarkably prescient:

* Pritchard, R. E., *Scandalous Liaisons: Charles II and His Court* (2015)

> She, though you catch the man upon her,
> Will swear not guilty 'pon her honour.

The 'Vision' of Lady Grey in the lampoon *Lady Grey's Ghost* had been supplied (anonymously) by one Aphra Behn. Aphra was certainly as guilty as the next London hack of exploiting the peccadilloes of the court in satires. In *Love Letters*, though, she was to give a voice to their victims, the tone of which proved as scathing and unrepentant as her own when she refused the prerogative claimed by her 'Brothers of the Pen' to hoard literary fame for themselves.

The men whom Aphra challenged were the products of immense privilege. Not all London's famous writers were aristocratic or wealthy, but many of them were. They had been educated at Oxford, Cambridge or the Inns of Court, they were familiar with Latin and Greek, they wrote in an erudite and sometimes arcane atmosphere of exclusive knowledge. Educated women and educated women writers were not necessarily admired, but they were not unknown. Yet women such as the Countess of Bath or the Duchess of Newcastle shared birth and breeding. They were, to a greater or lesser extent, people of 'quality'. So how did Aphra, a woman from nowhere, wrestle her way into the top rank?

Aphra Behn appears out of nowhere in the summer of 1666, brought into official existence by the stroke of a civil servant's pen. Before that, there is no documentation of her birth, her residence, her (possible) wedding. Between 1666 and the staging of her first play, *The Forc'd Marriage*, in September 1670 there is likewise absolutely no certain information. What facts there are have, as noted above, been assembled into a neat and believable life-story, whose only drawback is that it just doesn't make sense. Aphra was not, so far as is known, a person of 'quality', yet she ascended far enough socially to mix with and write about and for, those who were. Maybe the facts that are available can be considered in a different way, regarded from a different angle? If Aphra was indeed a woman who was constantly reconfiguring her own identity, perhaps it does no harm to remove one mask and try on another.

2

Before discussing the lives of either Aphra Behn or Harriet Berkeley, we need to understand the significance of the date which defined the courses of both. The year 1660 is an historical point of fission, the moment when the trajectory of national history fractured, swerving in a direction which to many contemporaries was quite unbelievable. England had been a republic for a decade, but now its banished King, Charles Stuart, had returned to reclaim a throne which had seemed irrevocably lost.

Just four years after his own succession to the crown, in 1629, the King's father, Charles I, had dissolved Parliament for eleven years, beset by religious and constitutional controversy. His attempt at sole government was perceived by an increasing number of his subjects as a tyrannical encroachment on their ancient rights, whilst his imposition of High Anglican church ceremony in Scotland had resulted in two invasions in 1639 and 1640. Whilst the King and his supporters pressured to maintain the royal prerogative, Parliament pushed back against what many of its members viewed as a tyrannical suppression of the ancient rights of that mysterious body 'the people'. In 1642, Charles I had felt his authority sufficiently threatened to raise the royal standard against those who sought to oppose him, thus inaugurating the First Civil War, in which the Royalist cause was defeated in 1646. The King surrendered to the Scots, who promptly delivered him up to his enemies in Parliament. A second phase of war ensued and after three years of intermittent captivity, Charles I was executed on 30 January 1649.

The subsequent ten years, known as the Interregnum, were an experiment with republicanism, first under the rule of Parliament and then the governance of Oliver Cromwell, the Parliamentary leader who was declared Lord Protector in 1653. Effectively, England, Scotland and Wales became a brutal military dictatorship. Most forms of public pleasure were officially outlawed, women were strictly policed and military spies sought out any sinful activity from adultery to dancing and, notoriously, the celebration of Christmas. More or less clandestine elements of the country's former cultural life did survive, at both folk and elite levels, but the Parliament were strict and joyless masters.

Charles II, who had learned of his father's death while in exile at the court of his sister Mary at The Hague, did make one last attempt to regain his rights, in 1651. After defeat at the Battle of Worcester and six weeks on the run in England, he escaped to Normandy in a fishing boat with almost nothing apart from hope to sustain his dreams of return.

Charming, cynical, seductive and entirely untrust-worthy, Charles II learned the hard way to rely only on the self-interest of others. Aged twelve when the Civil Wars broke out, a military commander at fourteen and a King at nineteen, Charles was a regal chancer, an incorrigible lover and a haunted boy, scarred by trauma and betrayal, obsessive in the pursuit of his inheritance, eventually triumphant over apparently impossible odds. For the Royalist supporters who joined Charles in exile, homeless adventurers roaming the Continent in search of allies and funds, the Interregnum was a period of poverty and humiliation, a quicksand game in which every player knew that today's penniless pretender might be tomorrow's King. For many, dis-possession was too much and conciliation with Cromwell's Republic too tempting. The boundaries between allegiance and treachery were stretched to the limit, and Charles's court in exile swarmed with spies. Even his own intelligence chief in London, Sir Richard Willys, warned that 'Charles Stuart can give nothing to the Royalists but leave to run mad when they please', and for many, including some of Charles's closest friends, the pursuit of a seemingly hopeless cause proved too difficult.

In contrast with life under the repressive regime of Puritan England, there were as many parties in the King's circle as there were plots. Charles's plate and jewels had been pawned, there was no money for the royal laundry and sometimes even the royal dinner, the scions of some of England's greatest aristocratic houses wore rags and slept on straw, yet if the court in exile knew it lived on the edge of a precipice it was determined to go out dancing. Cromwell's spies claimed that Charles's followers were 'better versed in begging than in fighting', but the Royalists were the most glamorous beggars Europe had ever seen.

As the bedraggled King wore out his Continental welcome, Parliament's spies reported a fresh mistress at every staging post. Charles was accused of extravagance, debauchery and, worst of all, Catholicism, charges which were (accurately) to dog him until the end of his life. Three of the eleven illegitimate children the King eventually acknowledged were born during the Interregnum, the first of whom, James, Duke of Monmouth, carried the Civil Wars into the next generation, and in so doing profoundly impacted the life of Harriet Berkeley and the career of Aphra Behn.

Oliver Cromwell had dynastic ambitions of his own. When he died in 1658, it was already determined that his son Richard would succeed him, but 'Tumble-down Dick', as he was nicknamed, proved hopelessly inadequate to the role and war loomed once more as the army made a bid to take over the government. Secret negotiations began to bring the King once more unto his own and in 1660 at Breda in Holland, Charles II was finally proclaimed.

On 25th May the former pride of Cromwell's fleet,

the *Naseby* (hastily renamed the *Royal Charles*), docked at Dover, where people had gathered in huge numbers to witness the King's arrival. His progress to London was an uproarious cavalcade of cannon fire and cheering crowds. Bonfires were lit, all the church bells pealed, girls in their best dresses pelted him with flowers. 'Nor so joyful a day and so bright ever seen in this nation' enthused the diarist John Evelyn, whilst the writer John Dryden, who would in future become a colleague, rival and friend of Aphra, celebrated with a panegyric poem to the handsome young King, *Astrea Redux*:

> Oh, happy Prince! Whom Heaven hath taught
>   the way,
> By paying vows to have more vows to pay!
> Oh, happy age! Oh times like those alone,
> By fate reserved for great Augustus' throne!
> When the joint growth of arms and arts
>   foreshow
> The world a monarch, and that monarch you.

'Astrea' was a familiar character from the Greek pantheon, a goddess of justice whose story was told by Ovid and Virgil. Astrea was the last of the Ancient Greek immortals to leave the earth at the end of the Iron Age and her return thus signified the beginning of a new cycle. 'Astrea' was also the codename used by Aphra during her employment as a spy and which she chose to retain as her professional pseudonym in literary London. Where Aphra herself actually was during the thrilling days of Charles's return is unknown. She may well have been amongst the crowds who lined the route of the royal procession, but equally she may have been on the other side of the world.

Shortly after Aphra's death in 1689 two 'biographies' appeared: the account of the *Life of the Incomparable Mrs Behn* and *The Life and Memoirs of Mrs Behn. Written By One of the Fair Sex*. Neither is particularly accurate; indeed the *Memoirs* is more a work of fiction, padded out by a collection of fake letters. Such concoctions were a common feature of the early publishing industry, particularly if their subjects were notorious or scandalous. For example, both Barbara Palmer, mistress to Charles II, and Athénaïs de Montespan, mistress to his cousin Louis XIV, had 'Memoirs' published in their names. Most of the supposedly biographical material in the *Life* and the *Memoirs* comes from Aphra's best-known work, her novel *Oroonoko*. Both agree that she was the daughter of a gentleman from Kent named Johnson, but beyond that there is nothing. Nevertheless, the theory of a Kentish birthplace is widely accepted, although it is compellingly likely that Aphra was born somewhere else entirely.

The task of looking for Aphra is respectively helped and hindered by two men named Thomas. One, Thomas Colepeper, provides some apparently plausible hints about her life which form the foundation on which the 'official' version has been erected. The ther, Thomas Killigrew, makes nonsense of it. Thomas Colepeper claims to have known Aphra Behn, Thomas Killigrew definitely did. If Thomas Colepeper was telling the truth, her relationship with Thomas Killigrew becomes extremely unlikely. Yet since we know that Thomas Killigrew and Aphra Behn met and corresponded, the presence of that second Thomas in her life casts doubt upon that of the first.

The most salient feature of Thomas Colepeper's claim to association with Aphra Behn is his date of birth. The only son of Lady Barbara Sidney and Sir Thomas Colepeper, Lieutenant of Dover Castle, was born in Kent on Christmas Day 1637. As an adult, Colepeper was loyal to the Stuart cause and active in promoting the Restoration of Charles II, for which he was imprisoned during the dying days of Oliver Cromwell's Protectorate. The picture left by accounts of his life is slightly eccentric – an impulsive, possibly reckless man, litigious, quarrelsome, careless of his own interest in the pursuit of his grudges. He died childless and poor in London in 1708, having devoted much of his life to dreaming up schemes for the improvement of everything from tax collection to the extraction of minerals. Such scientific interests were reflected in his membership of the Royal Society, to which he was admitted in 1668, and he was a prolific writer, leaving a large number of tracts, schemes and observations now held in the British Library, amongst which is the eighteen-volume work known as the *Adversaria* in which he records his knowledge of Aphra Behn.

Colepeper claimed that his wet nurse (whom he does not name), was Aphra Behn's mother. According to his *Adversaria*, Aphra was born, like him, in Kent 'At Sturry or Canterbury'. She was, he writes, 'a most beautiful woman and a most Excellent poet'. His account states further that Aphra had a sister, Frances, that their maiden name was 'Johnson', that Frances married a man whose name is smudgily rendered as 'Wrils' or 'Wrels', whilst Aphra became the bride of a 'Mr Beene'.

Given that he was a baby, Colepeper could only have been relying on information from his family as to the identity of his wet nurse. Still, his record of Aphra's maiden name and birthplace thus accords with the two biographies. On the whole, however, gentlemen's wives did not act as wet nurses (women paid to breastfeed the babies of others), so some discrepancy as to Aphra's social status might be observed. Enter the Countess of Winchilsea.

Like Aphra Behn, Anne Finch was a writer. Unlike her, she was an aristocrat, a fact that she was keen to point out to posterity. She had spent her young womanhood at St James's Palace as a maid of honour to the future Queen Mary of Modena, the second wife of the King's brother the Duke of York, later James II. Anne married Heneage Finch, one of the Duke's Grooms of the Bedchamber, but the couple withdrew from court in

1689 and lived for twenty-five years on the family estates in Kent. In 1694, one of Anne's poems was printed in an anthology, *Comes Amoris, Being a Choice Collection of the Newest Songs Now in Use in London.* The piece was a 'Session' poem, one of those imagined competitions between writers, entitled *The Circuit of Apollo.* In the poem, the god of poetry is ranging through the English countryside, seeking a writer worthy of his notice, but he has arrived too late for Aphra:

> And standing where sadly he now might descry,
> From the banks of the Stoure the desolate Wye,
> He lamented for Behn, o'er that place of her
>   birth . . .

That is, the poem clearly states that Aphra was born in Kent. In a manuscript version of the same poem, Lady Anne expressed a qualified admiration for Aphra's superiority 'in fancy, in language, or wit' but observed that she wrote 'loosely', that is, in a frank, even scandalous fashion, not a style to which a court lady would stoop. Moreover, Lady Anne sniffed in a handwritten annotation to the piece, Aphra was no gentlewoman but 'Daughter to a Barber, who lived formerly at Wye . . . in Kent.'

The first of the two hastily cobbled-together 'biographies' of Aphra Behn, the *Life* and the *Memoirs*, appeared respectively in 1696 and 1698, that is, *after* the *Circuit of Apollo* was issued to the public. The *Memoirs* state that Aphra was: 'a Gentlewoman by Birth, of a good Family in the city of Canterbury in Kent'. Anne Finch's marginal note was written later, in response to this statement, contradicting it with the information that Aphra was not a gentlewoman but a barber's daughter. It observes that:

> Though the account of her life before [i.e. at the beginning of] her Works pretends otherwise; some Persons now alive Do testify upon their Knowledge that to be her Original.

Who those Persons were or how they came by their knowledge of Aphra Behn Anne Finch did not add. Nor did she object to Aphra's maiden name being given in the *Life* as 'Johnson', but then there was only so much time, after all, that one could devote to a barber's daughter. Had Anne considered it a little further, she could have concluded that the statement that Aphra was born in Kent, as reproduced in the biographies, came from her own pen. The Kent birthplace was thus apparently confirmed in that the biographies accepted Anne's version, but she is the original source. The evidence is circular.

So, Anne, Countess of Winchilsea believed that Aphra was born in Kent and this was accepted. As the marginal note signals, the social position of 'Aphra Johnson' was less certain. Her rank, or lack of it, posed a problem to subsequent scholars.

Edmund Gosse was one of the great poets and critics of the Victorian age, or possibly a tremendous literary busybody. His curiosity was piqued by Aphra Behn. In 1884, two centuries after Aphra's death, Gosse determined to get to the bottom of the origins of this mysterious woman, who had competed as an equal against some of the most learned and ingenious writers of her age. To Gosse, the Countess of Winchilsea's contention simply made no sense. How could it have been possible for a barber's daughter to attain the level of education required for her to become a successful playwright? The difficulty was a real one, not (entirely) a product of snobbery. True, the Civil Wars had greatly disturbed the class system of the mid-seventeenth century, but nonetheless the hierarchy of rank obtained to a level almost incomprehensible to twenty-first century minds.

We have been conditioned by the sentimentality of historical TV dramas to believe in a cosy version of the past in which masters and servants lived relatively companionably, a forelock-tugging, *Downton Abbey* world where nobs and plebs rubbed along contentedly side by side. The world Aphra Behn lived in and wrote from was savage. It considered the lower classes, the working poor, as essentially sub-human, useful certainly, but having precious little in common with their betters as ordained by God. It seemed unlikely to Mr Gosse that the daughter of a provincial working man could have attained a level of literary fluency which allowed her to make a successful career amidst the vicious rivalries of the Restoration theatre. Moreover, the nineteenth century, like the seventeenth, was firmly convinced that people, particularly women, should 'know their place' and stick to the social station in which they were born. If Aphra had really been a barber's daughter, she had not kept to her place. Ergo, whatever the Countess of Winchilsea believed, Aphra *must* have been a lady.

Mr Gosse bustled down to Wye and consulted the parish register. There he struck gold, as he proudly announced in an article for the *Athenaeum* magazine. Aphra Behn was not born Aphra Johnson, but Aphra Amies, baptized by the curate of St Gregory and St Martin Church along with her twin brother Peter on 10 July 1640. Her father's name was John (hence perhaps the Johnson confusion), her mother was Amy. Mr Amies's 'Quality, Trade or Profession' was not stated, which made it easy to assume he was, indeed, a gentleman. It's a pity that Mr Gosse didn't bother turning over the pages of the register before rushing into print, as poor little Aphra and her brother were buried two days after their christening. Nonetheless, the Amies theory of Aphra's identity was accepted well into the following century.

Both Edmund Gosse and Lady Anne had made mistakes, in the way of a muddle rather than an outright error. Gosse had claimed Aphra's surname as 'Amies', whilst Lady Anne might well have heard from 'certain Persons' that an 'Aphra Behn' lived there in Kent, because she did. In September 1605, one Aphra

Smithet had married Thomas Amyes at the church of St John the Baptist at Barham in Kent. The couple went on to have at least eight children, including a daughter, Afra Amies. After Thomas Amyes died, his widow married Thomas Beane, described as a yeoman at Elmstead St James in 1632. Aphra Amies senior thus became Aphra Behn, which is the name used in her will, proved at the Prerogative Court of Canterbury in 1651. 'Afra Behn, Widow' left small legacies to all her children, including her daughter Afra, who was made executor. What a mess.

The salient point here is that the 'evidence' of the woman who became famous as Aphra Behn having been born in Kent at all rests on a case of mistaken identity. Lady Anne and Edmund Gosse both had the wrong woman, but scholars nonetheless continued to look for Aphra in Kent. Frustratingly, though, no 'Aphra Johnson' was to be found.

The Christian name itself was fairly common in Kent in the seventeenth century. It derives from St Aphra, a fourth-century reformed prostitute who was reputedly martyred after refusing to perform a pagan sacrifice during the reign of the Roman Emperor Diocletian. 'Affra', 'Ayfara', 'Afra', 'Affry' all appear frequently in the parish registers, and as we see from the records above, the same person could often have their name spelt differently across the documents.

In the 1970s, playwright and scholar Maureen Duffy made a pivotal discovery in the village of

Bishopsbourne near Canterbury. On 25 August 1638 a local man named Bartholomew Johnson married Elizabeth Denham of Smeeth, another nearby village, at St Paul's Church, Canterbury. Their first child, Frances, was baptized in her mother's home village on 6 December 1638. A second daughter, Eaffrey Johnson, was baptized at another nearby church in the hamlet of Harbledown in December 1640. At his wedding, the twenty-three-year-old Bartholomew was described as 'Yeoman'. In 1648, however, a Bartholomew Johnson was granted the freedom of the city of Canterbury. The document confirming his payment of £5 for the honour gives his profession as 'this city barber'. Bingo. An Eaffrey/Aphra Johnson, born in Kent, daughter of a barber. It had to be her. And indeed the Eaffrey Johnson persona has now become the accepted version of the true identity of Aphra Behn.

The Eaffrey Johnson story seems so thrillingly perfect that biographers have had difficulty letting it go. Except that there are just too many holes in the story of Eaffrey Johnson to make it fit, despite the documentary contortions of two generations of scholars. We know that Anne, Countess of Winchilsea believed Aphra Behn to have been the daughter of a Kent barber, but she was possibly thinking of Aphra née Smithet Amies/Behn. We know that Bartholomew Johnson married Elizabeth Denham and had a daughter named Eaffrey. We don't know that the 'city barber' of Canterbury was the same Bartholomew Johnson.

Re-enter Thomas Colepeper. The information he proffers in his book pertaining to Aphra's birthplace and maiden name was a matter of public record before Colepeper wrote it down at some point before 1708. (The Kent birthplace from Lady Anne, repeated in the *Life* and *Memoirs*; 'Johnson' in the two latter, uncontested by Lady Anne.) Colepeper's account accords with the Canterbury birthplace, adding that Aphra may have been born at Sturry. The only fresh information he adds is that Aphra's mother was his wet nurse and that she had a sister called Frances.

If Eaffrey is Aphra, then Colepeper is wrong about her precise birthplace, but perhaps that can be dismissed as an error, given that the Johnsons were married in Canterbury and had moved back there by 1648. The wet-nurse theory is rather less plausible.

Eaffrey Johnson's mother gave birth to her first child at the end of 1638. Since she was married the preceding August, she would have been about five months pregnant as a bride. This in itself was not at all uncommon in the seventeenth-century countryside, but it would mean that Elizabeth Denham must have had another baby before Christmas Day 1637, when Colepeper was born, in order to be able to breast-feed him. No record of such a child exists, but perhaps Elizabeth had given birth to a bastard who had then died. She must however have stopped feeding Thomas early in 1638 in order to be able to fall pregnant by Bartholomew Johnson. (Breast-feeding is not a guaranteed contraceptive, but it is effective, and one reason why pregnancy rates for the period amongst wealthy women who put their children out to nurse were considerably higher than amongst their breast-feeding sisters lower down the social scale.) Still, as children were not weaned until about the age of two, Elizabeth might have fed Colepeper at a later date, between the birth of her daughter Frances and the conception of Eaffrey, i.e. December 1638 to the spring of 1640.

Eaffrey Johnson's birth was registered at Harbledown. Hackington Manor, the Colepeper home, is two and a half miles from Harbledown, hardly a great distance, but not one to be walked several times a day in order to breast-feed a baby. Wet nurses would usually be expected to live with their employers during their service, which would mean that Elizabeth and her one or possibly two small children would have stayed there for a time. Not impossible. Colepeper does not give the Christian name of his nurse, but Maureen Duffy connected the name Johnson and the barber statements to identify Elizabeth Johnson. Given the number of Elizabeth Johnsons in the Canterbury records, however, Thomas Colepeper may have been wet-nursed by a woman of that name who had nothing whatsoever to do with the woman who became Aphra Behn.

Attempts have been made to present Elizabeth Denham as a member of a gentry family, but if so Bartholomew Johnson wasn't exactly a catch. A possible father has been proposed for him in another Bartholomew, 'a poore man' buried at Smeeth in 1617. Perhaps Elizabeth Denham was married off to Yeoman Johnson after disgracing herself with an illegitimate child. The Canterbury records do show *a* Bartholomew who had *perhaps* reinvented himself as a barber, since he is recorded there in 1648, though he was unable to pay his £5 fee for the freedom of the city for some time. By 1654, he had presumably done so since he had become one of the Overseers of the Poor at the church of St Margaret's. After that no more is heard of him.

There is no particular reason to believe that Eaffrey Johnson's father was the same Bartholomew Johnson who appears as a barber in Canterbury in 1648 except for the fact that a barber was required for the role. Assuming that Bartholomew had successfully abandoned farming for hairdressing, his daughter Eaffrey was thirteen when her father is last mentioned in the Kent public records. Had the family still been living in Canterbury, Bartholomew ought to have appeared in the 1664 Returns of the city, but he is not mentioned. Of Eaffrey's mother Elizabeth there is similarly little trace. She may have been widowed and died in Kent (twenty-five Elizabeth Johnsons were buried there between 1645 and 1664), or she may have left the county with her husband and children. What little Aphra Behn herself had to say about her parents was presented in the fiction of her later career and makes no allusions to Kent or barbers and certainly not to wet nurses.

In Aphra's secret service letters and her story *Oroonoko*, she mentions a younger brother. Bartholomew and Elizabeth did have another son, George, who was buried at St Margaret's in 1656. It has therefore been assumed that there must have been a second, unnamed boy.

However, in May 1657, the funeral of an Edward Johnson, son of Elizabeth and Bartholomew Johnson, took place at St Botolph's Church at Aldersgate in London. Another piece of evidence is therefore added to the story – possibly mourning the death of their child, Bartholomew and Elizabeth had relocated from Canterbury to London. This would explain Bartholomew's absence from the Canterbury Returns. (It would also require a third son to appear later as Aphra's younger brother, but we can return to him.)

In 2019, the scholar Karen Britland published a paper which included a further discovery. Some months after Edward Johnson's death, marriage banns were published for 'John Halse, gentleman and Aphara Johnson daughter of Bartholomew Johnson, both of this parish'. The banns were read on the 19th and 26th of July and the 2nd of August, but no wedding between the couple was recorded in the church. As Britland points out, this does not necessarily mean that their marriage did not take place. In 1653 the church of St Botolph's opened a new register for marriage banns in accordance with a recent Act of Parliament which decreed that a couple wishing to marry must first publish their banns three times, then appear to formalize their union before a Justice of the Peace (effectively a civil wedding). Of the twenty-six records of banns recorded in the new register, only half the couples then went on to marry in the church, but this does not preclude the weddings being solemnized elsewhere. It is perfectly possible, therefore, that Aphara Johnson, daughter of Bartholomew, did marry John Halse. So in moving to London, the Johnsons had achieved sufficient standing for Eaffrey/Aphara to be betrothed to a 'gentleman'.

Britland's discovery allows us to make further tentative additions to the chronology. So far, we have Eaffrey Johnson born at Harbledown in 1640, moving with her family first to Canterbury and then to London by 1657, her name now spelt as 'Aphara'. In London she becomes engaged to be married. If a marriage took place, the bridegroom died before Eaffrey/Aphara/Aphra left England for Surinam, as the narrator of the novel *Oroonoko* claims she did. The novel further claims that the narrator's father died on the voyage to the West Indies, leaving Aphra with her mother, sister and younger brother. Some time before returning to London, she acquired and then mislaid a husband, 'Mr Beene'.

In the early 1660s, a woman who there is good reason to believe was Aphra Behn was described as living near to Suffolk Street in the Haymarket near the church of St Martin-in-the-Fields. One house in the street was occupied by an Elizabeth Johnson, presumed to be a widow. So Aphra, also widowed, may have been sharing a house with her mother.

This is all quite convincing, but it does not come close to explaining the presence of the second Thomas in Aphra's life, Thomas Killigrew. Suffolk Street, where Aphra may have lived with Elizabeth, was a few minutes' walk from Drury Lane, home from 1663 to the Theatre Royal, managed by Thomas Killigrew. The first extant letter signed by Aphra Behn dates from 31 August 1666 and was written to Killigrew. It concerns her recruitment as a spy for the English government, which Killigrew had engineered. How did the two come to know one another? Or rather, how did Eaffrey Johnson, the daughter of a Kentish barber, come to be corresponding with one of the most prominent figures at the Restoration court?

3

The Killigrews were a huge family and a staunchly Royalist one. There were Killigrews all over the West Country and Cornwall, where Thomas Killigrew's father, Sir Robert, served as Member of Parliament for six boroughs between 1601–9 and was appointed Lieutenant of the county in 1621. Vice Chamberlain to Queen Henrietta Maria, and ambassador to the Dutch United Provinces, Sir Robert, like many of his contemporaries, also had family and commercial interests in the New World. He was one of the signatories of the second charter of Virginia in 1609 along with Sir Maurice Berkeley, who married Sir Robert's sister Elizabeth. Their son William Berkeley became Governor of Virginia in 1642, while their daughter Jane married Henry Killigrew, a Barbados sugar-planter. Sir Robert's wife, Mary Woodhouse, was sister to a future Governor of Bermuda.

Of Robert and Mary's twelve children, Thomas was born in 1612. As the governor of the Queen's household, Sir Robert could easily place his children at court; Thomas arrived as a page to Charles I in about 1625, accompanying his older sister Anne, a lady in waiting to the Queen. Thomas Killigrew was the first to admit he hadn't had much of an education, describing himself as an 'illiterate courtier' who could barely decipher the scrawl of his own handwriting; nonetheless it seemed that the Killigrews had writing and theatre in their blood. All the Killigrew brothers wrote (more or less successful) plays, and Thomas's niece Anne was to become a noted court poet in the next generation. Thomas himself was mad about theatre, volunteering as an 'extra' or 'demon' in order to get in to plays for free and writing at least three of his own before the First Civil War.

As an adult, Thomas Killigrew's loyalty to the Stuarts was unwavering. He followed Charles II into exile and spent the first years of the Interregnum as a peripatetic diplomat, travelling through France and Switzerland in an attempt to rally political support and funds for his master. In 1650–2 he was in Venice, where he lived in great splendour on Piazza San Marco, before falling foul of the authorities when it was discovered that he had been allowing his servants to use his official residence as a smuggling depot. Drummed out of Italy, he rejoined Charles's court in Holland, where he married a wealthy Dutch wife and became involved in the network of spies and secret agents which was to enmesh Aphra Behn in 1665.

Described as Charles II's 'fool or jester', Killigrew enjoyed a relationship of exceptional closeness and familiar licence with the King. (They were, in a sense, related by blood, as Killigrew's sister Elizabeth had given birth to Charlotte Fitzroy, one of Charles's numerous bastards, whilst in exile with the Royalist court in 1650.) At the Restoration, he was amongst the earliest of Charles's supporters to be rewarded for his loyalty. In August 1660, the King granted a duopoly over control of London's reopening theatres to Killigrew and his fellow Royalist rake, Sir William Davenant. Killigrew was to have charge of the King's Company, which first staged productions at his child-hood haunt, the Red Bull Theatre, before moving to more splendid premises at Drury Lane in 1663.

The connection between theatre and royalty is one of the enduring images of Charles II's reign. As Davenant put it in a new prologue to the first play to be officially performed before the Restoration court:

> This truth we can to our advantage say,
> They that would have no King, would have
> no Play.
> The Laurel and the Crown together went,
> Had the same Foes and the same Banishment.

Killigrew was to prove an effective if somewhat erratic theatrical manager, but he didn't entirely depend on the stage for his income. As well as occupying the lucrative and influential post of Groom of the Bedchamber to the King, he continued the family concerns on the plantations of the West Indies. A letter of May 1657 from Lord Willoughby, the Governor of Barbados, mentions the 'disorder' on the island and numbers Tom Killigrew amongst those tasked with alerting the King to it: 'if Tom Killigrew fails on his part, I shall [have] him of his sugar. Found his two sons here, they are loyal subjects . . .'

We know that the West Indies were also a significant location for Aphra Behn. Most Behn scholars presently concur that Aphra spent time in the early 1660s in Surinam, a short-lived English colony on the Atlantic coast of South America. Almost all the detail about her time there comes from the short novel *Oroonoko*, corroborated by letters from the governor of the island which correspond with the most documented period of her life in the middle of the same decade. What is not clear is how she came to be there. When Aphra returned from Surinam, she either already knew or quickly came to know Thomas Killigrew. The new London theatres needed material, but they also needed scripts, handwritten copies of the 'books' from which the actors learned their parts. There is evidence that Aphra worked as a copyist in a 'scriptorium' in the 1660s and 1680s, and Killigrew was apparently amongst the admirers of her clear, confident handwriting. So how and where did Aphra acquire such a hand and how did Killigrew come to see it?

That Eaffrey Johnson somehow made the acquaintance of Thomas Killigrew, who somehow decided to employ her on sensitive government business and then to encourage her literary career, is perhaps the most pertinent question provoked by this theory of

Aphra Behn's biography, yet it has received comparatively little attention. The social gulf between them was vast. Moreover, perhaps the first reason to think that Eaffrey Johnson was not Aphra Behn is that Eaffrey's mother couldn't write. Possibly Elizabeth could read, but she signed the marriage register at St Paul's Canterbury with only her initial.

All kinds of ingenious theories have been posited as to how Eaffrey could have acquired a polished education, mainly based on convoluted and tenuous connections with Thomas Colepeper. Despite the latter's claim to being her foster-brother, Aphra herself left no evidence of ever having met or corresponded with Colepeper, yet it is his connections amongst people of 'quality' which supposedly provided her with her significant intellectual accomplishments.

Literacy rates were increasing rapidly in the mid-seventeenth century, but only an estimated 10 per cent of women, rising to 20 per cent in London, were able to read and write in 1650–60. The daughter of a country barber whose mother was at best semi-literate might well have learned basic letters and arithmetic, suitable to her station in life, but it was hardly the kind of education that would have prepared her for swapping quips with the Poet Laureate. Furthermore, Aphra Behn spoke fluent Dutch and French. In *Oroonoko*, the narrator mentions that she is able to converse with the enslaved hero in both English and French, whilst Aphra's correspondence from her spying mission in Antwerp frequently uses French words amongst the English ('malgré' instead of 'despite' is one example). Peppering English with French and Italian words was a fashionable affectation, one that Aphra satirized in her 1679 play *The Feign'd Curtizans*, but in the early 1660s a provincial girl from the lower orders would have had little exposure to such conversational flourishes. Aphra Behn was later to prove herself an excellent translator from French, but Eaffrey Johnson did not come from a milieu where it was spoken. Thomas Killigrew does seem to have played Professor Higgins to Aphra's Eliza Doolittle, yet did her genius really gleam so brightly that he overlooked her status and her sex to select her for a sensitive political mission on the basis of her handwriting?

The skeins of Aphra's semi-imagined life are as convoluted as they are barely visible. Somehow she supposedly got herself from Kent (possibly via London) to Surinam, after which she was entrusted with a spying mission to Holland by an intimate of the King himself. Everywhere one looks in the biographical theories of the years before Aphra was established as a writer, Thomas Killigrew pops up, but with no satisfactory explanation as to how he got there. He is the springboard which catapults a mysterious young woman with connections in the colonies from one existence to another. Put simply, how did Aphra end up in Surinam and how did she know Killigrew? Somehow, the two questions must be related.

As many scholars have noted, one of the numerous problems with constructing a biography for Aphra is the extent to which information on her real life must be extrapolated from her fictional life, from her works. Such inferences are necessarily compromised, but they are frequently all we have. Aphra herself stated that her first play was *The Young King*, written in the first years of Charles II's Restoration. In the dedication to the piece, which was not performed until 1679, Aphra suggested that her Muse might be thought of as 'an American'. Throughout her career, Aphra was interested in the colonies, the Eastern seaboard of the United States and the Caribbean. Perhaps, just perhaps, this interest stemmed from the fact that along with her imagined muse, she too was 'American'. If Aphra Behn was not Eaffrey Johnson, it is possible that she was someone else altogether, someone who appeared in London from the other side of the known world.

Oroonoko, or, The Royal Slave was published at the end of Aphra's life, in 1688. In the story, Prince Oroonoko of Coramantien, a noble and brilliant general, is in love with the beautiful and virtuous Imoinda. They marry in secret, but before they can consummate their relationship Oroonoko's lustful grandfather the King forces Imoinda into his Otan, or harem. The King is elderly and impotent and the couple contrive to be together before the King discovers them and orders

Imoinda to be sold as a slave. Oroonoko is then tricked by an unscrupulous sea captain and is enslaved himself. Transported to Surinam, he is re-named Caesar by his owners and reunited with Imoinda, who has been sold in the same colony. She is soon pregnant, which prompts Caesar to exhort his fellow slaves to rebel. The revolt is crushed and Caesar kills a willing Imoinda, planning to follow her to the grave rather than endure the degradation of slavery, but he is captured and put to an obscenely horrible death.

It was later claimed that Aphra had written her most famous story in a single draft, whilst in company with others, her pen never rising from the page. Such fluency endorses her narrator's conceit that the account is a 'true' recollection. Given how unproblematic we now find novels which pose as true accounts, it is surprising that scholars have wrangled for years over whether or not *Oroonoko* can be taken literally in its entirety. Behn's narrator is no more recounting the 'truth' than Daniel Defoe's castaway hero Robinson Crusoe; nonetheless there are many indisputably real elements of the story which have been effectively observed as corroborating Aphra's stay in Surinam.

The European characters in the novel were drawn from life. They include one who never actually appears onstage in *Oroonoko*, Francis, Lord Willoughby of Parham, the governor of the colony and long-time acquaintance of Thomas Killigrew. They were the same age (Willoughby was born in 1613) and like Killigrew, Willoughby inherited economic connections with the Caribbean, as his wife was descended from the Noell family, who were amongst the first investors in the territories of the New World. Unlike Killigrew, Willoughby declared against the crown in the Civil War, commanding the Parliamentarian forces in Lincolnshire in 1643. In 1647, Willoughby leased the island of Barbados from the Earl of Carlisle for twenty-one years. He was granted a charter which declared the intent of 'better securing and settling it', but his allegiance wavered when it became clear that Cromwell intended to execute King Charles I. Willoughby was a moderate, amongst those who had attempted to seek a compromise with the crown, but the Parliamentary leaders had set their course for revolution and there was no place for moderation within a regime which declared that 'the office of a King in this Nation and to have the power thereof in any single person is unnecessary, burdensome and dangerous to the Liberty, Safety and Public Interest.'

Charles I's death had not been the wish of the majority and was achieved by a military coup. Parliamentary procedure was dismissed, the House of Commons swept free of opposition in the aggressive rejection of opposition MPs in what became known as 'Pride's Purge' and the House of Lords simply ignored. Shocked by the turn events had taken, Willoughby declared for the Royalists and as a consequence his

English landholdings were sequestered by the new government in 1649. Like many other Cavaliers, he sailed for Barbados.

Barbados was flourishing in the 1640s and had remained largely though not uncontentiously neutral in the war on the other side of the Atlantic. By 1649, though, the island was 'awash' with Stuart supporters and the treasurer of the Barbados assembly was overthrown and replaced with a 'fervent monarchist' named William Byam. On 3 May 1650, Barbados declared a formal oath of loyalty to the exiled King Charles II. In an attempt to restore order, Lord Willoughby sent a merchant planter named George Marten to London in order to negotiate with the Parliamentary regime. The Marten family were to become key players in the story of Aphra Behn.

George Marten failed to reach an agreement with Cromwell, but Lord Willoughby hoped Barbados could still be held for the Royalists. He also had a Plan B, the possibility of developing the settlements on the mainland around the Surinam River, where he sent an exploratory force of forty men. Writing to his wife, he described the country as 'the sweetest place that was ever seen'. Previous English attempts at monetizing the territory had come to little, but Willoughby, 'the most ambitious and aggressive' of governors, planned to change this. Communities of French, Dutch and Jewish settlers were already living in the area, but with Willoughby's encouragement a significant diaspora from Barbados came to dominate Surinam in the 1650s. The inhabitants of Barbados had quadrupled between 1640–70; hence the island possessed wealth, expertise and a surplus population eager for more land to exploit. Surinam, or 'Willoughbyland' as it was briefly known, grew rapidly, from 600 men and an unknown number of women and children in 1654, to over 1,000 white inhabitants in 1661 and 5,000 by 1663. By this time there were 500 members of the 'Barbados gentry' or planter class, who owned between 40 and 50 sugar mills. The colony's capital, Torarica, had over 100 houses and a chapel. Freedom of conscience was permitted and there may also have been a small Catholic presence there. The gruelling physical work of planting sugar encouraged the slavers to trade in Surinam, and the first ship to bring enslaved Africans to the colony, the *Swallow*, arrived in 1663, during the time that Aphra Behn was living there. It carried 130 people, 54 having died on the voyage from Africa.

In *Oroonoko*, Aphra takes care to ground her story in the 'real-life' verisimilitude of her narrator. At the beginning she declares, 'I was myself an eye-witness to a great part of what you will find here set down.' Her account of Prince Oroonoko's life before his arrival in Surinam she claims to have heard in numerous conversations with him (in French and English). Thus far, so conventional within the fictitious 'true story' model. After his capture, Oroonoko then arrives in Surinam, 'where I chanced to be' and is sold to 'our' overseer, one Mr Trefry, at Parham House, Lord Willoughby's mansion. John Trefry was a real person, Parham House a real place, where the narrator implies that she is staying. She then explains a little of her presence in Surinam:

> My stay was to be short in that country, because my father died at sea and never arrived to possess the honour which was assigned to him (which was lieutenant general of six and thirty islands besides the continent of Surinam) . . . so that we were obliged to continue on our voyage.

In 1927 the author, adventurer and model for Virginia Woolf's *Orlando*, Vita Sackville-West, began a biography of Aphra Behn. She had been a fan of what she perceived as Aphra's Restoration raunchiness for some years, writing to Virginia 'a course of A.B. has turned me into the complete ruffling rake. No more than Mrs A.B. do I approve of chastity.' During her research, Sackville-West found a passage in a comprehensive if somewhat dry Victorian history book, James Rodway's *History of the Discovery and Settlement of Guiana*, which in part foreshadowed the Eaffrey Johnson theory:

> Lord Willoughby, having been released from the Tower with permission to proceed to Surinam, deputed a relation of his named Johnson as governor of that colony . . . Taking with him his wife

and children and also an adopted daughter named Afra or Aphra Johnson, he sailed for Surinam towards the end of this or the beginning of the following year. He did not, however, live to reach his government, but fell sick and died on the voyage. His widow and children proceeded to Surinam, where they remained for two or three years, living on one of Lord Willoughby's plantations which was under the management of Mr Trefry, who acted as estate attorney for the lord proprietor.

The source given by Rodway for this story is Aphra Behn herself and her posthumous editors – that is, in substance it is derived from the novel *Oroonoko* and the *Memoir*. Disappointingly then, it's a red herring. Lord Willoughby had no relative named Johnson and no Johnson is recorded amongst the English emigrants to Surinam. Willoughby did however die at sea in 1666, twenty-two years before *Oroonoko*'s publication, a fact which the narrator alludes to.

In the novel, the narrator continues that when she arrived in Surinam she was presented with 'the best house' in the colony, St John's Hill. This too was a real place, owned first by Robert Harley and then by Lord Willoughby. The action of the story takes place while the colonists are waiting for Willoughby's arrival and in the meantime the authority is the deputy governor, Byam, the same William Byam who had been prominent in the Royalist coup on Barbados and who was indeed appointed Deputy Governor of Surinam. Amongst their pastimes, they go on a tiger safari, in the company of George Martin, 'brother to Harry Martin'. George and his brother were also real, the former having come to Surinam from Barbados in the early 1660s. A further real character is James Bannister, a villainous Irishman who in the story executes Caesar/Oroonoko. Byam was Deputy Governor of Surinam from 1662–7 and the projected visit of Lord Willoughby took place in 1663, which places the real-time frame of the novel in 1662/3.

In *Oroonoko*, Aphra's narrator gives out that she is a lady, a 'person of quality'. She has a woman or female servant, 'a maid of good courage', and a brother, with whom she appears in great splendour on an excursion up-country. The narrator, whose hair, she notes, is cut short, wears a taffeta cap adorned with black feathers; her brother is got up in a 'stuff suit with silver loops and buttons and an abundance of green ribbon'. A barber's daughter was certainly no lady, but Aphra could easily have been in Surinam in a more lowly capacity, which she subsequently fictionalized. In addition to her narrator's knowledge of real men and places present there, there is much in the descriptions of the landscape and customs which has the vividness of memory.

On the first page, barely has the story begun before the narrator launches into a description of Surinam's fauna – marmosets, tiny parakeets and 'great parrots' and 'a little beast in form and fashion of a lion as big as a kitten'. The climate of 'eternal spring', the abundant and exotic fruits, flowers, trees, the perfumed candles made from 'aromatic gum' are described with the same curiosity with which the narrator includes the six-foot-long leaf used as a tablecloth for a picnic, where the food was good but 'too high seasoned with pepper'. Aphra was subsequently accused by hostile critics of furnishing her Surinam background from travel accounts, a suggestion which has been painstakingly disproved, but considering just the words on the page, they are so alight with colour and enthusiasm, possessed of such freshness and arranged in such naturalistic combination as to carry her memories from recollections set down in a smoky London parlour twenty years after the fact to the immediacy of the reader's imagination three centuries later with a vivacity which is truly delightful.

There is significant evidence of Aphra's presence in Surinam which does *not* make its way into *Oroonoko*, though there is one deliciously slight hint. We recall that in the summer of 1666, Thomas Killigrew got Aphra Behn a job and that this is the first time she appears by name in any public document which has emerged to date. Aphra's task was to go to Holland to spy on a man named William Scot.

During the latter part of the Interregnum Killigrew had been closely involved in intelligence work in connection with Charles II's rackety court-in-exile in the

Netherlands. After the Restoration he continued to work with the head of the secret service, Lord Arlington. We know from Aphra's correspondence that it was Killigrew who personally recommended her for the Scot mission three years after she returned from Surinam to London. Killigrew might well have noted her talents as a copyist for the theatre, but a stronger reason for choosing Aphra for such delicate and dangerous work was that she had met William Scot in Surinam.

William Scot was the son of Thomas Scot, who had served two terms as the spymaster or head of intelligence for Cromwell's government in 1649–53 and again in 1659–60. Thomas Scot was a 'regicide', one of the men who had signed the warrant for the execution of Charles I. He was executed on 17 October 1660. His son William appears to have been a highly intelligent man – a fellow of All Souls, Oxford, and a lawyer at the Inner Temple – and something of a ne'er do well – he had been employed by his father but sacked in 1657, suspected of being a double agent for Charles II. William dodged prison by raising money on his estate 'for the securing of his person', i.e. a large fine, and disappeared for a time to France. He soon sent his wife Joanna and their child back to England, where Joanna found herself in such a desperate financial position that she was obliged to petition the government for a meagre pension. William returned at the end of the Interregnum, but his position grew even worse as the regime his father had served collapsed and the King was restored. In early 1660 a warrant was issued for his arrest and another for the recovery of £1,000 he owed to his father's official employer, the Post Office.

Just as the colonies had offered a haven for Royalists on the run during the Interregnum, Parliamentarians who could expect no quarter from the King sought refuge there. Scot turned up in Surinam in 1663. There he seems to have formed some sort of relationship with the woman who became Aphra Behn. Surinam's Deputy Governor, William Byam, corresponded with Robert Harley, the Chancellor of Barbados, whose home, St John's Hill, is mentioned in *Oroonoko* as being where the narrator stayed. A letter to the absent Lord Willoughby reports the presence of a party of 'Ladies' in the house in January 1664, which doesn't prove much either way, but in a letter to Harley dated February, William Byam reports on the departure of a lady from the colony:

> I found a ship full freighted and bound for London, on whom I sent off the fair shepherdess … with what reluctance and regret you may conjecture.

A second letter from Byam dated a month later notes that 'Celadon' has also departed Surinam:

> I need not enlarge But to advise you of the sympatheticall passion of the Grand Shepherd Celadon

who is fled after Astrea, being resolved to espouse all distress or felicities of Fortune with her.

This is rather bewildering at first, but 'Astrea' and 'Celadon' were the names of characters from a windy romance by the French writer Honoré d'Urfé, published and translated between 1607 and 1627. A hugely popular seventeenth-century bestseller, *L'Astrée* is the story of a pair of lovers, Astrea and Celadon, who enjoy a (seemingly endless), and chaste love affair in an idealized Arcadian world.

'Astrea' and 'Celadon' were also the codenames given to Aphra Behn and William Scot during the mission to Holland for which Thomas Killigrew chose Aphra in 1666. It has been accepted by many scholars that Byam's letter thus refers to Aphra Behn, prefiguring the pseudonym she employed for her secret work.

This puts a very different complexion on Aphra's time in Surinam. Either she could have been a spy when she went there or she became one during her stay. Scot was a wanted man with deep and longstanding connections in the secret world, and on the evidence of Byam's letters, Aphra had a connection with him. Perhaps they had begun a relationship? Or perhaps, since Byam's sardonic tone suggests that he doesn't care very much for 'Astrea', his reference to 'Celadon' following her is ironic, a reference to Scot's dubious character and the fact that the missing £1,000 he owed was a more likely motivation to get out of town.

As noted above, a document filed with the state papers of 1666, undated and recovered from a Dutch spy, instructs the bearer to go to the house of 'Scot's shee-correspondent' near the house in Suffolk Street, close by the residence of Elizabeth Johnson and Killigrew's theatre. If the woman referred to is Aphra Behn, who was that year set to spy upon Scot, it implies that a correspondence, at least, was maintained between Scot and Aphra *between* Surinam and Aphra's departure for Holland and further that the Dutch authorities were aware of this. Aphra was a person of interest to them. So, the choice of 'Astrea' and 'Celadon' as codenames strongly suggests that when Thomas Killigrew chose Aphra to spy on Scot he was aware of the nicknames applied to them in Surinam. What still remains unclear is what Aphra was doing in the colony in the first place.

Reviewing the Eaffrey Johnson theory, the barber's daughter from Canterbury may have moved to London in the 1650s, where as 'Aphara' Johnson she may have become engaged, or even possibly married. She then travels to Surinam, possibly as a settler's partner (though there is no evidence for that), or possibly to begin a new life with her family (though there is no evidence for that either). We know that the account in *Oroonoko* of her father dying on the way to his post is an invention which for a time was accepted as fact, but this does not preclude Eaffrey Johnson from making the journey.

Aphra's principal biographer suggests that: 'It seems most plausible . . . that Aphra Behn went to Surinam as a spy or agent.'

On the contrary, it is positively incredible, if Aphra Behn was Eaffrey Johnson. Why on earth would a barber's daughter be sent all the way to Surinam and who could have conceived of sending her? Aphra claimed that she had begun to write her first play whilst in Surinam, which may or may not be true, but we do know that by the 1660s she spoke languages unlikely to have been acquired in Canterbury: fluent French and Dutch. What few facts there are just don't fit Eaffrey Johnson, however laboriously they are stretched.

What if Aphra Behn's journey to Surinam began not in Kent but in Barbados, or even mainland America? In her dedication of *Oroonoko* to Lord Maitland, Behn claimed to have 'known' her hero 'in my travels to the other world', continuing that 'if there be anything that seems Romantic, I beseech your Lordship to consider these countries do, in all things, so far differ from ours that they produce unconceivable wonders'. It would be a very typical Aphra joke if one such exotic 'wonder' was herself.

4

We have progressed a little with the mystery. To investigate the possibility of an American Aphra further, we need to accompany her to that 'other world' across the Atlantic. The colony of Virginia, governed by Thomas Killigrew's cousin William Berkeley, was a crown property, ruled directly from London. Its neighbour, Maryland, was established in 1632 as a 'proprietary colony', that is, by virtue of its charter from Charles I, it was granted in perpetuity to George Calvert, first Baron Baltimore. The Baltimore family were Catholic, and they defiantly continued to profess their faith in the New World.

To be a Catholic in the 1630s was effectively to proclaim you were a terrorist. Catholicism had been proscribed in England since Queen Elizabeth's reign, during which 189 people had been executed for their adherence to the 'Old Faith'. A further forty went to the scaffold under Elizabeth's successor James I, and many more suffered imprisonment and torture. The English hatred of 'Popery' would shape the fortunes of the Stuart dynasty and directly impact the lives of Aphra Behn and Harriet Berkeley, but in the seventeenth century Maryland offered a somewhat unlikely refuge for those who remained loyal to the doctrines of Rome. Lord Baltimore and his descendants held the colony in absolute authority, which meant that they were able to offer a greater degree of religious toleration to settlers than neighbouring Virginia.

The second Lord Baltimore continued the policy of freedom of conscience established by his father. Puritans and Catholics may have been at one another's throats back in England, but in Maryland, they were prepared to co-operate since neither confession wished to come under the increasingly strict regulation of Church of England orthodoxy. In the 1640s, William Berkeley was attempting to enforce the Church of England's rules for worship in Virginia. One man who fell foul of Berkeley's drive for religious conformity was Edward Lloyd. Born in 1620, Lloyd had been one of the many Puritans who set out for the New World in the first half of the seventeenth century. In Virginia in the mid-1640s, he was charged with refusing to attend Anglican services or to accept the Book of Common Prayer. In 1649, he moved to Maryland, where he offered his support to the Catholic Lord Baltimore and obtained several important posts, including parliamentary commissioner.

A significant degree of 'geographic mobility' has been confirmed within the English colonial community of the Western Atlantic. Lloyd's first home in Virginia was a port of call for cargo travelling between New England and the Caribbean. Livestock, corn, tobacco, naval supplies, timber, furs and, ever increasingly, slaves travelled along the network of routes which connected Barbados, Surinam, Massachusetts Bay, Maryland, Virginia and Providence Island off the coast of Nicaragua and further afield to Brazil, Europe and of course Africa. The reality of Western Atlantic life was considerably more cosmopolitan (for good and ill) than the stereotypical image of dour-faced fanatics in white shirt bands and black hats screeching about witches.

The Lloyd family became one of the greatest landholders – and slave owners – on the Eastern shore of North America. Their base was the 600-acre Wye Plantation in the county of Kent. Situated on the Chesapeake Bay, Kent was enrolled as a county in 1632 and merged with Talbot county in 1661. Cecil county was part of Kent until 1659. The local tobacco crop, a lesser quality leaf kept for domestic use rather than export, was of a type named 'Oronoco'.

Suppose that all the information about Aphra Behn was both right and wrong? Suppose that her mother was Thomas Colepeper's wet nurse and that the Countess of Winchilsea was correct in claiming that she was from Wye in Kent? Supposing she was a lady, of a sort? How might that story look?

Colepeper says that Aphra's mother was his wet nurse, not that her name was Elizabeth Johnson or even Elizabeth Denham. So a woman who was nursing at the end of 1637 when Colepeper was born could have subsequently left Kent, England and travelled to Kent, Maryland. Initially male settlers considerably outnumbered female, but many women did make the long, daunting journey, which one account describes thus:

> all was darkness, stench, lamentation, disease and death . . . more than one fifth of those shipped were flung to the sharks before the end of the voyage.*

Those who survived included the white population who came to be known on Barbados as 'Redlegs' and convicts who had been transported under the Cromwell regime as well as indentured servants. These latter went to the New World in small but significant numbers. Almost all the women who emigrated to Maryland did so in this fashion, though family groups did come to settle increasingly in the mid-century. 'Indenture' meant that a person contracted to work for a period of four to five years without pay in return for their passage. In 1650 there were 400 men registered in Maryland and 200 women, the majority of whom were aged 18–25, with half being 20–22. However, servants under the age of 21 were frequently not registered.

For women who survived the journey and the harsh working conditions, a further risk as an indentured servant was giving birth to a bastard. One fifth of the

---

* John Cod, quoted in Macaulay, T. B., *The History of England from the Accession of James the Second* (1848)

indentured women arraigned at Charles county court for the period were charged with pregnancies out of wedlock. Indentured servants could not legally marry unless the remainder of their service was paid off, and helpless mothers could be fined, whipped or have up to two years added to their service if they were unable to pay. It was hardly an enticing opportunity, but some English-born women were prepared to risk it. Poverty, criminality, the shame of an illegitimate pregnancy or destitution due to the loss of fathers, brothers or husbands in the Civil War were all motives to start afresh.

Yet once released from indenture, the colonies offered more opportunities than many women might perhaps have found at home. A woman could reinvent herself, much to the disgust of some commentators. The colonies were 'the Dunghill whereon England doth cast forth its . . . rubbish. A Bawd brought over puts on a demure comportment, a whore if handsome makes a wife for some rich planter.'* In Maryland, high male mortality rates (70 per cent of men died before the age of fifty), along with a high ratio of men to women and a legal age of majority for women of sixteen meant that women had plenty of opportunity for marriage and, better still, for widowhood, which

* 'Extracts from Henry Whistler's Journal of the West India Expedition [1654-1655]', Charles H. Firth, ed., *The Narrative of General Venables, with an Append of Papers Relating to the Expedition to the West Indies and the Conquest of Jamaica, 1654–1655* (1900)

meant legal independence and perhaps inheritance. Most of the early generation of female settlers in Maryland married in their mid-twenties, and 'serial polyandry' was common. A woman could thus move up the social scale through a succession of marriages, acquiring property and wealth husband by husband.

This is precisely the tactic of the Widow Ranter, the heroine of another work from the end of Aphra Behn's career, *The Widow Ranter, or, The History of Bacon in Virginia*. The piece echoes the suspicion of the potential for crooks to fraudulently re-invent themselves in the New World:

> They say your Honour was but a broken Excise-Man, who spent the King's money to buy your wife fine Petticoats, and at last not worth a Groat, you came over a poor servant, though now a justice of the Peace, and of the Honourable Council.

The Widow has also arrived as an indentured servant, 'bought from the ship by Colonel Ranter', who she persuades to marry her after six months. A year more and the Colonel is dead and his widow a rich woman, with 'Fifty Thousand Pounds Sterling, besides Plate and Jewels'.

(Incidentally, Philemon, the son of Edward Lloyd of Wye, Kent, married a rich Catholic widow named Henrietta Maria Nede Bennett.)

The mystery of Aphra Behn's identity might be beginning to look rather different, especially when considering that Anne Finch, Countess of Winchilsea, was a close friend of Thomas Killigrew's niece, Anne Killigrew. Born a year apart, both Annes were amongst the six Maids of Honour appointed to the Duchess of York, Mary of Modena after her marriage to Charles II's brother James. Both women wrote poetry, though Anne Finch did not make her talent public until the end of her life. Anne Killigrew circulated her poems in manuscript at court and was also a highly accomplished painter. A self-portrait hangs in Berkeley Castle, while another painting, *Venus Attired by the Graces*, features her friend Anne Finch. Anne Killigrew died of small-pox aged just twenty-five, eulogized in a celebrated poem by John Dryden; Anne Finch retired from court to her husband's seat in Kent when James II lost his crown in 1689. The connection between the two Annes suggests another possibility for the note in the Countess of Winchilsea's manuscript. She may have been thinking of another local Aphra Behn entirely when she wrote of the barber's daughter from Wye, England. Or she *may* have been reporting what 'some Persons now alive' had heard from her lost friend Anne Killigrew and her uncle Thomas, that the playwright Aphra Behn had been born in Wye, Kent. It would be natural for her to assume that it was the English, rather than the American village.

Colepeper does state (though it was already public knowledge), that Aphra's maiden name was Johnson, a fact that Anne, Countess of Winchilsea did not contest. There were lots of Johnsons in Cecil and Kent counties in Maryland, including a David Johnson, a Cornelius Johnson and a John Johnson who all died in the 1680s. There were also lots of Aphras (or variant spellings), and the name persists in the records until the nineteenth century. There were also lots of Behns in Maryland and at least one, Abraham Behn, who died in 1704, on Barbados.

Colepeper's wet-nurse story doesn't quite, as we have seen, fit Eaffrey Johnson's mother. Colepeper may have simply presumed that the woman who suckled him was Aphra's mother, inferring it from the name Johnson and the biographical information already available. Or perhaps he just wanted to believe it. It's an odd fib to tell, but then Colepeper was an odd man – the *Adversaria* has a touch of celebrity mania to it in its obsessive attempts to aggrandize its author's genealogy. The lure of what we now term 'parasocial' relationships – connections or imagined connections between an individual and a fictional character, celebrity or other public figure – may have been as strong in the seventeenth century as it is in the twenty-first. Aphra Behn was famous and Thomas Colepeper thought he should be, which may have been enough.

Indeed there is a slight, a very slight hint in Aphra's play *The Feign'd Curtizans* that Colepeper might have tried to claim acquaintance with her when she had become successful and well known in London. The comic butt of the plot, Sir Credulous, is a Kent land-owner making the Grand Tour to Italy. His newly acquired Continental pretensions include renaming his valet 'Jack Pepper' as a more glamorous Giovanni. If this is a faint allusion to the Kentish Colepeper it's a bit of a slap-down, a poke at someone who made a life's work of namedropping. More pertinent perhaps is that Aphra never drew on the Colepeper connection, even in her not-infrequent moments of financial desperation. Colepeper's mother, Lady Barbara Sidney, had been the daughter of the Earl of Leicester, with kinship ties to some of the greatest families in the land, yet Aphra never once called on her supposed foster-brother's contacts for funds or commissions.

The name Johnson, however, does seem to some-how stick.

An alternative version of Aphra's story, then, might go like this: a young woman leaves England, possibly after an unwanted pregnancy which permitted her to act as a wet nurse. She arrives in Maryland, where she marries and gives birth to a daughter, and then per-haps remarries, ascending the social ladder in the process. Moving in the fluid world of the Western Atlantic colonies, she leaves Wye, Kent, possibly via Barbados, for Surinam.

Like the Eaffrey Johnson theory, this is of course no more than speculation, but there are various bio-graphical suggestions which fit this version better than the Canterbury origin story. The first is Aphra Behn's fascination with Catholicism. She possessed an 'extraordinary knowledge of Catholic institutions and rituals not easily explained by a Kentish childhood'.* Convents feature frequently in her writing, and whilst as a consequence of anti-Catholic prejudice the cloister in seventeenth-century writing is often the locus for a fascination with depravity, the scenery of an exotic, corrupting Europe, Aphra's knowledge of how they functioned is more detailed than most. Her story *The Fair Jilt* includes a knowledgeable list of the various orders of Catholic nuns, including more obscure communities such as the 'Jesuitesses' (Dominicans), and her story *The History of the Nun* has its narrator declare herself to have once 'been design'd a humble Votary in the House of Devotion'. In her novel *Love Letters*, Aphra pokes fun at the lavishness of an aristocratic monastery whose luxuries are the inverse of ascetic spirituality:

> In my opinion 'tis here a man may hope to become a Saint sooner than in any other, more perplex'd with Want, Cold and all the necessaries of life which takes the thought too much from Heaven and afflicts it with the cares of the World.

An early knowledge of Catholicism does not indeed sit easily with an upbringing in Kent, England, where

---

* Todd, ibid.

Catholics were practically outlaws under Cromwell's regime. In Kent, Maryland the opposite was true. The colony was named after Henrietta Maria, Charles I's Catholic Queen; the governor's active promotion of Catholics (as enshrined in the 1649 Maryland Act of Toleration) attracted an immigrant Catholic gentry class, and the Catholic tradition of the colony was to produce the first convent for women on American soil, founded by Marylander Ann Matthews in the following century. Similar though unofficial toleration of Catholics was also the practice in Barbados and Surinam. Confessional intermarriages, such as that of the heir to the Wye plantation, did take place, and exposure to Catholic doctrine and custom, if not the glories of devotional art and music present on the European Continent, was therefore far more probable.

The second reason to query the Eaffrey Johnson theory is that whilst much of Aphra's poetry celebrates the pastoral idyll of a lost golden age, she didn't locate it in Kent. She does not reference the beauties of the Kentish countryside or of Canterbury's architecture. If she did grow up there, it has left very little impression in her work as compared with the New World of *Oroonoko* and *The Widow Ranter*.

A third and perhaps the most significant reason is Aphra's connection with the Marten family. The George Marten who is mentioned so warmly in *Oroonoko* was born in London in 1608. He chose the

Parliamentary side in the Civil War, serving as the captain of his family-owned boat, the *Marten*, and attaining the rank of Colonel. In 1644 he was employed as a spy for the Parliamentarians in France – Marten spoke and wrote French fluently. George married his wife Frances Weld, a member of a successful City merchant family with Catholic connections, in 1638. Like the Killigrews, the Weld family had interests in the colonies; Frances's grandfather, Sir Humfrey Weld, served as a lord mayor of London and, along with Sir Robert Killigrew, was one of the signatories to the second Charter of Virginia. The American branch of the Weld family was a significant presence in Massachusetts from the early seventeenth century. In partnership with his brother Henry, George made several visits to the colonies and in 1646 sailed for Barbados, where he set up as a sugar planter, working an estate of 259 acres with the labour of sixty slaves.

Politically, the playwriting Aphra Behn was firmly Royalist, but this did nothing to diminish her expressed early fondness for Marten, despite the fact that his elder brother Henry, described in *Oroonoko* as 'Harry Marten the great Oliverian', was one of the most politically prominent signatories to Charles I's death warrant. Like Thomas Scot, the father of William, Aphra's mark on her spying mission, he was a regicide. George Marten's impeccably loyal Parliamentary connection had thus made him the obvious choice as envoy for Lord Willoughby in 1650, when Royalist

Barbados had to renegotiate its status within the new republican regime.

Henry Marten was a brilliant, uncompromising character, a committed republican MP who in 1643 had been banned from attending Parliament for advocating the eradication of the monarchy in the House of Commons. In the early years of the Civil Wars this was unpardonable extremism, but as the political barometer under Cromwell began to swing towards precisely that resolution, Marten found himself once more in favour. In 1649 he was made a member of the Council of State and awarded £1,000 per year as a reward for his commitment to the republican cause. This didn't prevent him from getting hopelessly into debt and by 1655 he was languishing in the Upper Bench prison in Southwark, owing his creditors the astronomical sum of £35,000. Unlike his fellow regicide Thomas Scot, Henry Marten managed almost incredibly to escape execution at the Restoration. He had remained true to his principles, claiming he should not have agreed to the execution of King Charles had he known he was paving the way for King Cromwell, but it was his very un-Puritanical lifestyle which contributed to his reprieve. The judge, Lord Falkland, was reported to have commented, 'Gentlemen, ye here talk of making a sacrifice, it was the old Lawe, all Sacrifices were to be without spot or blemish; and now you are going to make an old Rotten Rascal a Sacrifice. This Wit took in the House, and saved his life.'

Writing to his brother Henry from Barbados in 1652, George Marten confirmed that the island was 'in a willing and cheerful obedience to the Parliament, the supreme authority of England'. The brothers had much in common besides their political beliefs, as by 1658 George too was bankrupt. Apparently, both Martens loved a party. According to the diarist John Aubrey, Henry had squandered half of his estate on 'pretty girls', and both he and George spent with reckless extravagance on drink and finery. George moved to Surinam in an attempt to re-establish himself but died in an outbreak of plague there in 1666.

Aphra's comments on George Marten in *Oroonoko* bear out his reputation as a charming womanizer:

> a man of great gallantry, wit and goodness and whom I have celebrated in a character of my new comedy by his own name in memory of so brave a man. He was wise and eloquent, and, from the fineness of his parts, bore a great sway over the hearts of all the colony.

Caesar/Oroonoko expresses 'great respect' for Colonel Marten, which makes his end all the more horrible. The royal slave is slowly cut to pieces, a torture which he endures by smoking his pipe of (oronoko?) tobacco to the end. His body is quartered and in the penultimate paragraph one of the pieces sent to George Marten, who swears 'he had rather see the quarters of . . . the governor himself, than those of Caesar, on his plantations and that he could govern his Negroes without terrifying and grieving them with the spectacle of a mangled king.' Such a spectacle was precisely what Henry Marten had given his consent to at the execution of Charles I, yet Aphra does not condemn him.

The Marten brothers were anti-monarchist yet their religious views did not tally simplistically with the strict Protestantism of many of their fellow Parliamentary republicans. John Aubrey described Henry Marten as 'as far from a Puritan as light from darkness'. Henry loathed royalty, but he championed religious freedom, including for Catholics. George's wife Frances Weld was from a family of Catholic sympathizers; three of her brothers were prominent recusants (Catholics who practised in secret), with one of them, Humphrey, founding a Catholic dynasty at Lulworth Castle in Dorset, which he purchased in 1641. George and Frances had twelve children, the first of whom, their daughter Frances, was born in 1638, the year of their marriage. Frances senior herself died (presumably of exhaustion) in London in 1650. It is not clear whether she had accompanied her husband to Barbados, but it seems unlikely, as George was an indiscreetly unfaithful husband. On Barbados he lived openly with a woman to whom he gave the jolly nickname 'butter box', though no more than that is known about her.

The affable gallant of Aphra Behn's portrait of

George Marten does not tally with other contemporary accounts, one of which describes him as 'old, overgrown, desperate and malignant'. Beyond the sympathetic lens of *Oroonoko*, George Marten emerges as a hard-drinking spendthrift, a disillusioned and ruined Parliamentarian with treacherous views on the Restoration regime. He did not entirely neglect his family responsibilities, however, as amongst the five letters he wrote to his brother Henry whilst the latter was imprisoned for debt in 1657 is a request for help in bringing another daughter, Susan, out to Barbados.

A close reading of *Oroonoko* throws up the concern of its narrator to emphasize her social status. Along with the descriptions in the story of fine clothes and servants including a maid and a footman (who comes to a most unfortunate end), Aphra writes in her dedication that she herself was unable to intervene in Caesar/Oroonoko's terrible fate despite the fact that 'though I had none above me in that country, yet I wanted power to preserve that great man'. It is also notable that the narrator makes a point of her absence during Caesar/Oroonoko's demise, as she herself is up-country with Colonel Marten, unlike her mother and sister. She stresses her intimacy with this man whose political views were anathema to her and whose real-life habits and character were not as appealing as her depiction.

The Eaffrey Johnson identification for Aphra has established her birth year as well as her birthplace

Quite possibly the latter may be erroneous, but what about the former? In 1913 a very bad-tempered academic named Ernest Bernbaum published a paper entitled *Mrs Behn's Biography: A Fiction*. Professor Bernbaum's portrait of Aphra's character stops just short of loathing and he is particularly scathing about the 'underestimation' of Aphra's age presented in the *Memoir*, which states of *Oroonoko* that the author could not have been expected to be in love with the 'real-life' Caesar/Oroonoko as at the time the story takes place she was hardly out of childhood. The *Memoir* is in no way reliable, but if the Eaffrey Johnson story is rejected, then the date of Aphra's birth becomes more flexible – it is possible that she was born somewhat later than 1640 and (just) possible that George Marten was her father.

Martens, Welds, Killigrews, Berkeleys, all English gentry families with connections in the West Atlantic and the London theatre. George Marten, a French-speaking former spy, brother to a regicide. A young woman with a sister called Frances, who meets the son of another regicide in Surinam and is then set to spy on him. A plantation at Wye, Kent, with a strong connection to Catholicism and links to Barbados. Maryland registers full of Johnsons and Behns. A novel whose educated narrator has pretensions to a high but indeterminate social rank. A writer who returns at the end of her career to stories set in the colonies. Behind the accepted version of Aphra's biography waits another, a network of ghosts, frail to be sure, but none-theless compelling.

George Marten does appear in *The Younger Brother*, the 'next comedy' to which Aphra refers in the introduction of *Oroonoko*. He is the first character to enter, explaining to his valet that despite the 'slavery' of his status as a second son he needs a splendid coach and rich liveries for his servants, 'for 'tis Appearance only passes in the world'. Aphra's *The Widow Ranter*, set in Virginia, was dedicated posthumously at the author's request to a 'Madame Welldon', whose identity remains unknown to date.

Aphra Behn as the bastard daughter of an English planter born in America and brought up in the West Indies is no more *implausible* than Aphra Behn the barber's daughter from Canterbury. If Aphra were the product of a relationship between George Marten and a Maryland immigrant mother who remained attached to his household, it would explain not only her familiarity with Surinam and her language skills (for Dutch was spoken there as well as French), but her attraction to Catholicism, the curious appearances and vanishings of her mother and 'younger brother', her opportunity for education and her almost fanatical secretiveness about her past. Crucially it also sheds light on Aphra's appointment by Thomas Killigrew to spy on William Scot. She didn't arrive in Surinam as a spy, but she left as one.

George Marten's business had gone no better there than on Barbados and by the early 1660s the English position in 'Willoughbyland' was increasingly precarious. Perhaps it went something like this – Aphra's father was finding it increasingly hard to provide for his family and Aphra had formed some sort of relationship with Scot. It may have been a useful moment for the natural daughter of a struggling Parliamentarian planter to prove her loyalty to the English King, so Aphra agreed to leave for London, possibly even to lure Scot there after her. Her visit may have been planned as temporary, with the intention of her returning home, but events intervened – in 1665 London was consumed by the Great Plague, then Scot left for Holland, where Aphra followed him, but by the time she had returned to London, Surinam had fallen to the Dutch and George Marten was dead. Aphra found herself alone and unconnected in the great city and turned to what was possibly her only marketable talent, perhaps a cherished secret ambition, and became a writer.

It is by no means a perfect story but it is just as probable, or improbable, as that of Eaffrey Johnson. However it was contrived, Aphra did go to London from Surinam and when she arrived she was sent directly to Thomas Killigrew.

(NOTE: It has been beyond the scope of this book to prove a definitive connection between Aphra and George Marten and, obviously, this suggestion raises as many questions as it (tentatively) answers. Who was Aphra's mother and why did the name 'Johnson' hover so persistently? Did Anne Finch mix up Wye in England with Wye in Maryland? Was she referring to

another Aphra whose father was a barber? Conversely, what would have persuaded a young woman living in respectable circumstances in the colonies to travel across the world as a secret agent? Consultation with professional archivists has revealed that the Eaffrey Johnson theory does not meet what is known as the 'Genealogical Proof Standard', that is, it would be inadmissible for legal purposes. If Eaffrey was not Aphra, then the possibilities for further research and discoveries about her life are absolutely thrilling.)

5

Aphra was fascinated by the relationship between writing and painting. Hers was an intensely visual age, where sight, for good or bad, was believed to have a visceral effect. The poet, she wrote, was a type of painter, in that she depicted reality, but unlike artists, writers could summon 'the nobler part, the soul and mind' in addition to the material image. A poem could be an incorporeal painting, a painting a corporeal poem, but in the dedication to *Oroonoko* Aphra boldly asserts that 'the pictures of the pen shall outlast those of the pencil'. In her stories, Aphra is sensuously alert to colour and texture, to the gleam of silk or the rich patina of stone. Her description of the 'unconceivable tinctures' of the feathers used by the Surinam Indians to make 'glorious wreaths for their heads, necks, arms and legs' is confirmed by a manuscript note at Worcester College, Oxford, which describes the effect of a set of these 'speckled plumes' on a London theatre audience. The feathers in question were a gift from Aphra to Killigrew at the King's Theatre, where they were used in a production of a play by John Dryden and Robert Howard, *The Indian Queen*. Aphra was delighted with their reception, remarking that they were 'unimitable' and 'greatly admired by persons of quality'.

The use of the feathers in Killigrew's production helps to determine the date of Aphra's arrival in London. *The Indian Queen* was first performed in January 1664. Aphra departed from Surinam around February that year. The play was revived in 1667 with the feathers making another appearance in its sequel, *The Indian Emperor*, which was watched by Samuel Pepys and his wife in November that year. Assuming Aphra was telling the truth about the provenance of the feathers, they must have featured in this second production, and the interesting question is what happened to them in between. Of course, they could have been stored anywhere until they were brought into use, but Aphra's life was peripatetic between 1664 and 1667, not to mention at times gravely impoverished. How could she have taken care of such precious and delicate items, or at least not be tempted to sell them? Perhaps the feathers had another purpose.

When Lord Willoughby wrote back to England from Barbados mentioning Tom Killigrew's two sons, he had made a mistake. Thomas Killigrew had one son, Henry, born of his first marriage to Cecilia Crofts in 1637, and three boys by his second wife, Charlotte de Hesse, the eldest of whom was just two years old when Willoughby made his report. Henry was on Barbados by 1655 when he joined the clan of Killigrews already resident there, which included the family of another Henry Killigrew, who possessed a substantial estate. Willoughby may have been mistaking Killigrew cousins for Killigrew sons or he may have been referring to an illegitimate child. What matters is that within the small planter class of Barbados gentry, the Killigrews and the Martens knew one another.

Thomas Killigrew was aware that William Scot was in Surinam at the same time as Aphra. He knew that some sort of relationship had developed between them and he chose the codenames 'Astrea' and 'Celadon', used in the letters documenting their departure, for the mission he later gave to Aphra. There doesn't seem to be any particular reason for Eaffrey Johnson to have been selected to travel to Surinam as a honeytrap for Scot, but there was quite a good one for a young woman already present there and familiarly associated with the Parliamentarian Martens to have been persuaded to get close to him. Scot would have trusted Aphra if she came from a similarly compromised political background to his own. When Aphra returned to London it appears that she remained in contact with Scot before following him to the Netherlands (as suggested by the reference to the 'Shee-correspondent', see p. 71), and in between she met Thomas Killigrew. It's interesting to think that the 'unimitable' Indian feathers could have acted as a sort of passport or proof of identity between her and Thomas Killigrew, a rare and unusual object, expensive and unobtainable in London, which would prove to Killigrew that 'Astrea' was who she claimed to be.

Picture Aphra then, disembarking with relief from the cramped and stinking ship in the spring of 1664. It was probably raining. It was certainly shockingly cold after the climate of Surinam. The city in which Aphra Behn arrived was one of the most exciting and dynamic in the world. It was also one of the loudest and smelliest. London *roared*. Bells from the 130 parish churches within and without the ancient City walls, shouting footmen running beside the coaches of the 'quality', trumpets, coach-horns, goats, pigs, dogs, cows scattering through unpaved streets where foundries, smithies, mills thumped and hammered, ironmongers, coopers, coppersmiths, armourers banged and bellowed, watchmen shouting the hour, chairmen jostling, street vendors crying the peculiar argot of their wares, alehouses spilling boisterous drinkers, singers and sermonizers on the corners, acrobats tumbling, hawkers shrieking, knifegrinders sawing and everywhere at once the clacking trip of three hundred and seventy thousand and growing inhabitants rushing to business or pleasure in the 'hideous din' of the 'Noisie Town'.

Add the filth, the pall of smog and smuts that hung across the medieval streets, the smoke that lingered in cellars and spewed from garrets, twining the town between ghost-grey fingers. Add the stench, human and animal excrement from gutters and 'boghouses', stewing rubbish piled in middens, the sweat of horses, the foul bubblings of the tanneries, acrid coal-dust, thick river slime.

Then add pleasure and profit, the twin poles between which London dances on a tightrope of luxury. Below is the morass of ruin, the prisons where the debtors loll in mouldering silks and the divines shake their heads over where this craze for grandeur will end. London is dizzy for excitement, for balls and masquerades, for china and chocolate, for dancing masters, hairdressers, exquisite furniture, delicate perfumes, everything that is novel and fine. The East India Company combs every corner of the known world to produce the gown and accessories of a single fine lady. Greedy London is bursting its boundaries, swelling westwards from the confines of the old City to the elegant squares and red-brick facades of the new homes of the rich. Great draughts of luxury flow into London's maw; the city bulges, insatiable. And if there is no ready money to supply its wants, London can satisfy its cravings on credit. The ladies and gentlemen of the court find the milliner or the silversmith to be most accommodating, so why resist the new silk bonnet or the latest sword, what matter if the coal merchant is unpaid or the butcher's children go hungry? The King himself is the greatest debtor of them all, so what matter if one can appear in splendour at the play?

London was an assault on the senses. Picture Aphra then, crossing its vastness from the docks, making for the fashionable quarter of the West End. We know absolutely nothing about her circumstances at the time, whether she had the funds to take a boat up the river or hire a hackney carriage, or whether she would have trudged through the fringes of the City towards Whitehall clutching the precious plumes in her bundle.

The *Memoirs* claim that Aphra had an interview with the King himself on her return to London, during which she pleased him with a 'pleasant and rational Account of his Affairs there'. As ever, they are not to be trusted, particularly as the first part of the account is largely a puff for *Oroonoko*, but it does observe that Charles expressed himself 'satisfied of her abilities in the Management of Business and the Fidelity of our Heroine to his Interest'. Charles's restless intellect was always excited by novelty, and he was definitely not averse to meeting young ladies, so the prospect of inspecting a potential recruit for his intelligence service fresh off the boat from Surinam might well have piqued his interest.

Whitehall Palace was a city within the city, a huge complex of state rooms and galleries, gardens and apartments which had been the principal residence of English royalty since Henry VIII's time. Neglected since the death of its last inhabitant, Oliver Cromwell, in 1658, £8,000 had been spent on restoring Whitehall before Charles returned. The restored King had plans to rebuild the palace, remodelling it on the splendid lines of the house his cousin Louis XIV was constructing at Versailles, but the cash-strapped crown never did get around to it, and until it was destroyed by fire in 1698 Whitehall retained a ramshackle air, where regal magnificence contrasted with makeshift accommodations which were never quite adequate to house the thousands of people – members of the royal family, courtiers and their servants – who lived there.

By the time of Aphra's supposed visit, the private royal theatre, the Cockpit, had been restored, as had the Privy Garden with its sundial and the King's bedroom, floored in chequered marble, its great canopied bed topped with golden eagles. Charles's apartments, later known as the Volary building after the aviary which had once stood there, were a positive bazaar of precious objects – lacquered cabinets, silver chandeliers, huge gold candlesticks, tables and chairs in rare, imported woods, carved mirrors, draperies, tapestries and paintings – whose lavishness astonished onlookers – 'massy pieces of plate, whole tables, stands &co of incredible value'. Even the King's beloved spaniel dogs had specially made cushions of Venetian damask. The impression made by such surroundings on someone from a simple background would have been, as it was intended to be, utterly stupefying.

In her later writing, Aphra displayed unswerving respect, even reverence for the House of Stuart, and given her attraction to the sumptuous it is tempting to think that the source of this devotion might have been this first overwhelming visual encounter with majesty in all its mystical splendour. Later events however suggest that if Aphra did meet Charles in person she never felt confident enough to approach him again. If she did glimpse the King in the early 1660s it was far more likely to have been at the theatre.

The playhouse was the nexus for London's profligacy and dissipation, the moralists warned, encouraging pretensions to grandeur whilst distracting citizens from the honest business of getting and spending. The theatre was a flimsy, transient reality, where apprentices could lord it with the lords in the pit and ladies coquetted from the boxes, masked, patched and painted like the whores touting for custom beneath them. If the play was slow, there was always the alternative of peering into the royal box to snatch a peek at the city's greatest showman.

Charles II was always a performer, a player king. More than any other monarch's, his reign is associated with the theatre, with the thrilling glamour of its artifice and disguise. His decade-long struggle to regain his throne had marked his personality profoundly; there was a darkness within him, an inscrutable sadness that no amount of parties or pleasure could ever quite chase away. Charles had experienced diplomatic disloyalty and political treachery during the years of his exile, but he had also known a real poverty which was entirely beyond the experience of any of his fellow rulers. Somehow he never quite seemed to believe that his was not merely a tinsel crown. In the spring of 1660, he had been advised by the Duke of

Newcastle that he should display himself before his people 'like a God', for 'nothing keeps up a King like ceremony and order, which makes Distance and this brings respect and Duty', yet however dazzling the court which Charles created, it retained a gimcrack quality, perhaps because its leading actor was never quite able to believe entirely in his role.

The King's return to London had been an extended piece of theatre, designed to awe and impress the crowds which gathered to witness it. After his landing in Dover, Charles had first proceeded to Canterbury to pay his respects to the memory of his father in a three-day visit during which the city's mayor presented him with a solid gold tankard. Eaffrey Johnson of Harbledown may likely have been amongst the crowds who celebrated his return to the joyous chorus of church bells, dancing along streets decorated with flags and pennants where the public fountains ran with wine. The King's entry into London had been timed to coincide with his thirtieth birthday on 29th May (significantly, thirty was, according to the Gospel of St Luke, the age at which Christ had begun his ministry), and as he progressed towards the capital his minister Edward Hyde recollected that it seemed as though the whole kingdom had turned out to greet him.

The diarist John Evelyn described the seven hours it took for Charles's escort of 20,000 cheering soldiers to accompany him from Blackheath into London, with 'The Mayor, Aldermen, all the Companies in their Liveries, Chains of Gold, banners, Lords and Nobles, Cloth of Silver gold and velvet everybody clad in, the windows and balconies all set with Ladies, Trumpets and people flocking the streets.' The 'shouting and joy' wrote Samuel Pepys, 'were beyond all imagination.'

To many, the Restoration was nothing short of miraculous, so improbable had it seemed just a few years earlier, but Charles was aware that beneath the public rejoicing dissent still lurked between hastily turned coats. The re-establishment of London's theatres might not have seemed a particularly important priority for a new monarch, but Charles was aware of the power of the stage to influence opinion, and when he granted the patents of London's two theatre companies to Thomas Killigrew and William Davenant in 1662, he was not only rewarding them for their loyalty but effectively instituting the PR branch of the throne. The playhouses served to underline the difference between the old and new regimes, enhancing the new monarch's reputation for cultivated liberality. (That the theatres also emphasized Charles's reputation as an incorrigible philanderer was perhaps not quite part of the original brief.)

Davenant and Killigrew have often been portrayed as deadly rivals, but their relationship over the ensuing seven years was demonstrably business-like and collegiate. Certainly, they were to compete for writers, actors and of course audiences, but the duopoly of their two companies, the Duke's and the King's, functioned of necessity in tandem, offering the choice and fluctuations of fashionability which kept playgoers coming back for more.

Davenant had been a fixture of London's theatre world long before the Restoration. Born the son of a wine merchant in 1606, he was by far Killigrew's social inferior, but his links to the glory days of the early seventeenth-century stage lent him a roguish authority. His parents had been great friends with William Shakespeare, and Davenant did nothing to dispel the myth that his mother had been very close indeed to England's greatest playwright. He was a talented and ambitious writer who at the age of twenty-two had attained the post of Vice Chamberlain to Charles II's mother Queen Henrietta Maria (recalling that Thomas Killigrew's father also became a Vice Chamberlain, it is clear how closely both theatrical dynasties were allied with the court) and before the Civil Wars had created many of the 'masques' – gorgeous productions involving music, elaborate scenery and ingenious stage machinery – in which the otherwise rather sedate court of Charles I rejoiced. Charles II had performed in one such spectacle with both his parents, the last masque of the old world, before the wars came to claim them.

Davenant naturally elected for the Royalists during the wars and, after receiving a knighthood from the King for his services, was imprisoned in the Tower by Cromwell in the mid-1650s, whence the circumstances of his release were to prove significant for the career of Aphra Behn. Freed in 1655, Davenant had cautiously begun to experiment with means of getting round the strict laws against playhouses by reviving the masque-style performances which had been so popular before the wars.

The Cromwellian regime abhorred the licentiousness of the stage, but Cromwell himself adored music. Stories told with music, similar to the old court masques, were somehow less sinful than plays. Even the Lord Protector himself had taken a turn as Jove in a private production at Hampton Court. Davenant exploited the loophole this created by staging musical variety performances at his home near Smithfield, for which he charged five shillings a ticket. Government inspectors attended a performance and saw nothing immoral in it, after which Davenant became bolder. In 1656 his improvised theatre performed his work *The Siege of Rhodes*, described by the diarist Evelyn as consisting of 'recitative music and scenes' in the Italian fashion and considered to be the first English opera. The production was also notable in that it featured the first English woman, Catherine Coleman, to appear professionally on the stage. Despite this, Davenant convinced the fun police that opera was an entirely innocent pastime and three years later, as the incredible rumours of the King's return started to gather strength, he began to look for a real theatre of his own once more.

Aphra's first plays would be performed at what had formerly been Lisle's tennis court on the western side of Lincoln's Inn Fields. The brilliant and cruelly over-looked architect John Webb designed a wooden shell within the walls of the original space with a raised stage surmounted by Davenant's great innovation, the pro-scenium arch. Tiered boxes and galleries flanked and faced the stage, which had flies and wings to allow for scenery and 'machines' to be moved with maximum speed and efficiency. This grand, Italian-style model became the prototype for theatre building for the next three centuries. In 1671 the Duke's Company moved on to an even more splendid home, a purpose-built theatre at Dorset Garden on the banks of the Thames, with a deep apron stage on which flats of scenery could be moved, woodwork by Grinling Gibbons, marble col-umns and a huge backstage area where the 'machines' for special effects could be housed. Audiences could even arrive Venetian-style, stepping from their wherries or barges into a VIP water-gate.

Thomas Killigrew's King's Company had operated in its temporary space until the opening of the Theatre Royal on Drury Lane in May 1663. Samuel Pepys's com-ments on the new building suggest that London theatre-goers had become quite the connoisseurs in the three years they had been attending the playhouses. On the whole Pepys considered the building finished with 'good contrivance', but he knowledgeably criticized the narrowness of the passages leading to the pit and the excessive distance between the stage and the boxes. These deficiencies were corrected when the first Theatre Royal was destroyed by fire in January 1672 and rebuilt in 1674. Its new incarnation was, like Dorset Garden, influenced by fashionable Italian architecture, reached by a passageway which opened into a 'campo' where the theatre stood. The architecture was long attributed to Christopher Wren, the stuccoed interiors were definitely by Robert Adam (Pepys approved), while its ornate Baroque auditorium contrasted with a sprawling den of dressing rooms, rehearsal spaces, a script library and copying room, an accounting department and storage for props.

Such a backstage world would be Aphra's home for many years, a candlelit chaos of industry and craft, flirtation and gossip, an ongoing performance in itself with insolent 'wits' strolling in to watch the actresses dressing, writers hastily scribbling down altered lines, the bangs and grunts of machinery being assembled and hauled into place, the frantic bustle as the house prepared for the afternoon performance, quarrels and love affairs conducted in snatched moments between acts.

Aphra is invisible for the two years of her first stay in London. It is quite possible that she began to attend the theatre, assuming her funds allowed, but after presumably depositing her feathers with Thomas Killigrew in his more modest apartment at Whitehall her movements are unknown. She did, however, apparently acquire a husband.

6

The task of pinning down Aphra Behn looks positively simple when compared to that of identifying her spouse. To put it plainly, we can't. If there was a Mr Behn, his Christian name is unknown, there is no record of their marriage, or of his death. The easiest solution to this enigma is that he didn't exist. In the seventeenth century, 'Mrs', the abbreviation of mistress, did not necessarily apply only to married women; rather it was a courtesy title which could be used broadly to refer to any woman who had passed girlhood. Female servants and actresses were routinely addressed as 'Mrs', so the fact that Aphra Behn used the prefix doesn't necessarily mean that she was married at all.

If Aphra was George Marten's daughter (see p. 89) then the maiden name Johnson might have indeed come from her mother or simply have been selected at random, being as common as 'Smith'. Illegitimate children were seldom given the name of their fathers (unless they were royal Fitzroys or Fitzcharleses). Possibly Behn might have been her name all along. The Abraham Behn who died on Barbados in 1703 was baptized in Delft on 22 January 1645, and whilst it is going too far to suggest any connection between him and Aphra, it does reinforce the link between the name and the Western Atlantic where, as has been noted, it was relatively common. Interestingly, Abraham Behn was a cook, which was also the profession of one of the candidates for Aphra's husband.

The posthumous *Memoirs* state that there was a Mr Behn, an 'eminent' London merchant of 'Dutch extraction', while Thomas Colepeper's *Adversaria* states that Aphra had a sister, Frances, who married a sea captain and that Aphra herself married a 'Mr Beene' at the same time. In 1655 a ship named the *King David* was commandeered by the English off Barbados. Amongst the forty members of the crew was a certain Johan Behn. The name of the ship's captain was Erick Wrede. In the *Adversaria*, Colepeper's spelling of the name of Frances's husband is illegible: it looks like 'Wrils' or 'Write', or, as has been posited, 'Wrede'.

Working from the timings of the letters from Surinam which allude to 'Astrea', it can be surmised that Aphra arrived in London in May 1664 and a ship named the *King David* was anchored there the following August. It has been suggested that Johan and Aphra somehow met in Surinam, that they voyaged back together and that their marriage took place soon after. Perhaps it was a double wedding with Frances and Erick as the second couple. It's a charming idea, but the dates pose the first problem. If the bridegrooms' ship arrived on Barbados in 1655, they would have had to travel to Surinam and hang around for eight years before meeting the 'Johnson' girls. So maybe the *King David* was trading to and from the Caribbean and put in at a later date. If Aphra was already in the colony she could have met Johan at any time, but his presence is not mentioned in any of the letters which allude to 'Astrea' and 'Celadon'. *Oroonoko* is by no means a guide to her time there, but equally it is the only source we have and some elements are factual, yet the novel makes no mention of the narrator enjoying any sort of romance. The only man with whom Aphra seems to have formed an attachment in Surinam is William Scot, who according to Byam's scornful claim left the colony in pursuit of her.

Frances is another problem. Colepeper's account is little more than a sketch, based on recorded sources spiced with his own assumptions, hearsay, or outright inventions. There is mention of a 'younger sister' in *Oroonoko*, but no more is heard of her. If Colepeper's smudgily written name for Frances's sea captain is close enough to 'Wrede' it might equally be close enough to 'Weld'. Recall that George Marten and his wife Frances Weld numbered a Frances and a Susan amongst their daughters, and that George requested Susan be assisted in coming out to join him on Barbados the year before he quit the colony for Surinam. Whether Susan went or not and whether Frances was there has not been confirmed. But if the party of 'Ladies' recorded as staying at St John's Hill plantation included Aphra, possibly her mother and possibly one or more of the Marten girls, then might they not have been sent back to London together when their father's business began again to fail?

Colepeper's account contains some half-forgotten, over-written truths – if he believed Aphra's sister was Frances Johnson, then her name being Weld Marten could be explained away by the romantic assumption of a seaboard marriage. (And of course, the Marten men were naval captains by trade.)

(NOTE: Drowning in a sea of red herrings, I spent some time on trying to discover whether Susan Weld Marten had travelled to Surinam, with the theory that an English Aphra might have accompanied her as a companion or maid who had possibly shared her mistress's education and the family inclination to Catholicism on the maternal side. The Weld girls' mother had died in 1650 and George Marten in 1666. Their uncle Henry Marten was living under arrest, so I investigated their three maternal uncles, Catholic recusants all, focusing particularly on Humphrey Weld of Lulworth. I had a fancy of finding Aphra amongst the Lulworth parish registers, a local Dorset girl who had gone into service with the squire's nieces, but nothing useful emerged.)

The next difficulty is Mr Behn's profession. There is very little evidence of him engaging in any commercial activities, which is hardly surprising if he were actually a cook. If Aphra had married a member of such a lowly profession, it's no wonder she wanted to keep it quiet in the status-obsessed arena of literary London, elevating him to a 'merchant' in later conversations.

An alternative Jochim Behn, who was indeed a master ship owner and merchant, born in Hamburg in 1611, has been proposed as Aphra's husband. They can't be the same man, as this would require them to have been in different ships at the same time, but Jochim could have met her in Surinam or on Aphra's return to London. This Mr Behn would have been fifty-three years old in 1664, considerably Aphra's senior, but he does seem a more likely fit.

In August 1667 an Italian ship's captain, Antonio Basso of Genoa, petitioned for the removal of English soldiers from his ship, the *Abraham's Sacrifice*. The vessel had been seized and taken into port at Galway where the goods it was carrying were unloaded and some of them stolen, on the grounds that the cargo belonged to the Dutch, with whom England had been at war at the time of the incident. Two years later, Mr Blathwayt, a representative of the English government, was sent to Amsterdam to settle the case at the admiralty court. The issue was one of compensation: if the goods were Dutch they were legitimate booty, but if they could be proven to be Genoese the King would be obliged to recompense their owners. The amount of money at stake was large enough for the English government to warn William Temple, the ambassador to The Hague, that 'if it should prove so His Majesty would be obliged to refund a great sum . . . to them'.

The case was a tremendous hassle for hardworking Mr Blathwayt, who wrote two letters back to London reporting on his frustrating progress, complaining that 'after so many proofs and testimonies of the goods belonging to Dutchmen they can have little to say for themselves'. One of them, undated, refers to 'the factor or the person that looks after the business of the Widow Behn'. This individual, whose name may have been Will (it is written next to the factor but it is not clear if the two are the same), was questioned by Blathwayt about the insurance of the goods. He refused to name anyone but confirmed that 'if this person should call any of the cargo theirs it is more probable it was so than that W Behn had any commission from Genoa for landing such goods.' Since the Widow Behn had no evidence of permission for loading her share of the cargo on to the *Abraham's Sacrifice* at Genoa, the goods were deemed to be Dutch and Blathwayt succeeded in settling the case.

No more is known about the 'Widow Behn'. If she was Aphra, the letters confirm that she was indeed married to a merchant, widowed, and involved through her husband in the shipping business. Further, the *Abraham's Sacrifice* papers connect her with the Dutch after her spying mission to Antwerp had ended. The Widow Behn was not present in Amsterdam to be questioned by Mr Blathwayt in 1669, but as we shall see, there may have been a good reason for her unavailability: that she was in prison for debt.

7

At the end of April 1664, around the moment when Aphra arrived in London from Surinam, Samuel Pepys confided to his diary that 'All the news now is of what will become of the Dutch business, whether war or peace. We all seem to desire it, as thinking ourselves to have advantages over them, but for my part I dread it.' War against Holland would directly touch Aphra in her upcoming spying mission, and its political repercussions would also cast a long shadow over her writing and her beliefs.

'Holland', as it was usually termed at the time, was a somewhat nebulous name. Until the sixteenth century, the Netherlands or Low Countries (covering modern-day Holland, Belgium, Luxembourg and parts of northern France) had been a patchwork of states, duchies and principalities controlled by the Hapsburg Empire. After a long series of revolts and war, the area was divided under the Peace of Westphalia in 1648, which confirmed the Seven United Provinces (Guelders, Holland, Zeeland, Utrecht, Overijssel, Frisia and Groningen) as a confederate republic whilst the remaining territories, collectively known as Flanders or the Spanish Netherlands, remained under Hapsburg control. The division reflected confessional differences: the United Provinces were (broadly) Protestant, Flanders (largely) Catholic. The government of the United Provinces was intimately bound with that of England, as Charles II's sister Princess Mary had been married at the age of nine to William II, Prince of Orange.

Nominally, the United Provinces were governed by elected 'stadtholders'; practically for many years this meant the rulers of the royal house of Orange. Elite and particularly royal marriages in the seventeenth century were affairs between families rather than individuals, instruments of policy rather than passion. Educated to believe in the power and precedence accorded her as Princess Royal, Mary had resented being pushed into the marriage with the fifteen-year-old William but had taken comfort in the plan that she would be permitted to remain with her parents until she was old enough for it to be consummated. In 1641, however, she had become the first Stuart exile of the Civil Wars, fleeing to the United Provinces with her mother, Queen Henrietta Maria (and the Crown Jewels), in an escape disguised as a royal progress. When her brother Charles joined her nine years later, Mary was the widowed head of a ruling dynasty while he, the boy born to rule England, was a bedraggled pauper living under an alias.

On her nineteenth birthday in 1650, Mary gave birth to a son, the future William III of England. Over the ensuing years, while she battled against her mother-in-law for her right to act as regent for her child, the United Provinces were fighting a war against the new Parliamentarian government. One of the conditions of the settlement of that conflict, in 1653, was that the House of Orange (and by proxy that of Stuart), should no longer be permitted to occupy the position of stadtholder. Mary lived to see Charles regain his crown and his kingdom, but she died of smallpox in December 1660, leaving instructions that her brother should be guardian to her ten-year-old boy. The United Provinces were at the time governed by Johan de Witt, since 1653 the leader of the Republican faction, and as was the case in the Caribbean, the respective exiles from the government in England swapped places. During the Interregnum, Charles II and his court had sought refuge in Holland, but now positions were reversed it became a safe haven for Parliamentarians on the run from the King. Even before the second Dutch War began, the United Provinces were swarming with anti-Royalist plotters.

In the early 1660s, anti-Dutch feeling was running high. The brilliant commercial successes of the United Provinces were viewed as an affront to re-royalized England, whilst the squabbles over colonial territories in West Africa and the Caribbean were intensifying. A form of unofficial proxy war was taking place, with Dutch and English ships attacking one another and raiding their respective overseas territories. Charles wrote to his younger sister Henriette about one such raid on the island of Manhattan: 'a very good town, but we have now got the better of it and 'tis now called New York.' The 'naval' faction of the English government, headed by the Duke of York, were keen for the English to augment their maritime domination, whilst the powerful East India Company had its eye on Dutch trade routes and overseas territories. Hawkish feeling was stoked by Sir George Downing, since 1657 ambassador to The Hague, who in alliance with Charles's close friend the Duke of Buckingham was pressuring him towards conflict. Downing's dispatches encouraged Charles to declare war, assuring him that the 'Hollanders' would quickly surrender. Charles was reluctant, and delayed as long as he could, but in March 1665 he gave in. On 13th June that year, the Battle of Lowestoft marked the first major encounter with the enemy, and while both sides claimed victory, the English had the better of it.

Jubilation at the promising start to the war was short-lived. A more ominous threat than Dutch warships was looming over England. Fleas, the carriers of bubonic plague, abounded in seaports and English fleas were believed to be particularly aggressive. The summer of 1665 was one of the hottest in living memory; Samuel Pepys recorded in his diary that the week of the 7th June was the warmest he had ever known. The fleas were on the move, circling London from the crowded docks to the inner slums, feasting on tightly packed, unwashed bodies in stifling rooms. Soon, the first symptoms began to appear: swelling in the groin, neck and armpits as the bacteria carried by the fleas attacked the lymph nodes, followed by fever, vomiting, blackened patches on the skin and death. There was no remedy and no defence. As Pepys wrote up his diary, seventeen people in London had already died of the plague; by the next week the figure was forty-three.

An urgent meeting of the King's Privy Council was called as wagons were drawing up at Whitehall, preparing to carry Charles and his court beyond the pestilence. Fifteen 'Rules and Orders' were issued, which included the banning of public gatherings and forbidding freedom of movement between towns for anyone not furnished with an authorized health certificate. The houses of the infected were to be closed up for forty days; permission was given for parishes to levy new taxes to support those unable to work. As red crosses began to appear on London's doors, the King left for Hampton Court and anyone who could fled to the country. Slowly the teeming capital churned to a halt, with the theatres, shops and businesses closed and the streets eerily empty. By September the court (including Killigrew and his theatre company) had retreated further, to Oxford, and the death toll had reached 1,000 per day. Quacks soon began to exploit those fearful, desperate inhabitants who had stayed behind, advertising 'Charms, Philters, Exorcisms and Amulets' at inflated prices. With few suppliers willing to send provisions into London, many people began to starve.

(The plague does put an end to the inconvenience of Mr Behn. If he ever existed at all, it may be safely assumed that he died of it. The whereabouts of Aphra herself during the pandemic remain unknown.)

In Bowling Green Lane in Clerkenwell on the edge of the City, the servants of Lord Berkeley hastily packed up the household's belongings. Unlike many of his fellow aristocrats, Lord Berkeley had resisted the temptation to move across London to the newly fashionable district of the West End. Berkeley House had been constructed by an earlier Baron Berkeley in the sixteenth century, a capacious brick and wood building with a large garden, more impressive for its size than its architectural polish. Named for the 'well' or spring whose water was believed to be healthful, Clerkenwell in the 1660s was still green and open, a pleasant spot for Londoners to take Sunday walks, and the district retained much of the mixed character of old London, where the different social classes lived side by side. Berkeley House was grand, but nearby was 'one of those mountain heaps of cinders and rubbish which disgraced old London' and a whipping post for the punishment of petty offenders still stood at the corner of the street. Lord Berkeley had remained in town in early summer for meetings about plague measures, but as the noisome rubbish heap by his garden wall steamed and stewed, he prepared to move his family, including his baby daughter Harriet, to safety.

The 9th Baron Berkeley had married Elizabeth Massingberd in 1646 when they were both in their teens and together they had eight children, of whom Harriet, born in 1664, was the last. Unlike the majority of aristocratic couples, the Berkeleys' marriage seems to have begun with genuine affection. A letter in the Berkeley Castle archives dating from just before their wedding addresses Elizabeth as 'Sweet Lady', and though the subject is practical – a recommendation for a servant – Lord Berkeley takes the opportunity to write that 'my very Soule honours you' and promises that 'if I may be so blessed as to have a return of your affection' his whole life will be a 'constant testimony' to his love. Parents who loved each other was one of the many unusual blessings with which Harriet was born.

Lord Berkeley was at the heart of the Royalist establishment. He had been amongst the commissioners sent to The Hague to negotiate the return of King Charles in 1660 and was a powerful advocate of the economic opportunities of colonialism. In 1661 he served as a member of the council for foreign plantations, and from 1663 as a commissioner of the Royal African Company, to which he added the Levant Company in 1680 and the East India (Lady Berkeley was the daughter of its Treasurer) in 1681. He was made Privy Councillor and created first Earl of

Berkeley in 1679. Another letter in the family archive, written in perfect French, attests to one of his nicknames, 'George the Linguist', and he was also known as 'George the Traveller'. Lord Berkeley was in his mid-thirties when his youngest daughter was born and was very much a man of his time, curious (he was a member of the new scientific association the Royal Society), cultured (he published a book of philosophy) and cosmopolitan. He also had a reputation for a ferocious temper.

The Berkeley family's destination that terrifying summer of the plague was Durdans, Lord Berkeley's seat at Epsom in Surrey. Sixteen miles from Guildford, the tiny village had become something of a resort in the mid-seventeenth century due to Epsom Well on the common, whose magnesia-rich water could supposedly cure all manner of ailments. Long before Bath became England's smartest spa, Epsom along with Tunbridge Wells in Kent attracted wealthy visitors in search of a healthful course of 'the waters' or simply a good time. The diarist John Aubrey took the cure there in 1654 and ten years later Epsom had become so popular that Samuel Pepys, visiting for the first time, grumbled that he was unable to find a lodging. Epsom was close to Hampton Court, the King's first place of refuge from the plague, and he had already visited the town along with Queen Catherine and the Duke of York.

In 1617 Harriet's great-grandmother Elizabeth

bought 'a messuage, with a dovecote, two gardens and 12 acres of land with meadow, pasture and wood' from Sir William Mynne of Hoton. Elizabeth had married Thomas Berkeley in 1596 and her wedding at Blackfriars is considered as the probable event at which Shakespeare's *A Midsummer Night's Dream* was staged. By the time Elizabeth began to build Durdans, the Jacobean palace she erected on her twelve Surrey acres, she had been managing the Berkeley finances for some years. Her husband Thomas was such a hopeless spendthrift that in 1606 Elizabeth had been forced to sell off part of her own lands to pay his debts, and in 1609 Thomas signed a formal agreement ceding the management of the Berkeley estates to his wife. A god-daughter of Queen Elizabeth I, Elizabeth Berkeley was a renowned scholar who owned thousands of books as well as an astute businesswoman. She was clearly of the view that women needed education and independence and she provided both for her own daughter, Theophilia, who was taught French, Italian, Latin and Greek and was bequeathed Durdans in her own right.

Theophilia maintained the family connection with the royal court, sharing her education with King James I's daughter Elizabeth and serving as a bridesmaid at her wedding. She married Sir Robert Coke in 1634 and the couple added a fashionable long gallery in the latest classical style to the house, which was known for its size (it had twenty-nine fireplaces), elegant formal gardens and extensive library. As well as architecture and botany, the cultivated Theophilia enjoyed the theatre, as a little boy named Samuel Pepys was given the starring role of Arethusa in a production at Durdans of Beaumont and Fletcher's *Philaster, or Love Lies a Bleeding*. Nine-year-old Sam was so captivated by the experience of this enchanting house, 'where I have seen so much mirth' that he could still remember his lines a quarter of a century later.

Durdans, which seemed such a paradise to little Sam, was occupied by Theophilia's husband until her death. In 1652, the year before Coke himself died, it was made over to her brother George, Harriet's father. Charles II dined there with the Berkeleys in the large paved hall in 1662 and again in 1664 around the time of Harriet's birth. Lord Berkeley was to alter the house substantially in the 1680s, but the Hearth Tax Returns for 1664 and 1673 show that Durdans was not extended during that period. A picture by Jacob Knyff from 1673 thus shows the house as Harriet would have known it as a child, the house from which she was to escape in the summer of 1682.

As the atmosphere at Durdans attested, Harriet's aunt and grandmother had been able to benefit from a tradition of women's learning which had developed around the scholar Queen, Elizabeth I. Education had become positively fashionable for upper-class women for a brief period at the end of her reign, but by the mid-century the attitude that women were unfit for study was firmly in the ascendant. 'Silence in a woman is the most persuading oratory', Sir Thomas Overbury had written in his tract *A Good Woman*, and despite the protests of elite women such as Margaret Cavendish, Duchess of Newcastle, that 'in Nature we have as clear an understanding as Men, if we were bred in Schools to mature our Brains', women who were seen and not heard had once again become the ideal. Elizabeth Josceline's advice in her guidebook, *The Mother's Legacy to Her Unborn Child*, that the Bible, housekeeping and good works were all the education a woman required was typical of the prevailing view of women's capacities and duties.

For most English women the chance of education was a matter of luck. If the family were well-off enough to educate their sons, daughters might be included in lessons with tutors, but dancing, music and French were more desirable accomplishments for well-born girls than Latin or mathematics. The effortful letters written by Lady Jemima Montagu, the wife of Samuel Pepys's patron, scrawled and wildly misspelt even by the standards of the time, are an indication of how sloppy girls' education could be, and how little was expected of them. The Berkeley sons Charles and George were born in 1649 and 1657, so the elder girls, Elizabeth, Theophilia and Arabella, might have had some opportunity to share their classes, but Mary, Arethusa (known as Lucy) and Harriet would have been too young. Harriet could certainly write, as letters were to play a hugely important part in her story. Like Aphra, she spoke French and she knew enough arithmetic to cast accounts, which activity she used as a cover when corresponding with her lover, but along with every other girl of her class her destiny was marriage.

Until she joined her sister Mary at court in 1680, Harriet spent much of her childhood at Durdans. The estate was a luxurious, protected environment, but beyond its elegant walls Epsom had been acquiring a racy reputation. When Samuel Pepys visited again in the summer of 1667 he stayed at the King's Head inn, where he heard all the gossip about a *ménage-à-trois* being conducted next door. Sir Charles Sedley and Lord Buckhurst, the court rakes who had behaved so dreadfully on the balcony of the Cock tavern (see p. 23), had moved in with the latest star of the London stage, an actress named Nell Gwynn, and the three were keeping 'a merry house'. Pepys was amazed that so many people seemed to have money to squander at 'the wells', but spa towns offered plenty of distractions besides the water. Epsom and Tunbridge Wells competed to tempt visitors with bowling lawns, assembly rooms for balls, coffee houses and gambling tables, and the spas swiftly became associated with another favourite seventeenth-century pastime, adultery. A cure of the waters could be used as an excuse for assignations, in a more socially mixed and relaxed atmosphere than London.

Aphra Behn visited Tunbridge Wells at some point during the late 1660s, commemorating it in a poem, *To Mrs Harsenet*, where the narrator admires a beautiful young woman for whom she suspects her own lover is yearning. Aphra's poem is conventional, if wryly resigned on the subject of men's faithlessness. The picture of Tunbridge Wells painted by her friend the Earl of Rochester is more realistic, a scathing vignette of the kind of society which the spas attracted. Frequented by fools and buffoons, cuckolds and whores, spas were places of social anarchy where countesses mixed with sewing women and lords with chandlers. Hooded young women lie in wait for vapid fops, army cadets pass themselves off as colonels, barren wives hoping to conceive slyly elide the truly effective remedy for infertility on offer at the spa – lower-class young men 'with brawny back and legs and potent prick' who are the real reason the 'waters got the reputation / Of good assistants unto generation'. Like the theatres, the wells were places of disguise and transgression, gaudy melting pots where vice flourished and the proper order of society dissolved.

8

Early next year, the plague had subsided sufficiently for the royal court to return to London. The disease nonetheless claimed a further 2,000 victims that year and Parliament was not recalled until September, whilst the theatres remained dark until November. If Aphra already had her first play ready as she later claimed, there could be no hope of its finding an audience. She needed a job and Thomas Killigrew found her one. So finally we see her. Aphra Behn makes her first entrance on the public stage in late July 1666.

A successful state needed spies. In the seventeenth century, Europe was a continent in flux; as nations expanded, consolidating and competing in their emergence as discrete states, espionage was one of the most crucial tools confirmed or aspiring rulers had at their disposal. Nonetheless, 'it is impossible to understand the early modern state without appreciating how fragile the lines of communication on which intelligence networks depended could be.'* The spoken word or the sealed letter were the only means of

* Akkerman, Nadine, *Invisible Agents: Women and Espionage in Seventeenth Century Britain* (2018)

imparting (relatively) secret information; neither could travel faster than a galloping horse. Security was precarious – subject to the vagaries of the weather and poor roads, letters went astray, missed their recipients, lay unopened in saddle bags or mouldering in ships' chests. Their senders, the inhabitants of the secret world, existed in a state of extreme precariousness, never quite certain who exactly they served or when and by whom they might be betrayed.

Secrets in the seventeenth century were not protected by official acts and spying was not precisely a separate category of profession. Diplomats, messengers, couriers and merchants were all potential sources of information, and men like Thomas Killigrew and George Marten could dip in and out of the hidden world. Ambassadors were expected to learn all they could about the governments to which they were posted, hence the usefulness of their dispatches to historians – they were the respectable face of intelligence gathering beneath which more clandestine activity was concealed and formalized. In the previous century, an organized, coherent secret service had been established under Elizabeth I by her spymasters Francis Walsingham and William Cecil, but the apparatus of their system began to fall apart at the beginning of the Civil Wars. It was only in July 1649, five months after the execution of Charles I, that the new Council of State appointed the regicide Thomas Scot as head of a committee for 'the businesses of Intelligence'.

Scot was, of course, the father of Aphra Behn's Surinam connection, William. In 1653, Thomas Scot was replaced as bureau chief by John Thurloe, who as Secretary to the Council and Postmaster General came to command a budget of £150,000 per year. The system developed by Scot and perfected by Thurloe was so efficient that, as one agent boasted, a letter from Cardinal Mazarin in France could be copied, deciphered and on Oliver Cromwell's desk within just four or five days.

Thomas Scot returned to his post during the last year of the Protectorate, fleeing to Brussels at the Restoration. In a cruel irony, he was identified by his own agents and by July 1660 was imprisoned in the Tower. As a regicide, Scot was excluded from Charles II's Act of Oblivion; he knew he could expect no mercy and he got none. He was executed in October, leaving his son William to continue in the intelligence trade as best he might. William Scot's career had already taken him to Surinam, where he had encountered Aphra Behn: they were now to meet again.

During the Civil Wars, female spies, or 'she-intelligencers' as they were known, proved useful as rarely before. Both Royalists and Parliamentarians were hungry for information and had to adapt their methods to conditions which encouraged the advance of women agents. Aristocratic women were active in support of Charles I, and the Royalists also made use of women lower down the social scale. A London bookseller named John Barwick, himself a spy, employed a group of 'adventurous women' to carry messages between the capital and the court at Oxford. Since women were seen as unimportant, they were less likely to be stopped and interrogated – 'faithful and honest Messengers, but such for the most part as were in Circumstances not much to be envied, and were consequently through the Mediocrity or rather the Meanness of their Condition less conspicuous and more safe.'* On the Parliament side, a woman called Susan Bowen was granted three payments of £10 by the Council of State between 1650–1 'in consideration of her giving intelligence' and the Council also made payments to Elizabeth Alkin, who became known as 'Parliament Joan'. Using this not particularly thrilling alias, her speciality was investigating the location of hidden printing presses which were turning out anti-Parliament propaganda. Women could more easily gain access to private spaces such as closets or bedrooms (indeed 'secret service' payments were often but not always a euphemism for the services of a prostitute) and they were less noticeable in the domestic arena, mingling with the maids in the kitchens or laundry rooms of great houses. Women could also conceal papers beneath their skirts or in their 'pockets' – handbags worn under their dresses – and were less likely to be intimately searched or physically attacked.

* Barwick, Peter, *Life of the Reverend John Barwick* (1724)

In laying the groundwork for Aphra's mission, Killigrew had noted that 'Astrea' had caught 'Celadon's' fancy in Surinam and had perhaps recruited her as early as 1664, with the presentation of the feathered head-dress to confirm her identity. Aphra's prior relationship with Scot, her intelligence, language skills and (possible) cover in seeing after her (possible) late husband's business affairs made her ideally suited to the job. Like Barwick's 'adventurous women' she was not so grand as to be noticeable, a young widow travelling to the Low Countries to resolve her business.

Prior to this date, there is no actual mention of Aphra by name. In the 1664 letter from the Deputy Governor of Surinam William Byam she was likely referenced as 'Astrea', whilst the remaining details of her possible early life have been pieced together long afterwards from evidence which is, as we have seen, flimsy to say the least. However, in the handwriting of Joseph Williamson, the keeper of the King's Library at Whitehall, Aphra emerges on to the page. Almost. Fourteen documents entitled *Memorialls for Mrs Affora** set out her mission to Antwerp on His Majesty's Secret Service. A letter of 31 August 1666 to Thomas Killigrew finally confirms 'Mrs Affora's' identity – as here Aphra Behn writes that he, Killigrew, was the person who approached her to become an agent. It's a suitably dramatic and mysterious appearance. A woman

See Marshall, Alan, *Memorialls for Mrs Affora* (2015).

from nowhere, with no official past, barely even a consistent name, is suddenly engaged on behalf of the English government for a highly sensitive undercover task.

After skedaddling from Surinam, pursued by debt, and unable to return to England where he was still a wanted man, Scot had offered his services as a spy to the Dutch government at The Hague. In April 1666, the King had issued an edict, the *Proclamation Requiring Some of His Majesties Subjects in Parts Beyond the Seas, to Return into England.* The proclamation aimed at scooping up the potentially disloyal or outright treacherous numbers of disaffected Royalists or former Parliamentary operatives who were still knocking around on the Continent. Scot's name was on the list of twelve men named. The penalty for those who did not return was a charge of high treason. Aphra's task was to turn Scot as a double agent for the English, an offer sweetened by a reward and a pardon.

Scot had officially left Surinam for the United Provinces, yet he had in fact recently been in England, visiting in disguise in October 1665. In order to rehabilitate himself with Charles's government, Scot would be required to send information which would be useful to the English in the war. During the visit he had been shown an anti-Dutch tract authored by Killigrew himself. Presumably Scot could use his knowledge of such propaganda to cement his loyalty to the Dutch and convince them that he was well-connected, the better to cover his projected activities on behalf of the English. Given the note about the 'shee-correspondent' of Suffolk Street, Aphra may well have continued her contact with Scot and even have seen him that autumn before her trip to the Netherlands.

The fourteen-point *Memorialls* itemized Aphra's objectives, which included learning from Scot how many ships the Dutch presently had, how many they had lost during the last battle against the English, the location of their East India fleet, their intentions towards their allies the French and their projections for an invasion. Scot himself was to be encouraged to 'come over and serve the King' in return for which he would receive the pardon and a sufficient reward to allow him to live 'plentifully'. Aphra was also provided with a basic numerical code in which she was 159 and Scot 160 as well as a passport from Lord Arlington. She was enjoined to 'use all secrecy imaginable'.

The situation which Aphra was entering was both complex and highly perilous. Aside from Scot himself, there were several key characters whose flexibly loyal backgrounds and opaque motivations Aphra would need to penetrate.

The first of these was Scot's controller, Colonel Bampfield (number 38 in Aphra's code), an Englishman whom the Royalists had accused of spying for Parliament in the 1650s. In an attempt to save his own life, William Scot's spymaster father had named

Bampfield as one of his informers before his death in 1660. Bampfield fled to Holland in 1661, from where he attempted to restore himself in the eyes of Charles II's government by offering information against the Dutch. Officially, Bampfield was the leader of an English regiment in the Dutch army; unofficially he had been working for Johan de Witt, the *de facto* leader of the Dutch Republic, since 1665, there gleaning the information that he hoped would see him able to return home. Bampfield was an extremely slippery character and Scot, whose own official job was as a cavalry officer in Bampfield's regiment, was terrified of him.

The second character in this double-crossed web was another Englishman, Thomas Corney. Based as a merchant in Amsterdam, Corney was also a spy, who had offered intelligence on Scot to Lord Arlington's network. He planned to undertake, on his own initiative, the task that would be Aphra's, that is to turn Scot as a double agent, but it failed horribly. Corney had developed a friendship with Scot, who saw straight through the ruse and supplied him with a stream of misinformation on Colonel Bampfield's orders. Corney's attempts to betray the Dutch to the English were thus exposed to Johan de Witt, who ordered his arrest. Corney was identified to the Dutch by Scot tapping him on the shoulder in a crowded place. He was imprisoned for six months and tortured on the rack. Physically and financially broken, Corney escaped over the border to Flanders on his release, where he continued to send information to Lord Arlington and plot revenge on Scot.

A third actor was Major James Halsall, who was to be Aphra's handler. She was to communicate her movements to him as she attempted to inveigle Scot back into the Royalist fold, and he provided her with an initial expenses bill for £50.

For a woman who so skilfully concealed the most elemental information on her own life, Aphra Behn proved an absolutely rotten spy. She sailed for Ostend at the end of July 1666 on the frigate *Castel Rodrigo*, accompanied by various English dignitaries who included Viscount Stafford and Sir Anthony Desmarches, an experienced informer who had worked in France for the Royalist cause during the Interregnum. Ostend was in the grip of the plague, so the party detoured to Passchendaele where they changed boats for Bruges before travelling on to Antwerp in early August.

Though not so large as London, Antwerp was an impressive city. It had been one of the primary cultural centres for the Counter-Reformation, the sixteenth-century movement which had emerged as a response to the growth in Protestantism. Art and architecture had been at the centre of this movement, a means of powerful visual propaganda which aimed to reinforce wavering faith with the might and beauty of the Church, and Antwerp had become a glorious, cosmopolitan beacon for some of the finest artists in Europe.

Dominated by its Gothic cathedral, the largest structure in the Netherlands, crammed in one traveller's description with 'rich church-stuff, shining with gold, silver, diamonds, pearls, rubies and other precious stones', Antwerp could also boast the Jesuit church of St Ignatius, decorated by Rubens and described by John Evelyn as 'sumptuous and most magnificent'. Any remains of Catholicism's visual legacy had been stripped from London by Cromwell's soldiers, so for the pro-Catholic Aphra, Antwerp's loveliness and grandeur would have been intoxicating, as well as a reminder of how the mean, pinched doctrines of the Puritans had impoverished London. In her novel *Love Letters*, Aphra declares that 'sure there is nothing gives the Idea of real Heaven like a Church all adorned with Rare pictures and the other Ornaments of it which Charm the Eyes, and Music to Ravish the ear.' These were just the sights and sounds she would have first encountered in Antwerp.

Lord Stafford was Catholic, with a daughter in the convent at Louvain. His journey may have been connected with relocating her, as the next year she was moved to Antwerp, which her father considered safer due to the war. Aphra obviously found him sympathetic since they appear to have conversed along her journey. If Aphra had known that Stafford was in contact with Thomas Corney, she might not have been so keen to tell him its purpose. As it was, by the time Aphra had moved on from Bruges to Antwerp in mid-August, Corney was waiting for her. On the 31st he described her arrival at the Rosa Noble inn on Kateynevest street to a fellow agent:

> 'a fair lady whose name is Affera Beene accompanied with her brother one Mr Cheney and a Mayd.

According to Corney, the other clients had not been fooled for a moment and were already referring to Aphra as the 'shee-spy'.

(NOTE: Mr Cheney is an enigmatic character. It has usually been assumed that Aphra was travelling with her brother and him, though given the lack of punctuation Corney's comment could equally be read as meaning that her brother's name was Cheney. Indeed, the younger brother is an altogether confusing presence in Aphra's life. He is mentioned in his finery in Oroonoko *and in the Antwerp correspondence, and supposedly held a position in the Coldstream Guards, though no 'Johnson' is listed amongst its officers. Commanded by the Duke of Albemarle, the regiment, known in the 1660s as The Lord General's Regiment of Foot, had been the primary military force in Charles II's Restoration. It does seem rather unlikely that the unnamed younger brother should have been conveniently released from his duties whilst the country was at war.*

The younger brother is another snag in the Eaffrey Johnson story. As mentioned above, Bartholomew and Elizabeth Johnson of Canterbury had one son, George, who died in 1656, and possibly, if they then relocated to London, another, Edward, who died in 1657. The younger brother present in Surinam and Antwerp with Aphra can therefore have been neither of them.

Conceivably, if Aphra was from the New World, her brother could have had a different surname as a consequence of their mother's remarriage. Again, it has been beyond the scope of this book to investigate this idea thoroughly, but a look through the birth registers of Maryland did reveal that the name Cheney and variant spellings appear reasonably frequently for the appropriate period.

There is also one very slight connection between the name 'Cheney' and the Martens. In 1658, Henry Marten received a letter from a Samuel Bathhurst requesting twenty pounds to send the writer's cousin 'Chane' on a voyage to Barbados. The Rye and Hereford Archives also contain a note from an Esther Chambre, living on Barbados, to her brother Chambre or Chane. She has written six letters already to which she has received no reply. All this tells us is that Henry Marten was presumed to have some interest in an unknown family which would incline him to help one of its members join another in Barbados. The spelling though is interesting. Corney would have transcribed the name orthographically, as it sounded, in his letter and as in the case of Wrils / Wrede and, why not, Weld, 'Cheney', 'Chambre' and 'Chane' are not dissimilar.

A respectable young woman in the seventeenth century could not travel unchaperoned, so the younger brother and Mr Cheney may have been socially suitable male companions, or convenient ciphers for other agents. 'Mr Cheney', whoever he was, seemed to serve no purpose whatsoever in Antwerp and disappears from Aphra's story as mysteriously as he arrives in it. Nor does the younger brother seem to play any further part in her life until he appears in the story of Oroonoko.)

On the same day Corney blew her cover, Aphra wrote a pot-and-kettle letter to Thomas Killigrew, giving her impression of Corney:

> this Mr Corney is a strange kind of prating fellow . . .
> I fear his tongue will Undo all his will would per-
> form; he makes as if he were his Majesty's right hand,
> but I fear he is not to be employed, because of that
> talking quality, so that I never heard such a Roda-
> mantad in all my life.

Corney was still in pursuit of Scot, desperate for revenge for the punishments he had endured. Clearly he and Aphra had recognized one another as rivals. Corney took to calling on her every day at her lodgings and incredibly, despite her mistrust of him and the necessity of absolute discretion, within a week Aphra had shown him her pass from Lord Arlington. Of all places, as Corney wrote to his colleague on 4th September, she had chosen a church to make this revelation. This was all very peculiar – whether Aphra knew Corney was a fellow agent or not, exposing herself to him in this manner was directly contrary to her orders. The two were using the same courier for their letters, an agent named Jerome Nipho, and they each appeared to have spent more time persuading Lord Arlington to oust the other from the job than they did spying on Scot.

Corney did have some sympathy for Aphra. Despite claiming that she did not understand her business, he conceded that Aphra 'hath a great deal of wit'; moreover, he knew that she was strapped for cash. In his 4th September letter he describes Aphra as having been three weeks 'wind bound' at the Rosa Noble for want of funds to settle her bill, a fact which Aphra herself pointed out to Killigrew in a letter of 17th September.

Still, there was work to be done and at first Aphra appeared to be doing her best to go about it professionally, though without much success. She contacted Scot when she arrived in Antwerp and suggested they meet. Scot was very nervous of being found out by Colonel Bampfield, 'he is so extremely watched . . . that he is not suffered to go out of his sight', explained Aphra, and so she had ordered a coach for a day's outing which would allow them some privacy. The outing was costly and useless in terms of secrecy, for two weeks later Corney was writing that since Scot was afraid to stay long in Antwerp for fear of meeting Corney himself 'they took Coach and went out of Town and stayed out all night and returned again the next morning.'

In Corney's view, Aphra and Scot were up to something. Scot was of very little value as an agent to England, since as a consequence of his ratting on Corney he was no longer trusted by the English dissidents in Holland. In fact, Corney said, everyone hated Scot, who could speak no Dutch and therefore was unable to pick up or overhear news, besides which he was so heavily in debt that he couldn't go anywhere there might be any, as the major cities were full of his creditors. Aphra, he said, was claiming that Scot was in a position to 'do much' for the English government, but this was all a 'Cheat'. The two were in league, spinning out her mission for financial gain.

Corney was right about Scot's uselessness, but there wasn't much financial gain to be had for anyone. Agents of the secret world were expected to work for expenses and the possibility of a future reward, but even the former were not sufficiently forthcoming and Aphra had swiftly found herself with serious money worries. Her landlord Jacomyna Huyckx was pressing her to settle her outstanding bill and she owed money all over Antwerp. Pawning a ring helped a little, but she urgently needed some serious funds. She wrote to Killigrew that her debts now amounted to over £100. Scot, now back over the border in Holland, was also badgering her for cash. Scot was refusing to return to Antwerp for a further meeting, whilst her lack of funds prevented her from crossing to enemy territory to find him.

Aphra didn't have anything more to offer Scot. The promised pardon and reward showed no sign of appearing. Scot was still on the payroll of his official employer, Johann de Witt, who was supposedly paying him £1,000 per year. What motivation had he to come across? There are two ways to read what happened next. One is that Aphra struggled on through what seemed a thorough impasse of miscommunication, absent funds and mercurial fellow agents. This is the view taken by Aphra's principal biographer, who painstakingly elaborates Aphra's attempt to serve the English government in accordance with her own stated desire that she receive 'no ill opinion from His Majesty, who would give my life to serve him in never so little a degree'. The other, posited by the espionage historian Nadine Akkerman, is that Aphra made it all up.

In her letter to Killigrew of 31st August, Aphra declared that her reports would be written in her own hand, i.e. that she would copy the intelligence she received from Scot. Using his codename, she explained that 'Celadon is afraid to have anything go in his own hand and therefore for the future will make me write all.' As with so much of Aphra's character, taking this statement at face value 'raises too many questions to which there are no logical answers'. In theory, Scot was sending his letters from Holland to Antwerp, where Aphra was copying them out in order to protect him. However, the mail boat from Holland to England was no longer sailing because of the war, so all letters had to come through Flanders. Aphra was claiming that for security Scot would send letters in his own hand from Holland, which was extremely dangerous, which she had then to copy from Antwerp, which was quite safe.

Akkerman argues that no such letters existed. Scot was no longer corresponding with Aphra; she was simply inventing his 'reports' in order to maintain herself in good standing (and vital funds) with her superiors in London. Unlike Scot, Aphra actually spoke Dutch. She could eavesdrop, she could read the gazettes and pamphlets and thereby relay information which appeared to come from Scot, with whom she pretended to be in regular communication. The snippets Aphra sent to London as Scot's 'reports' are fairly meagre – a plan to block the Thames which was already familiar, the illness of a Dutch military commander, an outbreak of plague in the Dutch navy, a meeting of English rebels in Utrecht. Nothing that couldn't be gleaned by someone who understood Dutch and kept an ear to the ground. At the end of September, Scot 'wrote' of the reception of the news of the Great Fire in London – unsurprisingly this had caused much rejoicing among the Dutch, which again was hardly a revelation. Aphra's own reports were of just as much, or little, value as those she invented from Scot, but it is interesting that she manipulated his masculine persona to endorse their authority. As Nadine Akkerman confirms, 'Like her employers in England, we have bought into the romantic notion that she was a spy, never having stopped to consider that the soon-to-be playwright and novelist might simply have been feeding her eager reader fictional intelligence . . . from factual sources.'

It has also been suggested that Aphra was 'ruthlessly pillaged' by Scot, who was stringing her along to squeeze money out of her, and that her plight in Antwerp was the fault of a careless, misogynist government who laughed aloud at her attempts at intelligence. Women spies had already demonstrated their usefulness and why should Arlington and Killigrew have bothered to send Aphra to Antwerp to waste their money unless they believed she was up to the task? This picture of Aphra as a beleaguered maiden, beset on all sides by callous and conniving men, is the opposite of the intrepid character Aphra would prove herself to be. Again and again in her plays, it is the women who are the most intelligent and resourceful characters, who manipulate the prejudices and conventions of their time to get what they want.

Just because Aphra was a good writer doesn't make her a spotless heroine. She was reputed to be extravagant all her life (perhaps it was the Marten genes), and may have been compensating for her overspending by fabricating information to keep the money coming. Or possibly, she may have learned of George Marten's death from plague. News took months to arrive from Surinam to Europe, but towards the end of the year Aphra could have known of it. Assuming the strong connection with Marten, Aphra would have known she was now on her own and needed to improvise while she worked out what to do next.

Corney put a stop to the scheme. Scot had been betrayed and captured (in church again!) at The Hague in early October. According to Corney, this was a consequence of Aphra's having made him so conspicuous at the Rosa Noble inn. She had failed spectacularly:

instead of recruiting Scot as a double agent, she'd managed to get him arrested. Corney gloated that 'That Rogue Scot is catched at last', adding that the despairing landlord of the Rosa Noble was now trying to evict Aphra. With Scot's imprisonment confirmed by Corney, Aphra could hardly go on pretending to be receiving reports from him, which left her to confront the dreadful morass of debt into which she had plunged herself. A begging missive to Lord Arlington saw some money authorized, but Aphra was told clearly that her posting had ended.

Frantic, she continued to work the grift. A fresh letter to her handler Halsall included a 'message' from Scot which he had somehow managed to convey to her from his cell. Naturally it came by word of mouth as it was too dangerous to write. Aphra also wrote again to Lord Arlington, assuring him that with patience, all could still be resolved:

> . . . where as tis thought my little Service are at an end: I am of another opinion and am very confident that I shall in a very few more weeks or days be able to do more than ever for, had I had those supplies for him which were promised . . . your Lordship had a better proof of my will and his ability . . . I do expect him [Scot] to have liberty in a few days, if he have it not by this time.

Scot had apparently promised much fresh intelligence, if only Aphra would not abandon him, and she has copied a little of one of his tantalizingly 'too long letters to me'.

Taken as a whole, this missive to Arlington becomes odder the more one reads it. Much of it is desperate and rambling, menial in tone, a grovelling servant's letter liberally scattered with 'Lordships'. However, Aphra also pointed out that she had not sought the position in which she found herself; she hadn't asked for the job and her expenditure had been caused only by Arlington's own tardiness with funds. She pleaded that she needed only another £100 and that she was almost 'killed' with grief at the thought of his having a poor opinion of her. Her tone is both humble and defiant, insisting over and over again on the need for money which is all Arlington's fault and yet begging as 'one who would venture her life to gain your favourable opinion'. It's spectacularly disingenuous and wonderfully audacious. Beneath her signature, A. Behne, Aphra added a postscript: 'I humbly beg your Lordship to be speedy least I eat out my head.' The letter whirls through the roles Aphra bestows upon herself – fragile woman in need of protection, dutiful supplicant, hard-done-by agent, reliable intelligencer. It feels deliberately overlong, wearisome and confusing for a busy official to digest and the conclusion hints at what could be a state of compromising mental disarray. Is it a desperate plea for help or a masterly performance by someone entirely in control of her ability to produce a bamboozling literary effect?

And what of Aphra's mark, the unfortunate Scot? Corney's sniping report that the two had spent the night together on their coach trip suggests that their relationship was intimate, if it hadn't already been so. Corney may have been trying to impugn his rival's morals, but Scot had been a presence in the life of Aphra Behn since Surinam; whatever the truth of her past, he was a connection to it. Aphra's letter to Lord Arlington could be read as a last attempt to relieve Scot from the position in which her own indiscretions had placed him, but there is nothing to suggest it succeeded as Scot simply vanishes from the records.

Aphra had hardly covered herself with glory on His Majesty's Secret Service, but her precarious experiences in Flanders foreshadowed those of that young woman, Harriet Berkeley, who was to play such an important part in her career.

9

Kinship networks were enormously important in seventeenth-century England. Connections were everything. Finding a job or a servant, planning a journey, pursuing a lawsuit or sourcing fresh butter all depended on who you knew and could call upon. Relationships with family members, however distant, and social superiors were maintained by letters, visits and the exchange of gifts. In a world where people in trouble could expect no recourse from the state, the difference between security and destitution was a matter of contacts. The idea that Aphra Behn arrived in London as in emigrant from the New World is, I think, supported by the fact that in times of need, she had almost no one to call on. Much attention has been paid to her possible or probable connections within the upper echelons of English society, for example through Thomas Colepeper, but very little practical assistance ever seems to have materialized from them.

Another instance of such mooted friends in high places has been extrapolated from the 'shee spy' note prior to Aphra's Antwerp mission. The woman mentioned by the Dutch writer in connection with William Scot was reported to be living near the residence of

Sir Philip Howard on Suffolk Street. Another resident there was the widowed Elizabeth Johnson, clearly a woman of means, as her home was taxed on the basis of it containing ten hearths – obviously a sizeable house. It is possible that this is the Elizabeth Johnson, wife (now widow) of Bartholomew Johnson, whose daughter was betrothed to John Halse in 1657 (see p. 50); that is, the mother of Eaffrey Johnson and possibly Aphra Behn. Leaving aside quite how the relict of a Canterbury barber came to be living in one of the most fashionable parts of London, why didn't Elizabeth Johnson help her daughter in 1668 when she was on the brink of being thrown into prison for debt?

Seeking a connection between this Elizabeth Johnson and the 'shee spy', up pops Thomas Killigrew. Elizabeth's neighbour, Philip Howard, a great-grandson of the 4th Duke of Norfolk, was acquainted with Killigrew through both the theatre and the intelligence service: via the former because he was having an affair with one of the King's Company actresses, Betty Hall, and via the latter because he had been involved in the interrogation of suspected anti-Royalist plotters along with James Halsall, the man appointed to be Aphra's handler on the spying mission. And, like Killigrew, Philip Howard had connections in the West Indies as the proprietor of a plantation in Jamaica, of which he was named governor in 1685. It has been suggested that it was through the neighbourly connection with Howard in London that Aphra was given her spying job, but it would be astonishing if a man of Philip Howard's rank paid attention to a barber's widow and her daughter. Much less so if the daughter in question had come over from Surinam as part of the secret service, extending as far as the Caribbean, in which he and Killigrew were engaged. The possible proximity of Aphra and her (possible) mother to Sir Philip makes much more sense if she had already been selected to spy on William Scot.

(Aphra did clearly have contact with the extended Howard clan before she left for Antwerp. The fabulous Surinam feathers she presented to Killigrew were, as noted above, used in the 1667 production of *The Indian Emperor*, Dryden's sequel to *The Indian Queen* by Sir Robert Howard, who was one of the shareholders in Killigrew's theatre company. Sir Robert and Sir Philip were second cousins and Robert was brother to Edward Howard, yet another writer member of the family, who just to make things simpler happened to be Dryden's brother-in-law. In 1671, Aphra's second play, *The Amorous Prince*, was to be performed in the same season as Edward Howard's *The Six Days' Adventure*, and whilst Aphra's work was not particularly well received, Edward Howard's was practically laughed off the stage. The two were friendly enough for Aphra to publish a poem in its defence, in which she advises Edward to:

> Consider and Consult your Wit,
> Despise those Ills you must endure,

> And raise your Scorn as great as it,
> Be Confident and then Secure.

However, such sage advice belonged to the future, when Aphra had begun to establish herself as a writer. She may have known the Howards through Killigrew in the mid-1660s, but when she found herself desperate for ready money towards the end of the decade she did not look to them any more than she did to Colepeper.)

The irregularity of the payments Aphra received from Arlington's office had caused her tremendous difficulties. After Scot's arrest she had somehow to make her way back to England, but what monies were provided were pathetically inadequate. This was partly policy as it was considered unwise to encourage agents to exaggerate their information by paying them too easily. Small, irregular payments were meant to keep them on their toes (in Aphra's case such precautions seem to have been entirely justified). To pay off her creditors and her passage home, Aphra had borrowed a considerable amount – £150 – from John Butler, a wealthy English cloth merchant in Antwerp. Along with practically every other inhabitant of the city, John Butler had once been a spy, using his business as a cover to transport documents between his home county of Devon and the Royalist community in Antwerp ten years before. He was also openly Catholic, a when he died in November 1667, he left money in his will to the English convent at Ghent. (Once again, the Butler debt connects Aphra with the secret world, with Catholicism and the Killigrew-dominated English West Country.)

Aphra finally sailed for England on 1 May 1667. She returned to an alien city. Most of the London she had known had been consumed in the Great Fire the preceding year, when for almost a week the flames which had spread from the house of Thomas Farriner, a baker who lived on Pudding Lane, had blazed their way through the medieval centre. Though remarkably few people lost their lives (just twenty, including Farriner's unfortunate maid), an estimated 65,000 were suddenly homeless. Over 13,000 houses had burned, along with 89 churches, the Navy and Tax offices and the Royal Exchange. St Paul's Cathedral was a charred shell. Crushing Londoners' spirits even further, the Dutch finally invaded a short time after Aphra's arrival, sailing boldly up the Medway River on 10th June.

The Medway was the route to the Chatham dockyards, where the Navy fleet was laid up for the winter, protected by a great chain stretched from bank to bank. In a raid lasting three days the Dutch burned thirteen ships and even more humiliatingly captured the *Royal Charles*, the flagship on which the King had sailed home in triumph in 1660. A warning from Holland had in fact been received the month before, a few weeks after Aphra's departure. One of Lord Arlington's many agents, Peter du Moulin, had sent word of the preparations for the attack. The news was greeted with complacency, as such rumours had been communicated many times since the Dutch war began, including by Aphra who had 'heard' them from William Scot, but that didn't stop the author of the *Memoirs* from giving her the credit for it, had the King only heeded her words. The shock of the attack and the symbolism of the capture of the *Royal Charles* were felt deeply. 'All our hearts do ache', wrote Pepys, whose misgivings about the war had been proved right. The Medway losses brought the conflict to a swift conclusion, with no advantages obtained for England. To compound the national shame, the King had apparently spent the evening of 10th June with his mistress Barbara Palmer in what sounds like an extremely tedious competition to catch a moth.

Where and how Aphra lived on her return to London is unknown, but her circumstances were clearly still compromised. Her creditor was closing in. After Butler's death in the autumn, his brother Edward was sent up to London to dun Aphra for the £150. He was 'a harsh, dour man with a heart of stone' who pressed Aphra pitilessly for the money. By the autumn of 1668 he had given her one more week to clear the debt. Aphra appealed in vain to Baptist May, the Keeper of the Privy Purse, and then to a character named William

Chiffinch, whose official position at court was Keeper of the King's Closet. Chiffinch was well known as Charles II's personal pimp, his job largely consisting of smuggling women up the back stairs of his lodgings at Whitehall to the royal bedroom. That Aphra should have approached Chiffinch implies she was familiar with the workings of the court. Could she even have imagined being conducted up those back stairs herself? Neither May nor Chiffinch would help her, so Aphra turned to Thomas Killigrew.

(NOTE: In the pleading letter Aphra wrote to Killigrew she mentioned her mother, who was obviously in no position herself to come to her aid. Returning to the Elizabeth Johnson recorded as living in Suffolk Street, her inability to assist Aphra co-ordinates with the timing of George Marten's death. Supposing Elizabeth had a relationship with Marten and had then accompanied Aphra back to England in 1664, it could have been possible for them to set up in a fine house. By the time Aphra returned from Antwerp though, George Marten was dead and whatever means he could have provided for his former mistress had ceased.)

The letter is a stark exposure of the paucity of Aphra's mooted connections, as amongst all the powerful people she 'may' have been connected with none stepped forward to help her. If she was closely connected with the Marten family, this might have been the time to ask for help, but George Marten's brother Henry, who had been living under house arrest after his pardon for regicide, had been moved from Windsor Castle to Chepstow in distant Wales that same year.

Taken at her word to Killigrew, Aphra was utterly desperate:

> Sir, if you could guess at the affliction of my soul you would I am sure Pity me, 'tis tomorrow I must submit myself to a prison the time being expired and though I endeavoured all day yesterday to get a few days more I can not because they say they see I am dallied with and so they say I shall be for ever: so I can not revoke my doom I have cried myself dead and could find in my heart to break through and get to the king and never rise till he were pleased to pay this; but I am sick and weak and unfit for it; or a Prison; I shall go tomorrow; But I will send my mother to the king with a Petition for I see every body are words & I will not perish in a Prison from whence he swears I shall not stir until the utmost farthing be paid and oh God who considers my misery and charge too, this is my reward for all my great promises and endeavours.

Aphra had every reason to be terrified of imprisonment for debt. There were six prisons in London used to incarcerate debtors: Newgate, the Fleet, Farringdon, Whitecross Street, the King's Bench and the Marshalsea. Following legislation dating from the fourteenth century, debtors could be locked up indefinitely until their creditors were satisfied. Damp, freezing, filthy, rife with fever and disease, debtors' prison often proved fatal to its unfortunate inhabitants. Conditions could be alleviated in return for steep fees, which of course debtors were unlikely to possess. A 1658 petition to Henry Marten illustrates their horrifying conditions:

> for many weeks (we) have fed on dogs, rats and ox-liver being festival food and (we) are allowed but 13 s 4d a week amongst a hundred persons.

For women, starvation and squalor were compounded by the risk of physical and sexual violence from fellow prisoners and guards. It was a prospect to make anyone run mad. Aphra ended her letter by repeating her plea that she had to have the money that evening. If Killigrew could not manage this 'you must send me something to keep me in Prison for I will not starve.'

Whoever Mr Behn might have been, he doesn't seem to have been much use as a husband, since he fizzled out without leaving Aphra anything much except, possibly, his name. Aphra's fear and isolation at this juncture also casts doubt on the ellipses and contradictions of the Eaffrey Johnson origin story. The links to gentry families who supposedly helped her to her education, her sister Frances or her mysterious younger brother in the Coldstream Guards seem to have vanished as suddenly as they appeared when required to explain her unlikely identity.

The vagaries of life in the seventeenth century were

extreme; poverty for many was only one misfortune away, and the after-shocks of the plague and the Great Fire may have rendered some of Aphra's friends or relatives unable to assist her. But there seems to have been no one at all. Aphra claims her creditors see she has been 'dallied' with; they are saying she has no meaningful network to call on. The anguish of Aphra's position will be shared by anyone who has ever experienced it – the humiliation of begging for help, the brush-offs and unreliable half-promises of friends anxious only to get away, the sense of absolute helplessness as the clock ticks down with nothing to do but hopelessly wait.

Was Aphra's predicament truly as desperate as she made out? The sum of £150 was a large amount of money (to put it into perspective, Sir Peter Lely's salary as painter to the King was £200), but she hadn't, quite, expended it on His Majesty's Secret Service. The Antwerp letters she had copied out claiming they had been from Scot, may well have been fictitious. The debt was real enough, but could Killigrew's refusal to lift a finger to aid his contact and former agent indicate that he suspected her of forging them? As ever with Aphra, her letter can be read another way. It is dramatic, extreme and subtly threatens Killigrew with a potentially embarrassing situation. Aphra says she is too weak to go to Whitehall to prostrate herself at Charles's feet but will send her mother. Killigrew would not wish to be responsible for old ladies troubling the King with petitions. Everybody is 'words', Aphra writes, including presumably Killigrew. She has been blandished and fobbed off and he ought to be ashamed of himself, but she is also defiant – 'I will not perish', 'I will not starve.' As she was frequently to do, Aphra plays with the conventions of her time, portraying herself as a weak, defenceless woman in need of help if that is what it takes to get her what she needs, but as with the Scot letters there is a toughness, a willingness to use her skill with words to exercise the only little power she has. Maybe her shivering, hysterical self-portrait in the letter wasn't altogether accurate. Even the threat to send her 'mother' to plead her cause was perhaps no more than a dramatic flourish.

The papers from the *Abraham's Sacrifice* dispute (see p. 111) also raise questions here. If Aphra was in a position to employ a factor to represent her as a widow in Amsterdam, she couldn't have been as poor as all that. If she was aware that the case was going to be heard, might she not have tried to promise Butler that he would be recompensed if it went her way? The absence of the Widow Behn from the hearing has been construed as evidence that she was in prison at the time, but there is in fact no firm evidence that she did go to jail. Killigrew did not help Aphra, but someone did. The prison claim is made in the fictional *Memoirs*, largely to set up their central portrait of Aphra as a talented, free-living writer who thoroughly enjoyed her membership of London's rackety bohemian set. On her release from jail, it claims, the remainder of Aphra's life was:

> entirely dedicated to Pleasure and Poetry; the success in which gain'd her the Friendship of the most Sensible Men of the Age, and the Love of not a few of different Characters.

10

The portrayal of England's first professional female playwright as a rambunctious literary party girl is a caricature, diminishing Aphra even as it praises her. Aside from the details of the Butler debt, there are no facts available for her life between her return from Antwerp and the autumn of 1670, when the first of her plays to be performed, *The Forc'd Marriage*, opened the season at the Duke's Theatre on the 20th September. It's a surprising turnaround, the pathetic debtor transformed into the West End's latest rising star, and it took more than 'Pleasure and Poetry' for Aphra to achieve it.

Given her personal history with Killigrew, the King's Company at the Theatre Royal on Drury Lane should have seemed the natural home for Aphra's debut production, yet it went to Davenant's at the Duke's. One suggestion is that Killigrew refused *The Forc'd Marriage* due to bad feeling over the Butler debt, but this is not borne out by the warmth of their subsequent relations. There were commercial reasons for the Duke's Company to take a play by a woman in 1670, but why Aphra's especially? *The Forc'd Marriage* is not a bad play but it is in no way outstanding – 'a run of the mill tragicomedy featuring the tried-and-tested formula in which lovers denied the objects of their true affections were finally united after many hiccups and all ended well' is as good a summary as any. The Duke's faced particularly strong competition from the King's that season. Jonson's *Every Man in His Humour* had been a huge success for Killigrew's men in March and for the winter showcase they were about to open Dryden's *The Conquest of Granada*, featuring Nell Gwynn returning to the stage as the working mother of the monarch's child. The play was a smash, running for a record-breaking two months, after which it was to be followed by Wycherley's *Love in a Wood*. With such competition, why would the Duke's risk a piece by an entirely unknown playwright?

Possibly the answer, like so much of Aphra's uncertain past, lay in the New World. In 1650 William Davenant embarked from the island of Jersey for the colonies. His destination was Maryland, where his official title was to be Treasurer to Thomas Killigrew's relative (and playwright) Sir William Berkeley, the Governor of Virginia. Under the tolerant regime of Lord Baltimore, Maryland had been welcoming religious dissidents of all confessions, including the Lloyds of Wye plantation in Kent county (as we have seen on p. 75). Davenant's brief was to aid Berkeley in bringing the 'Schismatics and Sectaries and other ill affected persons' protected by Baltimore into line. The exiled Cavaliers in Paris, who had a lot of time on their hands, came up with a little poem for the occasion:

> America must breed up the Brat,
> From where will return a West-Indy rat,
> For Will to Virginia is gone from among us
> With 32 slaves to plant Mundungus.

('Mundungus' was tobacco, the slaves were indentured artisans.)

Davenant didn't make it very far. His ship was captured by a Parliament vessel and he was taken to prison on the Isle of Wight from where in 1651 he was removed to the Tower. Ardent and active Royalist as he was, Davenant 'expected no mercy from Parliament . . . and had no hopes of escaping with his life'. Help came from where he might least have expected it. Henry Marten, the elder brother of George Marten, regicide and arch anti-monarchist, spoke up for him in Parliament, suggesting it had better grudges to pursue than concerning itself with such a 'rotten old rascal' as Davenant. It was the same argument subsequently made of Henry Marten himself when he was tried for regicide – that he was effectively already too wicked to be worth executing.

On 8 July 1652, Davenant wrote to Marten: 'I would it were worthy of you to know how often I have professed that I had rather owe my liberty to you than any man and *that the obligation you lay on me shall for ever be acknowledg'd.*' (Italics mine.) Davenant was eventually released in 1654 and went back to his house at Smith-field, where he built his secret theatre and contrived his way around Parliament regulations by staging 'operas' until the Restoration.

Davenant thus owed Henry Marten a favour. Aphra and George Marten were (in whatever manner), close. In Surinam in the early 1660s, if not before, Aphra could have learned of Davenant's reprieve. Whilst George Marten had died of plague in Surinam in 1666, soon after which Aphra Behn took the job as Kil-ligrew's agent, Henry Marten lived until 1680. There is no known correspondence between Aphra and Henry Marten, but it is not impossible that as someone close to George, Henry could have put in a word for her with Davenant. The only problem with this theory is that Davenant died in April 1668 and *The Forc'd Marriage* did not open until 1670.

There is no evidence of Aphra having a direct relationship with Davenant himself, but she was acquainted with his widow, Dame Mary, who had almost as much reason to be grateful to Henry Marten as her husband. Aphra's desperate petitions concerning the Butler debt date to the autumn after Davenant's death. What resources she had been able to call on previously were now exhausted, hence it is reasonable that she would now attempt to begin to earn a living from writing. Could she have approached Dame Mary and drawn on the Marten connection to persuade her to take a play? It is a very slight possibility, but again, slightly more probable one than Eaffrey the barber's daughter persuading the most powerful woman in London's theatre land to sponsor her first effort.

Aphra had obviously been attending the theatre. Her knowledge of the technicalities of the stage, of which she made assured use, must have come from somewhere. The division between actors and audience was far less strictly observed than nowadays and if Aphra joined the theatre fans who wandered in and out backstage and in the dressing rooms, she would have had the opportunity to meet Davenant. This free and easy atmosphere is captured in Samuel Pepys's diary, when he reports on hearing of Davenant's death. Pepys had just seen a play at Killigrew's Theatre Royal and was gossiping backstage with one of the actresses, Mrs Knepp, who was worrying about the effects of the louche theatrical atmosphere on the morals of her pretty young maid. They were interrupted by the news – 'Sir W Davenant is just now dead' recorded Pepys baldly.

Three days later, Davenant's coffin was carried to Westminster Abbey by his actors. The funeral drew crowds but was generally considered to be a somewhat rickety affair, with mourners arriving in hackney coaches and no crown of laurels to celebrate the doughty old stager's eminence. The Duke's Company was now to be officially fronted by Dame Mary, who took care of the business side with two of Davenant's leading actors, Thomas Betterton and Henry Harris, as artistic directors. Davenant had been loved and respected, but in order to keep up with the King's, the Duke's needed to introduce more modern, exciting plays, by 'wits' of the type which Davenant himself had dismissed as being 'not of the former age'. For the first time, their numbers might include women.

Killigrew had shrewdly observed the presence and influence of women in the theatre and from 1669 began actively to cater to it, setting a trend for prologues and epilogues spoken by actresses. Nell Gwynn was the first to attempt it: 'A Woman's Prologue! This is ventrous news!' she announced at the opening of Jonson's *Catiline, His Conspiracy* that year. In August, the King's went one step further, with a new play sensationally authored by a woman, Frances Boothby's *Marcelia*. The prologue attempted to capitalize on female support for the writer's boldness:

> I'm hither come, but what d'ye think to say?
> A Woman's Pen presents you with a Play . . .
> But still she hopes the Ladies out of Pride
> And Honour will not quit their sexes side.

It was the perfect moment for the Duke's to attempt something similar, but the staging of Aphra's play was perhaps stalled by political events. Early in 1670, the King had agreed to a secret treaty with his cousin Louis XIV. Ostensibly a new Anglo-French alliance against the Dutch, the unofficial version of the agreement was completed at Dover in the spring (with the public version following in December). In return for a huge cash payment of £160,000, Charles was to declare himself a Catholic. Neither the fact that his father had died a martyr to the Anglican church nor the knowledge that such an announcement would be political suicide appears to have weighed against the promise of French funds, but then Charles was nothing if not a pragmatist. The timing of his conversion was left to the royal discretion (he held out until the last minutes of his life), and in the meantime the Treasury desperately needed funds.

A visit from Charles's beloved sister Henriette-Anne, wife to Louis's younger brother the Duke of Orleans, was the pretext for the negotiations, and in May the court moved to the Kent coast for a fortnight of junketings, which included twelve consecutive nights of plays given by the Duke's Company. If Aphra had her play ready earlier, that is in 1669 when the Duke's were looking for a woman playwright and she needed funds, this would explain the hiatus. How and where she lived and on what between 1668 and the autumn of 1670 is unknown.

Theatre performances in the Restoration began in mid-afternoon. If Aphra was waiting backstage at Lincoln's Inn with the cast of *The Forc'd Marriage* on her first night, she would have seen the whole range of London society preparing to take their places. In 1698 a French visitor to London, Henri Misson, described the different strata of the audience:

The Pit is an Amphitheatre, fill'd with benches without Backboards and adorn'd and cover'd with green
Cloth. Men of Quality, particularly the younger Sort,
some Ladies of Reputation and Virtue and abundance of Damsels that haunt for prey, sit all together
in this Place, Higgledy-piggledy, chatter, toy, play,
hear not. Farther up against the Wall, under the first
Gallery and just opposite to the Stage, rises another
Amphitheatre, which is taken by the persons of the
best Quality, among whom are generally very few
Men. The Galleries . . . are fill'd with none but ordin-
ary people, particularly the Upper one.*

This was the audience Aphra needed to captivate,
sophisticated sensation-seekers, casually inattentive
and potentially rowdy. She could have smelled them as
she waited for the curtain to rise – unwashed clothes
and the smoky grease from tallow candles cut through
with Hungary-water scent and the sharp citrus tang
of oranges joined with the reek of her own adrenalin
Aphra could be confident in her experienced cast –
Mr and Mrs Betterton, the talented debutante Mary
Lee, seasoned actress Mrs Jennings – but it was her
words which would determine their success. If the
periwigged gallants in the pit turned against her play
she would be ruined. Given how much Aphra's future

* Misson, Henri, *Mémoires et observations faites par un voyageur en Angl*
terre (1698)

depended on the reception of *The Forc'd Marriage*, it's worth paying attention to the prologue, the first of Aphra's lines ever to be spoken on stage.

Like the 'damsels' of Misson's portrait, Aphra's opening is overtly predatory. She announces that women are developing a new weapon – wit, which will be effective long after their traditional foil, beauty, has declined. The actress who spoke the prologue appealed to the women in the audience, inviting their collusion:

> The Poetess too, they say, has spies abroad
> Which have dispos'd themselves in every road,
> In the Upper Box, Pit, Gallery, every face,
> You find disguis'd in a black Velvet-Case.

This refers to the masks employed at the theatre, which were worn by fashionable women, but also by prostitutes, so much so that 'vizard' became a noun for 'whore' as Aphra emphasizes next:

> There's not a Vizard in our whole Cabal,
> Those are but Pickaroons that scour for prey.

Aphra is here referring to her own spying life, whilst enjoining the women in the audience to distinguish between the skill of the clever writer and the flimsy allure of the whores. 'Pickaroon' is a Spanish-derived word, meaning 'pirate'; hence Aphra is suggesting that the women roaming for customers are thieves, entrapping their victims through deceit. Men are prepared to succumb to beauty, so why should they refuse 'the

Fetters of their Wit'? It's knowing and bold, setting up those who would criticize the play because it was by a woman as fools, incapable of proper discrimination.

In 1709, twenty years after Aphra's death, a periodical named *The Female Tatler* was launched. The first fifty-two editions were the work of the female playwright Delarivier Manley, who writing as 'Mrs Crackenthorpe' guided her readers through the pitfalls of London society. Mrs Crackenthorpe was particularly alert to the perils of 'masquerading', or appearing in disguise, which enabled rogues and adventurers to pass themselves off as their social superiors. Such chancers were in turn known as 'picaros', from 'pickaroon', a type characterized as 'ambitious, resourceful . . . who prided him [or her] self on his ability to dupe, swindle and steal from the unsuspecting'. Pirates, masks, spies, fetters: these are dark images to conjure at the opening of a comedy. They could be read as a warning – the anonymous 'Poetess' has brains on her side and she's coming for you. As a statement of intent there's a swagger to it, a hint of determination that the writer intends to conquer the pinnacle which the Harriet Berkeleys of the world occupied by right. Perhaps, hiding in the wings or concealed by a 'vizard' in the pit, Aphra wasn't sweating at all.

The theatre was full and the play enjoyed a respectable, if not sensational success, continuing its run for a week. If Aphra was hoping to repair her precarious finances with the play, what kind of reward could she expect? Audience sizes and takings in the 1670s are imprecise (no theatrical accounts are extant until 1714 and for the Theatre Royal until 1740), but according to one economic historian: 'No more than about 5 per cent of the total population of England and Wales could have had the discretionary spending capacity to indulge significantly in the purchase of elite culture.'* Ninety per cent of the population had an income of less than £50 per year, whilst 71,000 families had incomes exceeding £100. The threshold for a 'gentleman' was £500 per year (the sum received by Thomas Killigrew as a Gentleman of the Royal Bedchamber). London was the most expensive place to live, which also influenced spending on leisure – a labourer renting two rooms there with a wife and four children would need £55 to cover rent, food and clothes, whilst a family of the 'middling sort', six people plus two servants, was estimated to need £315, of which £16 might be available for entertainment.

Theatre boxes cost 4 shillings, the pit 2s 6d, the first gallery 1s 6d and the second gallery 1s. A play could be a pricey outing – a family of four who walked to and from the theatre could spend 4 shillings for seats in the second gallery, but if they made an evening of it, with a box, oranges, a hackney coach and dinner

* Hume, Robert D., 'The Economics of Culture in London 1660–1740', *Huntington Library Quarterly* (2006)

in a tavern, they might spend 25–30 shillings. Samuel Pepys kept careful accounts of his spending at the theatre. In 1661 he was embarrassed to find himself in the eighteenpence seats at the same performance as two underling clerks from his office who had splashed out two shillings and sixpence apiece. In 1664, his personal budget allotted £2 10 shillings for a year's worth of theatre tickets. King Charles spent £10 each time he went to the theatre, which he did on average twice a month.

Writers did not receive advances for plays. Instead they traditionally received the takings of the third night's performance. The maximum gross for the Duke's and King's companies could be £105 per night, which after the house charge of £25 would leave the writer a profit of £80. However, theatres tended to run at a 50 to 60 per cent capacity, giving an average take of £47–50 per day. This would be a reasonable expectation for Aphra then, but it was hardly a fortune. To survive in London, a writer would need a minimum of one original play per year, hence the 400 new pieces staged between 1660 and 1700. Compared with actors, whose pay ranged from £30 to £150 per year, writers fared poorly. There was no concept of royalties; writers would receive nothing after that third night, even if their work continued to be revived for decades.

Then as now, anyone who hoped to get rich by writing was an idiot, but the lack of financial rewards didn't stop writers competing to have their work staged. At the Duke's Company, Harris and Betterton acted like modern-day film executives, assessing and dismissing scripts with a brevity their authors found distressing. Harris claimed he could judge the quality of a play by reading a single act.

It has been estimated that Aphra made between £15 and £25 for *The Forc'd Marriage*, which wasn't going to last for long. Publishing plays was a useful form of supplementary income, as they remained the property of the author, rather than the theatre. Dedicating a printed play to a rich, prominent figure could also be useful – they might buy copies, give a cash present to the writer and support future productions. Aphra managed to get nearly all her plays into print, but though *The Forc'd Marriage* was brought out quickly by the firm of James Magnes, Aphra had, as yet, no one to dedicate it to. The work was released with just a poignant wish, fashionably expressed in French – 'Va mon enfant, prends ta fortune'.

11

Aphra's plays are the only 'children' she is known to have had. She never seemed very interested in or fond of children (though she could muster appropriate compliments when required), and they don't appear to have played much part in her life. There are more than enough gaps in her biography for her to have had several, in or out of wedlock, and the theatre world of Restoration London was not intolerant of bastards while the King himself was setting the example. There is one interesting and potentially shocking ellipsis, though, in Aphra's portrayal of Harriet Berkeley's alter ego Silvia in her novel *Love Letters*. Towards the end of the story, Silvia gives birth to a healthy child. Her pregnancy has been barely acknowledged until this point, and the child vanishes as quickly as it appears. Given that Silvia has by this point been transformed from an innocent girl to a rapacious and successful whore to whom motherhood would be most professionally inconvenient, there is a (slight) hint that she has disposed of the baby permanently.

Domesticity doesn't seem to have been Aphra's thing. She didn't own or lease a house of her own and her London life was spent in lodgings. Her professional and social life was based in the area between Holborn and the river, encompassing Lincoln's Inn and Covent Garden, with Whitehall to the west and the City to the east. The district with which Aphra was most strongly associated was Whitefriars, between modern-day Fleet Street and the Thames; not the most elegant of addresses. The name came from the Carmelite convent founded there by Edward I, which had been largely pulled down for redevelopment in the mid-sixteenth century. Until the Restoration, Whitefriars had retained a degree of respectability, but by Aphra's time it had become the home of 'the dregs of an age that was indeed full of dregs'. It contained the area known as the 'liberty of Alsatia', which had the uncertain legal status of a sanctuary, where debtors and criminals could legitimately take refuge, and Aphra's neighbours included 'degraded clergymen who would marry anyone for five shillings, broken lawyers, skulking bankrupts, sullen homicides, thievish money lenders and gaudy courtesans'. Some optimistic tour guides give Aphra an address in Dorset Street, perhaps because this was built on the site of Davenant's first theatre at Salisbury Court, hard by the Dorset Garden Theatre to which the company moved in 1671. Despite the presence of fashionable theatre audiences, Whitefriars was rackety, crowded, boisterous and more than a little dangerous, though Aphra may have seen it as vibrant and edgy.

Did she live alone? There is no more mention of family members after the Butler debacle. Aphra could order her life, so far as her resources allowed, as she chose. As an independent woman about town there was plenty of opportunity to enjoy the kind of clever company and conversation for which she herself became celebrated. Did she entertain in her rooms? Unless they were large enough to be equipped with a range and cooking equipment and a servant to deal with them, Aphra like many Londoners would have been dependent on takeaways from cookshops or taverns for dining. She had opinions on food: in *Oroonoko* she comments on the heavy spicing in the dishes of Surinam, which her narrator finds too strong, and rejoices in the abundance of fresh fruit. Looking back after twenty years in London, Surinam remembered was an Eden of plenty in comparison with the rather grim dietary options of the capital.

At its best, seventeenth-century food was everything that modern consumers aspire to, fresh, organic, locally sourced. At its worst, it was revolting and potentially deadly. Meat could be 'meazly' and diseased (eating pork in London was a game of Russian roulette); vegetables, increasingly brought in from the country now that London's gardens were being built over, were polluted with grime, soot and the human excrement which the barges carrying them into the city took on as return cargo; bread was contaminated with alum and reputedly chalk; butter often rancid and 'all kinds of horrors could be concealed in a pie'. Clean water was a rare commodity, food hygiene and obviously refrigeration unheard of. Sugar was added to all manner of dishes in wince-making quantities (the seventeenth century was the beginning of the end for British teeth). Commenting on the meals served at 'ordinaries', taverns which served fixed-price menus to busy Londoners like Aphra, Ned Ward described 'rotten Mutton, Beef that's turnip fed, Lean Meazly pork on London muck hills bred'. If the ingredients weren't bad enough, the cooking consisted of a basting 'with a Flux of mingl'd fat which greasily distils from this and that'. Those who could afford it carried their own utensils with them – the antibacterial properties of silver meant that not dying of food poisoning was one of the first advantages of the proverbial silver spoon.

The Aphra Behn signature dish was a concoction known as milk punch. Like so many other London commodities, the milk available in the city could be spectacularly nasty. Novelist Tobias Smollett described it in the early eighteenth century as being 'frothed with bruised snails, carried through the streets in open pails, exposed to foul rinsings . . . spittle, snot and tobacco quids, spatterings from coach wheels . . . the spewings of infants, and finally the vermin that drips from the rags of that nasty drab that vends this precious mixture.' Perhaps Aphra bought the milk for her punch not from a grimy-handed milkmaid but from one of the cows that were walked through the streets 'as mobile bovine vending machines', but the contents of her punch were enough to daunt even the most persistent bacteria. Aphra's recipe was recalled by one of the actors of the Duke's Company, John Bowman, who had never tried such a thing before. It included a gallon of brandy infused for two days with water, lemon rind and sugar after which it was mixed with the milk and boiled up with nutmeg before being strained ready to drink.

Within the fiction of the *Memoirs*, Aphra is painted as a *bon viveuse* who liked a drink, an image which fits the woman given over to 'Pleasure and Poetry'. Certainly, her circle of London friends included some of the most spectacular booze hounds of an epically boozy age, but her introduction of milk punch as a novelty recalls her connection with another Barbados character and suggests quite another aspect to her own.

Thomas Tryon has been neglected in Aphra Behn's biography, but her personal interest in him provides another instance of her connections with the New World. Originally from a farming family, Tryon had no formal education and taught himself to read from a primer. After an apprenticeship with a London hatter, Tryon tried his luck in Barbados, spending five years there from 1661. His observations on the indulgent lifestyle of the planters sparked an interest in the effects of diet on health and he went on to write more than twenty books on the subject. Tryon refuted the idea that the tropical climate was especially dangerous for Europeans in the colonies. The fevers and infections which made their lives so hazardous were exacerbated by 'the very frequent Tippling of that pernicious Drink called Punch'. Like Aphra in *Oroonoko*, Tryon celebrated the variety of 'fragrant Herbs, Roots and Grains' found in the islands, which 'far exceed those of cold countries in Quantity and Quality'. He was disgusted by the habits of the newly enriched English community, aping their betters back home, who 'gorge themselves with the grossest Foods, various dishes of Flesh, Fish and Fowls, whereof they daily eat to Gluttony, and the strongest liquors'. Tryon was an evangelistic vegetarian whose works advocated a diet rich in vitamins and fibre and the avoidance of excessive alcohol. Like Aphra, he was also preoccupied with the question of slavery, though his 1684 tract *Friendly Advice to the Gentlemen Planters of the East and West Indies* is far less ambivalent on the subject than Aphra's novel. Given the size of the European community on Barbados and Surinam and the frequency of contact between them, it is quite probable that Aphra knew Tryon before she arrived in London in the early 1660s. He was derided as a crank by many contemporaries, but Aphra was sufficiently convinced by his prescriptions to provide a poetic puff for his self-help diet book *The Way to Healthy Long Life and Happiness*, published in 1683. Praising his emphasis on 'harmless drink and wholesome food', Aphra encouraged Tryon to ignore his detractors, as she had tried his suggestions and found they worked: 'Let fools and mad-men thy great work condemn / I've tried thy Method and adore thy Theme.' Aphra didn't take all of Tryon's proposals to heart (he highly disapproved of the corrupting influence of poetry and the theatre), but she was sufficiently convinced to describe him as a 'Saving Angel'.

Aphra the teetotal vegetarian is a different person from the 'loose' woman of the *Memoirs*, but a degree of self-discipline accords with her professionalism as a writer. Deadlines and three-day hangovers don't mix, and unlike some of her hard-drinking aristocratic friends Aphra couldn't afford endless partying. One thing she did appear to indulge in though was fashion.

One of the features of Restoration theatre which can make it seem so clunky to modern audiences is the efficacity of disguise. Cross-dressing women in particular abound, if only because daring 'breeches parts' showed off actresses' legs, but many plots turn on the absolute conviction of their characters' belief in such concealment. No one ever seems to question the authenticity of the pretty pages and dashing bravos and the device is frankly tiresome. Yet in a strictly hierarchical, highly gendered culture, the visual signals of clothing were far more significant than today. The seventeenth century would be utterly bewildered by modern casual dress. What you seemed was what you were believed almost unquestioningly to be, hence the success of the disguise plots. Particularly in relation to class, dressing according to one's station was necessary to exact due deference from inferiors. Popular conduct manuals emphasized the importance of dressing according to one's 'Dignity' or risk having it insulted.

Great ladies flaunted their status with silk or velvet gowns worn over the finest peekaboo underlinens, their flimsiness and transparency displayed for maximum erotic allure. Samuel Pepys left a rather creepy description of spying on the washing line of the King's mistress Barbara Palmer in the Privy Garden at Whitehall: 'the finest smocks and linen petticoats . . . edged with rich lace at the bottom, that I ever see and it did me good to look upon them'. Gowns were further enhanced with drooping trains and sleeves in contrasting colours, braid, gold thread and embroidery. Amongst the fictionalized letters which make up the *Memoirs*, Aphra appears in character as 'Astrea' in a sequence set in Antwerp, where a fat old Dutch merchant makes her an offer to become his mistress. Her reply lists all the expenses on finery her acceptance will incur, including 'Ribbons and Hoods, Diamond Rings, Lockets, Pearl Necklaces, Silks, Holland, lawn, Gold and Silver Lace, Embroideries and Fringes, Perfume, Paint and Powder'. In her own writing, Aphra is attentive to the vivid lustre of bright silks or the luxurious sheen of rich velvet, but only the wealthy could afford such things. Outside the top echelon of society, most people bought their clothes second-hand from 'botchers' and remade them to fit. Acquiring clothes suitable for social dignity, let alone appearances at court or fashionable venues, would be a struggle on an income of £50 per year.

Astrea's itemization of the requirements of a well-dressed woman includes scent and make-up, and hygiene was another significant expense. The dirtiness of the seventeenth century is a hotly contested subject. Whitehall Palace is seen as little more than a gilded dungheap where exotic perfumes concealed foul odours, whilst after a period of residence at Oxford, the gorgeous ladies and gentlemen of the court were found to have left the fireplaces clogged with excrement. London fashions were set by those of France, and for comparison, a survey of conduct literature from 1500 to 1839 does indicate that the seventeenth century came off worst in terms of personal cleanliness. Only between 1600 to 1700 does the cleaning of the nails, mouth, head, teeth and ears remain unspecified, in comparison with 'morning and evening' in 1500–19 or 'morning and mealtimes' for 1700–19. Washing with water was not a frequent practice in London; instead the body was rubbed down with a cloth to dislodge lice and absorb dirt and grease from the hair and skin. Olive oil soap and perfumed washes for the hair and skin were available as were tooth powders and cleansing creams, permitting a peripheral cleanliness of the face and particularly the nails (as signifiers of status), but bathing was affordable only for the very rich. Versailles and Whitehall were equipped with bathrooms and even Turkish-style hammams, yet Aphra herself may conceivably never have had a bath indoors.

London was a particularly difficult place to stay clean. In dry weather, dust, rubbish and manure blew about the streets, in wet weather they became mires of filth, and in all weathers smuts and acrid smoke bogged the city. Walking in the middle of the street put pedestrians at risk from traffic, at the edge from gushing downpipes and oozing 'boghouses'. Seeing 'people of quality' get dirty was one of the delights of the urban poor 'when a well-dress'd person is dash'd over Head and Ears with dirt . . . a sorry Scoundrel with scarce shoes to his feet shall shake his sides.' Galoshes or high pattens and heavy cloaks protected precious garments; sedan chairs and hackney coaches, which Aphra made use of when she could, were used as much to spare clothes as for speedier transport. Tripping in the slippery, churned London mud could be extremely hazardous. Aphra grieved at the bathetic end of her friend the artist John Greenhill, who died after falling drunkenly into a gutter. A 1706 essay *Towards a School of English Painters*, notes that 'Mrs Behn' had been greatly won over by Greenhill's poetic and agreeable conversation, and her admiration is commemorated in the eulogy she wrote for him:

> Great master of the Noblest Mystery
> That ever happy knowledge did inspire,

Sacred as that of Poetry,
And which the wondering World does equally
    admire.

Before his muddy demise, John Greenhill has been
credited with producing the most accurate image of
Aphra as she wished to present herself when her
career as a writer began to take off. Known as the 'Yale
Portrait', the painting is a copy, reportedly by Greenhill, of an earlier work by his teacher, the royal painter
Sir Peter Lely. Lely died in 1680, so this lost work can
be placed in the 1670s. The provenance of the Greenhill copy can be traced to 'Mr Tho. Wright' from the
notes on its auction in 1717 where it is described as
'Mrs Behn the Poetess'. Thomas Wright was the chief
'Machinist', or stage engineer, at the Duke's Theatre
and the portrait is an example of 'lobby pictures' produced for publicity purposes.

(Aphra returned to her American roots in the
nineteenth century, when the picture was sold by Col-
naghi in 1888 to R. Hall McCormick. It was then sold
to Mr Arthur Schlecter, who bequeathed it to Yale
University.)

Aphra's light auburn hair is dressed in ringleted
waves and pinned up with two pearl clasps. Her features may have been slightly re-modelled to give them
the 'Lely look', languorous almond eyes, full rosebud
lips and a fashionable hint of double chin, yet it
remains very much the portrait of an individual. The

gaze is particularly notable, frank, steady, confident, and there is the slightest, slightest hint of a suppressed smile. Her low-cut russet gown worn over a foam of sparkling linen is slashed at the sleeve and bodice, fastened in front with another pearl, and she has a taupe silk shawl over her left shoulder. The impression is of 'a modest yet fashionable woman of her day, accessorized with fabrics and ornaments that speak to a genteel and prosperous status'.* This doesn't necessarily mean that Aphra had attained genteel prosperity. Artists customarily provided props and garments for their sitters, so Aphra's dress and valuable pearl clasps could have been borrowed or hired, but she very much looks the part. A modern fashion writer might describe Aphra's look as 'current' or 'relevant'; her dress is up to date and quite simple, not fussy or over-embellished, and the overall effect is fresh and accessible. This 'Poetess' has no superior-seeming symbols surrounding her, no heavy books or pretentious laurel wreaths, and there is nothing overtly sexy about it. As a publicity shot, it works, Aphra comes across as serious, professional and appealing without being pushy. Just the thing for the women who were attending the theatre in ever increasing numbers.

There are two more portraits of Aphra extant, one

---

* Van Hensbergen, Claudine, 'Aphra Behn: Portraiture and the Biographical Account', *Review of English Studies*, vol. 72 (2021)

engraved by Robert White from a lost picture by John Riley and the other, the 'St Hilda's Portrait', attributed to Greenhill's fellow student Mary Beale. It would be delightful if the only professional woman portraitist of the Restoration had indeed painted its only professional woman playwright, but 'the sheer desire to accept this portrait as an authentic image of Behn cannot compensate for the lack of evidence for doing so'. Aside from bearing very little resemblance to the two corroborated pictures, its date is too early, and it was rejected by the National Portrait Gallery in 1950. The 'Riley' portrait, by contrast, was supervised by Aphra herself as it was used as the frontispiece for her 1684 collection *Poems on Several Occasions*, which was sold by her publisher Jacob Tonson. The similarities of the gown, shawl and wry expression suggest that it may in part have been a reproduction of the Lely/Greenhill image, though the hairstyle has moved on and the features are harder, more mature and defined. Here Aphra is alert and intelligent, apparently at ease. Perhaps it is not going too far to say she looks frank and forceful or at least that she seems to have just thought up a very satisfactory joke.

Discrepancies between these available images of Aphra have suggested to some writers that she was concealing her racial origins, that is, that she was 'white passing'. If it is accepted that Aphra Behn was *not* Eaffrey Johnson and that she was born in either Maryland or Barbados, with a consequently uncertain birth date, does this theory merit attention? That is, could she have been the daughter of a white father and a black mother? In the case of Maryland it seems improbable, since labouring women in the colony were predominantly white indentured servants during the first decades of its establishment. Barbados, however, had been receiving slaves in growing numbers since 1627. Between 1641 and Lord Willoughby's first departure in 1652, slavers transported over 6,500 people to the island. By the 1660s, the slave population was estimated by some contemporaries to have attained 70,000.

One proponent of the theory suggests that Aphra's appearance in London without any apparent familial ties may be related to an attempt to conceal her past: 'Persons who engage in colour passing generally must sever all ties to the community of their birth, their families, and most importantly erase all social and cultural traces of a "pre-passing identity".'*

'Black' was used generally in the seventeenth century to designate a person with dark hair and eyes – Charles II, for example, was frequently described as a 'black man'. A posthumously published story of Aphra's, *The Black Lady*, uses the adjective in this manner. However, the heroine of the same story is named 'Bellamora' which can be read two ways, either (in the fashion of nominative determinism popular for

* Hendricks, Margo, *Race and Romance: Coloring the Past* (2022)

fictional characters) as 'beautiful love', or as 'beautiful moor'. The latter interpretation relates *The Black Lady* to another of Aphra's stories, *The Unfortunate Bride*, which features a 'Blackamoor Lady' known as Moorea. Moorea is a powerful character, the titled widow of a knight with a huge income of £6,000 whose charms divert the hero, Frankwit, from his betrothed Belvira.

That Aphra was highly alert to the horrors of slavery in the colonies and also to the presence of a significant black community in London does not really suggest that she was herself black. However, two comments on her appearance might be considered in this context. Back in Antwerp in 1666, Aphra's rival spy Thomas Corney had drawn attention to her 'Faire' looks. Corney is being sarcastic, intending to disparage Aphra, but how far does the sarcasm go? In the *Session of Apollo* poem of 1676, Aphra swears to her talent on her 'sweet face' and her 'black ace'. The latter refers crudely to the vulva, ace being slang for female genitals, the ace of spades in particular. As an inside joke, perhaps the poem takes a swipe at the auburn hair of the Yale portrait having received a little help, but even that seems to give too much importance to a convenient rhyme. Put simply, if Aphra was black as the term is presently used, why did no one mention it?

Such speculation does, however, draw attention to Aphra's attitude towards slavery in her novel *Oroonoko*. In terms of contemporary views, this is both complex and problematic. In his *Advice* to English planters, Aphra's friend Thomas Tryon recalls a conversation with 'Sambo', an archetypal slave character, who sets out the appalling conditions of life on Barbados in the most explicit terms. Sambo describes the slaves rising at daylight to go to the sugar fields where they work until dusk with only a brief break to eat yams or potatoes. While the greedy planters worship their 'Idol, Belly-God Paunch', the starving slaves are reduced to supplementing their rations with carrion, cats, rats or the exhumed corpses of horses. Exhaustion often leads to unnecessary accidents in which they are maimed or killed, but the 'Flint hearted Tyrants' allow them no respite from their 'continued drudgery' until 'our Heart strings crack and our Nerves are enfeebled and our Marrow is exhausted and our Bones fall under our Burdens and our Spirits are consumed and our souls in Weariness and Anguish wish for death rather than life.' Escapees are strung up from trees and whipped until their flesh falls off in ribbons. For many slaves, suicide seems the only way out of this torture.

Tryon is particularly condemnatory of the white women on Barbados, the planters' wives, who show no empathy or pity for slave mothers. Pregnant women must return to the fields days after giving birth. In noting the number of children born of women raped by their masters, Tryon wonders how the latter can be so cruel as to continue to perpetuate such horror on their own offspring. In *Oroonoko*, Caesar and Imoinda choose death rather than allow their child to be born a slave. Tryon does not go so far as to condemn the practice of slavery outright, but his *Advice* is considerably more condemnatory than Aphra's better known *Oroonoko*.

Aphra's story was popular from the moment it was published, adapted for the stage shortly after her death and translated into French where it went through seven editions in the following century. As the anti-slavery movement began slowly to gain momentum in Europe, *Oroonoko* was held up as an eyewitness account of the atrocities of the slave trade, yet though it is about slavery it is not exactly or entirely against it. As the book opens, the narrator explains that the native inhabitants of Surinam are both too numerous and too useful to be used for chattel labour and hence the colony is supplied by slaves from Coromantien, in modern-day Ghana. Prince Oroonoko is himself a slave owner and slave trader, having learned English and Spanish from traders to his country. He presents 150 fettered slaves to his beloved, Imoinda, during their courtship, and as a gesture of respect to a defeated but noble enemy does not 'put him amongst the rank of captives, as they used to do without distinction, for the common sale or market' but retains him at court as a friend. The English trader who (with the help of pernicious punch) traps Oroonoko into slavery is already known to him, as they have concluded sales of human cargo in the past, as Oroonoko is stated to have done with the merchant's predecessors. That is, the early pages of the novel insist on slavery as an African cultural practice and one from which Oroonoko himself profits without objection.

After he too has been enslaved, Oroonoko, renamed Caesar, incites a revolt against the Surinam planters. In his exhortation to his fellow slaves he makes the distinction between the commercial sale of people as property and the 'honourable' custom of enslaving enemies:

'Have they vanquished us nobly in a fight? Have they won us in honourable battle? And are we by chance of war become their slaves? This would not anger a noble heart, this would not animate a soldier's soul; no, but we are bought and sold like apes or monkeys, to be the sport of women, fools and cowards, and the support of rogues, runagates, that have abandoned their own countries for rapine, murders, thefts and villainies.'

It is intolerable, he continues, 'to render obedience to such a degenerate race, who have no one humane virtue to distinguish them from the vilest creatures'. He is not saying that one people have no right whatsoever to enslave another, but that the grounds for this cannot be sought as justification in the respective races of the peoples concerned, but rather in the more abstract quality of their 'honour'. It is just for Prince Oroonoko to enslave those he has captured in war and sell them to Europeans, but unjust for Europeans to enslave Caesar on the basis of the colour of his skin. That Oroonoko's conception of honour is derived from the European education he has received from those he counts as degenerate simultaneously reinforces and undercuts his argument.

Oroonoko has generated a vast quantity of academic studies, which have mined the text for its every nuance, but there is nothing in the narrator's role in the story which reasonably supports the idea that it is a narrative of 'white passing' on its creator's part. Indeed 'passing' in the seventeenth-century context may be seen as anachronistic, since the entrenched obscenity of imperialist racism had not yet cohered, nor was slavery at the time confined to the traffic of black people by white people. Slavery existed in the Ottoman Empire and its remains lingered in parts of Italy where the early Renaissance beauties of cities like Venice and Florence had been constructed on the backs of slaves from the Black Sea. The claim that 'Aphra was not alarmed by slavery as such' does not mean that she accepted or endorsed the practices of the Atlantic slave trade but that her interest in enslavement, in the exploitation of the weak by the strong, was informed by the politics, including gendered politics, of her time.

In September 1655 the first advertisement for a 'Freedom Seeker' appeared in the newsletter *Mercurius Politicus*. A 'Negro Boy' had escaped from the service of Lord Willoughby of Parham. A discreet reward was offered for information leading to his 'return', for which might be read 'capture'. In the future, 'Freedom Seekers' were to become a regular feature of the London press and, as in the case of the advertisement for Harriet in the *London Gazette* placed by the Earl of Berkeley in 1682, these notices were instances of an owner requesting the return of his property. Many literary scholars have observed a correlation between Aphra's interest in writing about slavery and her observations on the servitude imposed on women by Restoration culture. This is not to suggest that she saw the two conditions as equivalent, but that there were parallels between them. That Aphra was more alert than her fellow playwrights to the presence of the growing black community in London* might suggest the influence of a colonial upbringing, but in the 1670s most Londoners exercised their prejudice on confessional rather than racial grounds. That is not to say that black people were not already suffering discrimination, but that race was not yet a such a topical issue. The English hated foreigners in general, the Dutch and the French in particular

* Estimates of the number of people of African descent in London in the late seventeenth and eighteenth centuries vary widely according to the source. In 1794, *The Gentleman's Magazine* proposed that the black community numbered as many as 20,000 people, whilst figures from the Old Bailey suggest a lower number, between 5,000 to 10,000 by the last quarter of the eighteenth century.

and Catholics most of all. It was the political divisions engendered by such hatreds that would bring Aphra's life and writing ever closer to the story of Harriet Berkeley.

The terms of the Treaty of Dover had seen Charles II agree to an alliance with his cousin Louis XIV against the Dutch United Provinces, and what became known as the Third Dutch War was duly declared on 17 March 1672. It produced dissonance amongst the loyalties of the English, who despite popular anti-Dutch prejudice loathed the idea of joining a French Catholic force against a Protestant nation. In an attempt to appease Protestant non-conformists (those who like Edward Lloyd of Kent Maryland refused to adhere to the doctrine of the Anglican church), the King proposed passing an 'Act of Indulgence' which would guarantee their freedom of worship. The plan was shelved when it was pointed out that the terms of the Act would also permit Catholics to worship in private and was replaced by an alternative 'act for preventing dangers which may happen from Popish recusants', otherwise known as the Test Act. Anyone holding a government or military position would from now on be required to take Anglican communion within three months of obtaining their post and to wear an oath denying one of the primary tenets of the Roman church, that the bread and wine of the sacrament were truly the body and blood of Christ. A reluctant Parliament was thus persuaded to grant the funds for the war, but the Test Act created a huge problem within the royal family.

The King's brother and heir, the Duke of York, had himself converted to Catholicism some years previously. It is a measure of the extraordinarily blockheaded stubbornness of the Stuarts that he now earnestly resigned from his post as admiral of the fleet in accordance with the Test Act, making public what had until then been just about deniable. In an equally uncompromising insistence on the royal prerogative which had seen off his own father's head, Charles refused to concede until his death that his brother had thus renounced the right to succeed him. The Duke of York provoked scandal and consternation when he publicly refused to take Anglican communion at Easter 1673, but with the war against the Dutch in progress the government tried to suppress fears of a Catholic succession by emphasizing that York's children by his late wife, the Princesses Mary and Anne, were Protestants. Naturally the pig-headed Duke scotched this by marrying a Catholic, Mary of Modena, in September that year.

Charles had justified the war to some extent as concerning the rights of his dispossessed nephew, William of Orange, who had been excluded from the position of stadtholder of the United Provinces in 1653. William was, after all, a Protestant prince. Unfortunately for Charles, his restoration rhetoric had been undercut by William's appointment as admiral and captain general of the Dutch armies just a few months after the war had begun. Between the Duke of York's conversion, the public opposition to his marriage and William's acceptance of the position of stadtholder in July, the continuation of hostilities was no longer tenable. The war was brought to an inconclusive but face-saving end in 1674, but resolution within Charles's kingdom was to prove much more difficult to achieve.

Aphra wrote and produced four further plays between 1671 and 1677, *The Amorous Prince*, *The Dutch Lover*, *Abdelazer* and *The Town Fopp*, as well as collaborating with Thomas Killigrew on a verse anthology, *The Covent Garden Drolery*, which included four of her own poems. Of these works, the reception of *The Dutch Lover* provoked her into her most explicit statement yet as to how she viewed what was becoming not only her livelihood but her art. Despite the presence of the King in the audience, the play had been a flop. The script is frantically crowded with three competing narratives, too much use is made of darkness and mistaken identity, even by the patient standards of the time, and the 'beastly' Dutch lover fell flat. Aphra defiantly published the play, adding an 'Epistle' in which she addresses the reader directly. Her target is the pomposity of self-appointed critics who judge drama according to an abstract set of classical rules, rather than the overall effect it produces. Playwriting, she argues, merits a dignity of its own:

for surely they [plays] deserve a place among the middle, if not the better sort of Books, for I have heard the most of that which bears the name of Learning and which has abused such quantities of ink and Paper and continually employs so many ignorant unhappy souls for ten, twelve, twenty years in the University . . . as Logic and several other things (that should be nameless lest I misspell them) are much more absolutely nothing than the errantest Play that ever was writ.

Aphra goes on to explain that the reaction a playwright intends is emotional, not intellectual, and she expresses her own version of the 'show don't tell' doctrine used by modern-day screenwriters: 'for though you are told within a leaf or two of the Prologue that they are people of Wit, good Humour, good Manners and all that, yet if the authors did not kindly add their proper names, you'd never know them by their characters.' Claiming that the play is (note the French) 'the best divertissement that wise men have', Aphra dismisses those who are obsessed with form over content, concluding proudly that 'I studied only to make this as entertaining as I could, which whether I have been successful, gentle reader, you may for your shilling judge . . .'

That Aphra had a chip on her shoulder about her lack of formal education is painfully obvious, but in defending the emotional immediacy of the stage and refusing to conform to sterile strictures about what 'good' writing is, Aphra's 'Epistle' foreshadows a more famous statement by another independent-minded woman writer, Jane Austen:

> Oh! It is only a novel . . . only some work in which the greatest powers of the mind are displayed, in which the most thorough knowledge of human nature, the happiest delineation of its varieties, the liveliest effusions of wit and humour are conveyed to the world in the best chosen language.

In her writing life at least, Aphra had established a regular and productive routine. It was a busy time, working on her current production, dealing with actors, rewrites and rehearsals whilst carving out time to produce fresh work. Aphra was known for the speed and deftness with which she wrote, and her work often went on in the presence of others, even during conversations. There was no room in seventeenth-century London for the concept of writing as a sacred activity to be performed privately, in reverential silence. Like many writers today, tapping away on their laptops in coffee shops, Aphra wrote where she could, backstage at the theatre or at the corner table of a tavern. Public spaces provided warmth and especially light – candles, even cheap, foul-smelling tallow ones, were expensive and to be used sparingly. Aphra was earning her living, but as those coffee-shop freelancers also know, being self-employed is a highly unreliable business.

Wheedling what she was owed from publishers and the management at Dorset Garden was also a time-consuming affair. In one of her rare signed letters, Aphra effectively mortgages her next play to Zachary Baggs of the accounts department. She had received an advance of six pounds cash from her publisher Tonson which Baggs was to pay back to him in turn, in exchange for which, 'in case the said debt is not fully discharged before Michaelmas next' Aphra empowered Baggs to 'stop what money he shall here-after have in his hands of mine upon the playing of my first play till this aforesaid debt of six pound be discharged'. It was a painfully small amount of money to warrant such contortions. Recalling her fear as described to Lord Arlington from Antwerp – 'I shall eat out my head' – or the defiant pleading to Killigrew over the Butler debt, the Baggs note is a reminder of how perilously close Aphra often came to poverty and of how much discipline and determination it took for her to work on in the face of almost perennial financial anxiety.

The most obvious solution for a woman who needed help with the rent was to 'go into keeping' to take a lover who would, as was customary, expect to contribute to his mistress's upkeep. It wasn't quite so bald a transaction as charging a set fee for sex, but it was not an exchange among equals. In 1687 a nosey parker named Roger Morris published a *Register* of London gossip, in which he recorded that ten of twelve years earlier, 'Mrs Beane' had been in keeping with a Mr Hoyle. The couple had subsequently broken off their acquaintance due to a 'difference'. John, or 'Jack' Hoyle is the only confirmed relationship we know Aphra to have had. A Yorkshireman, Hoyle was a lifelong republican, the son of a Parliamentarian alderman who had supported the execution of Charles I and then hanged himself in remorse on the anniversary of the sentence. He was a lawyer, educated at Gray's Inn and a member of the Inner Temple, part of the raffish crowd on the fringes of literary London who were amongst Aphra's first friends when she began writing professionally.

Hoyle has not left a record as a particularly pleasant character. Amongst other drawbacks, he was a murderer, having stabbed a watchmaker to death in a fit of drunken aggression in 1663. He was tried but escaped the noose on the grounds of insufficient evidence. Hoyle was also more sexually interested in men than women; he was lampooned as a notorious 'bugger' and in 1687 he was on trial again for 'sodomy with a poulterer' (one wonders which was worse, the act or the profession). In 1692 he received his just desserts when he died of stab wounds incurred in yet another drunken brawl. In his favour, he was said to be extremely good-looking, and he owned a significant library, which he left to the Royal Society in his will.

From the hints that can be gleaned from Aphra's poetry, she was entirely comfortable with same sex attraction and admired beauty in men and women. Her name was associated with two younger men, a Jeffrey Boys and a Latin translator named John Cooper, but beyond the relationship with Hoyle there is no firm evidence concerning her private life. A series of letters, published along with the *Memoirs* as *Love Letters to a Gentleman by Mrs A. Behne* have been cautiously taken by some critics as being real, but in both their form and content they are patently fiction. If they were by Aphra at all, they read more as a draft for a short story in letters or perhaps part of a novel similar in style to *Love Letters*. They are not without value, as they capture with great immediacy the frustrations and contradictions of a love affair conducted more in words than deeds. The male character, called 'Lycidas', displays all the behaviours of which twenty-first century women on dating apps complain. He 'ghosts' the writer, 'Astrea', then complains when she doesn't contact him. He makes dates which he always cancels at the last moment but claims to be jealous if she sees other people. Frustrated, she spies on him and discovers he is hanging around in the coffee house at the end of her street; when she confronts him he says he needs space. Psychologically, 'Astrea's' voice is spot-on – the letters capture her self-contradictions and futile attempts at assertiveness as concisely as modern text messages: 'I am undone and will be free; I will tell you, you did not use me well; I am ruined and will rail at you – Come then.' Or, 'You would not be in Love for

all the world, yet wish I were so.' The more he with-
holds the harder she pursues, even while she knows
that treating him mean is the only way to entice him.
Concise and remarkably astute, the letters are a clever
and often poignant mini drama, but they reveal nothing about the reality of Aphra's relationship with
Hoyle.

Amongst his many other activities during the Interregnum, Thomas Killigrew had found the time to
write a long play, *Thomaso, or The Wanderer* in two parts
and ten acts, chronicling the adventures and amorous
scrapes of an exiled Royalist. Aphra's reworking of
his script, retitled *The Rover*, was to prove her most
successful play to date. The King was in the audience
at the Dorset Garden Theatre for its first performance on 24 March 1677. Aphra's timing was brilliant.
The generation of gallant Cavaliers who had loyally
followed their King from rags to riches were growing
old. Charles himself had become a terrible bore about
his escape from the Battle of Worcester, endlessly
recounting the story of his six weeks on the run across
England. The younger generation at court who had
taken no part in the Restoration were, for all their
drinking and roistering, diminished by its shadow. Setting *The Rover* in the past allowed the older men to
indulge their nostalgia and the younger ones the relief
of laughing at it.

Aphra's hero Willmore, still in the same breeches
in which he escaped Worcester, is washed up, in
every sense, in Naples. Poor, drunk and aimless, 'a

no-purchase, no-pay tatterdemalion, and English picaroon', he has somehow remained wildly sexy, attracting the attention of the city's most expensive courtesan, Angellica, then a well-born girl, Hellena, who is desperate to see life, and love, before submitting to the convent. Willmore tries to seduce Hellena by claiming true love needs no promises beyond itself – marriage he says is as certain a bane to love as lending money to a friendship. Hellena is having none of it. 'What shall I get?' she asks. 'A cradle full of noise and mischief with a pack of repentance at my back?' After the usual cross-dressings, misidentifications, duels and tricks, all comes right and the couple marry. So much was conventional, yet in the characters of Angellica and Hellena Aphra did something new. Angellica the whore calls out Willmore on the hypocrisy of men's sexual double standards, pointing out that marrying for money is the same 'mercenary crime' as prostitution. Hellena, a 'mad wench', is intelligent, funny, outspoken and as subtly cynical as her suitor. She accepts the marriage because she has no other way of avoiding a nun's veil, but she does not idealize it. Beneath the dashing dialogue and madcap action, Aphra is pointing out that the only choices available to most women – being supported as a wife or earning a living by selling their bodies – often amount to the same thing. The buffoonery of the male characters, hot Willmore included, makes both options seem less than appealing.

Willmore's character owed a good deal to one of the most meaningful relationships of Aphra's life, her friendship with John Wilmot, 2nd Earl of Rochester. Brilliant, beautiful and desperately flawed, Rochester embodied in his person all the promise and paradox of the Restoration. His father, Henry the first Earl, had been Charles II's closest companion after the flight from Worcester and the King's loyalty and affection for his son never entirely wavered, though they were often sorely tried. Born at Ditchley Park, Oxfordshire in 1647, Rochester made his first appearance at court in 1664, the year of Harriet Berkeley's birth and Aphra's arrival in the capital. How exactly she and he met is unknown, though it is likely to have been first on the page, through the rustling lampoons that connected London's writers, and then through the theatre. For a time they were neighbours, as from 1670 Rochester kept a lodging on Portugal Street, near Lincoln's Inn. He was also close to Thomas Killigrew, though their relationship was affected by the drunken jeering to which Rochester frequently descended. As Pepys described of an evening at the Dutch ambassador's house in February 1669 to celebrate the peace:

> The King dining yesterday at the Dutch ambassa-
> dor's, after dinner they drank and were pretty merry
> and among the rest of the King's company there was
> that worthy fellow my Lord of Rochester and Tom
> Killigrew, whose mirth and raillery offended the

former so much that he did give Tom Killigrew a box on the ear in the King's presence, which do give much offence to the people at court.

Giving offence was Rochester's speciality. He was a poet rather than a playwright, though he appeared onstage in practically every rakish hero of the 1670s, from Aphra's Wilmot to Don John in Thomas Shadwell's *The Libertine* in 1675 and Dorimant in Etherege's *The Man of Mode* in 1676. Their friendship was certainly established that year, when Aphra was included in the list of writers in *A Session of the Poets*. Like most of Aphra's professional colleagues, Rochester was a University man, but he despised intellectual pretension and pedantry, the 'frantic crowds of thinking fools' who claimed that only slavish devotion to classical models could result in good writing. This was precisely Aphra's view, though her work was seldom darkened by the contempt and deliberate crudeness of her friend's.

Appreciation of Rochester's genius as a poet is often occluded by the shock his verse still produces. His writing pinpoints the dismal realities of drunkenness and venereal disease, whose corruptions marred the glamour of the court, but it also exposes a desperate existential void, a despairing search for meaning in a futile world. Like many men of his generation, brought up on the romance of the Restoration, he was appalled and disgusted by the failure of Charles's regime to live up to its honourable promise. That this was often lightly expressed, as in his doggerel on the King:

> We have a pretty, witty king,
> Whose word no man relies on.
> He never said a foolish thing,
> And never did a wise one

does not deflect from the agonized complexity of poems such as *A Satire against Reason and Mankind* or *The Imperfect Enjoyment*. Rochester despised pretty much everything he saw around him, including himself. In an essay written after his death, Robert Parsons observed that Rochester:

> seemed to affect something singular and paradoxical in his impieties, as well as in his writings, above the reach and thought of other men . . . for this was the heightening and amazing circumstance of his sins, that he was so diligent and industrious to recommend and propagate them.

The *Session* poem of 1676 was the product of an enforced rustication the previous year after Rochester in a drunken paroxysm of loathing had smashed the King's precious sundial in the garden at Whitehall palace. A senseless piece of violence or a deeply symbolic gesture – Rochester's love and admiration for Charles were constantly in conflict with what he perceived (rather unfairly) as his weakness. As he wrote in his *Satire on Charles II* :

> All monarchs I hate and the thrones that they
>   sit on,
> From the hector of France to the cully of
>   Britain.

'Cully' referred to a man who was imposed upon, often with the implication of cuckold, a man whose wife was unfaithful. It would not be too much to suggest that the court culture of the Restoration was entrapped in Charles's personal sexual trauma, his inability to produce a legitimate heir. Charles had married the Infanta of Portugal, Catherine of Braganza, in 1662, and despite several miscarriages the Queen had been sadly unable to fulfil the primary function of her role, the birth of an heir, her humiliation compounded as bastard after bastard was born to her husband's mistresses. Catherine was by no means as dull or as timorous as many historians have assumed, but to contemporary eyes the emptiness of the royal cradle remained as incontrovertible evidence of the failure of the marriage.

Restoration poetry and plays alike are consumed, obsessed, with infidelity and impotence. Rochester made the correlation explicit when he described the royal sceptre and the royal penis being 'of a length', and the failure of one became the failure of the other. As the 1670s drew on, the monarchy was increasingly embroiled in a succession crisis, a series of humiliating political reversals and a compensatory turn to authoritarianism. The 'wit' so prized by Rochester and his circle ultimately 'feminized' them as described in his *Satire against Reason*:

> For wits are treated just like common whores,
> First they're enjoyed and then kicked out of
> doors.

Horner, the rakish hero of Wycherley's popular play *The Country Wife*, feigns impotence the better to pursue his amorous affairs amongst the ladies of London, but the joke was on the nation. The drinking, cursing, swaggering blades of the court were enacting the regime's futility in displays of exaggerated but ultimately fruitless virility.

Both Rochester and Aphra wrote explicitly about male impotence, he in *The Imperfect Enjoyment*, she in her poem *The Disappointment*. Rochester's piece is a raucous tirade against the failure of his penis to do its duty; Aphra's is more thoughtful, as she expresses the embarrassment and frustration of impotence from a female point of view. The woman's disappointment at her lover's failure is compounded by the fact that, obviously, he blames her. 'The Nymph's resentments none but I / Can well imagine or condole', Aphra wrote. Might she have been thinking of the inadequacies of her relationship with John Hoyle, who preferred male partners? There are hints that Aphra enjoyed sex with vigorous younger men and that she also had feelings for women (much of Rochester's work also expresses a relaxed, gender-fluid attitude to sex), but she remained ruthless when mocking masculine failure to perform. In *Love Letters,* the first full sexual encounter between Harriet and Lord Grey, imagined as Silvia and Philander, ends in farcical failure. Having stoked the sexual tension to its height, Aphra has the lovers come together only for Philander to fall 'just fainting before the surrendering gates'. Naturally, this has never happened to him before.

Rochester is often condemned as a misogynist writer, but it was his times he loathed, not women. It says much about his character that he appreciated two of the most brilliant professional women of his age, Aphra and the actress Elizabeth Barry. Aphra may have come to know Elizabeth through Rochester, or vice versa, but in either case the relationship between England's leading woman playwright and its first star actress deserves a book of its own. Like Aphra, Elizabeth's origins were made respectable by posterity – she had arrived in London aged about fifteen from no one quite knew where and though later accounts gave out that she was the daughter of a lawyer, she may well have been a runaway servant from Norfolk. The trajectory of her early career is equally ambiguous.

Supposedly, Elizabeth was taken up by Lady Davenant, Aphra's employer at the Duke's Company, though she showed no talent as an actress until Rochester got his hands on her. The Earl supposedly made a bet with the playwright Etherege that he could make this unpromising ingénue into a star in six months and that it was his training in a novel, naturalistic method of acting which was behind her success. As with so much of Aphra's work, Barry's was assumed only to be any good because there was a man behind it. In fact, the dates of her stage appearances don't match with Rochester's account, and though the two had an intense love affair which produced a daughter, Esther, it seems far more likely that it was Lady Davenant and Aphra herself who were behind Elizabeth Barry's ascent to fame.

A curious reference to Aphra's past, and her appearance, is made in one of Rochester's letters to Elizabeth. Theirs was a tumultuous affair, marred by his drunken outbursts and obsessive jealousy and culminating in his cold-hearted removal of their two-year-old child from her care. Rochester complained to Elizabeth about the interference of two of her women friends in the relationship, one 'fat', one 'lean'. He also refers to one of their meetings being interrupted by the arrival of Elizabeth's neighbour, the 'shee spy'. If it was Aphra she was probably the more curvaceous of the officious ladies.

Elizabeth starred in eight of Aphra's plays, and according to the Duke's Company actor John Bowman (who had such fond memories of Aphra's milk punch), Aphra coached her in the movements and gestures she had imagined for her heroines. Elizabeth created the role of Hellena in *The Rover*; from playing the virgin she switched to the fascinating whore, La Nuche, in *The Rover Part II*, possibly her greatest part. Her stage career continued until 1710, when she was in her fifties. Although she was notorious for her lovers, Elizabeth never married, remaining single and independent. The collaboration with Aphra was hugely important for them both and it continued long after Rochester himself was gone.

Rochester died at the age of thirty-three in July 1680, racked with syphilis. At least seven of his fellow poets commemorated the occasion, including Aphra. It says a great deal about her exceptionalism as both writer and personality that she should have grown close to a man who was not only leagues above her socially but who admired and respected almost no one. Rochester had no time for Dryden, who he saw as a puffed-up crowd pleaser, attacking him in *An Allusion to Horace* with a set of poetic instructions which the Laureate had failed to follow:

> Compare each phrase, examine every line,
> Weigh every word and every thought refine.
> Scorn all applause the vile rout can bestow
> And be content to please the few who know.

This was lofty advice, which Aphra herself could never afford to take, yet Rochester respected her as a professional and an equal on the page. The elegy Aphra wrote to mourn her friend rightly observed that her age had lost its greatest poetic talent:

His name's a genius that would wit dispense,
And give the theme a soul, the words a sense.
But all fine thought that ravished when it spoke,
With the soft youth eternal leave has took.

It was particularly cruel that Rochester died in the year when Aphra seemed to have attained such solid professional success. She had been included in a volume of translations of Ovid's *Heroides*, edited by Dryden, alongside several prominent writers, and despite her modest qualification that being of 'the Fair Sex' she had no Latin, her contribution was highly praised. Naturally Dryden couldn't resist mentioning in his preface that Aphra's oenone to Paris was a paraphrase rather than a strict translation, but he sweetened his patronizing pedantry with the observation that if Aphra didn't understand Latin 'I am afraid she has given us occasion to be ashamed who do'. In February and March, Aphra's plays *The Rover* and *The Feign'd Curtizans* were given at court. Perhaps if her aristocratic friend had lived, Aphra might have followed her characters into royal circles, but to her increasing frustration throughout the rest of her career, she never did. Her plays were themselves no more risky or shocking than those of her contemporaries, but they were men. A woman could make it to the top of the Restoration court on her back, but writing, however brilliantly, for a living was just too scandalous. Nonetheless, whoever Aphra really was and wherever she really came from, her friendship with Rochester had as its source an unquenchable talent which elevated Aphra in her own right far beyond the milieu of any countess or duchess. She had something that birth or wealth or both together could only aspire to. And when she had mourned her friend she put it once more to work in the sustained piece of bawdy brilliance which deserves to be celebrated as the first English novel.

PART TWO

. . . the true end of satire is the amendment of vices by correction

John Dryden, Preface to *Absalom and Achitophel* (1681)

PART TWO

13

Clerk of court: '. . . *for that they (with diverse other evil-disposed persons), the 20th day of August, in the 34th year of the reign of our sovereign lord the king that now is, and diverse other days and times, as well before as after at the parish of Epsom in the county of Surrey, falsely, unlawfully, unjustly, and wickedly, by unlawful and impure ways and means, contriving, practising and intending the final ruin of the lady Henrietta Berkeley, then a virgin unmarried . . .*'

'Quality' was a meaningful concept in Aphra Behn's world. It informs the romantic Cavalier heroes of her plays and the conduct of her gently born heroines. To be a 'person of quality' was not necessarily the same thing as being wealthy; social status could be bought but the innate characteristics which supposedly designated breeding presumed a different value structure than one based strictly on economic class. Above all, a 'person of quality' answered in their morals and behaviour to a code of honour whereby good name or reputation superseded money as an indication of worth. As ancient members of 'the quality' the Berkeley family compromised themselves severely by bringing Lord Grey to trial for the seduction of their daughter. Why were they prepared to take such a drastic step?

Until the 1640s, adultery cases had been prosecuted within the parallel justice system of the ecclesiastical courts, after which they were transferred to the King's Bench, where Harriet's case would be held. In 1684, a man named John Pledwell and his accomplice Mary Champion were arraigned for conspiring to rape one Mary Haysward at swordpoint, whilst in 1692 the Duke of Norfolk brought suit against John Jermaine for seducing his wife. The years between 1692 and 1730 saw fourteen such cases heard, but the 'Criminal Conversation' charge brought by the Earl of Berkeley was practically the first of its kind. Effectively, 'criminal conversation' was a crime of trespass against property, that is, the physical body of a woman who was the possession of her husband or father. Sixteen years after the case was prosecuted, its echoes could still be heard, not only in Aphra Behn's novel, but in William Congreve's celebrated marriage comedy *The Way of the World*.

At the end of the play Lady Wishfort is subjected to a blackmail threat involving her daughter Mrs Fainall, who has had an affair. Unless Lady Wishfort accedes to the fortune-hunters' plotting, her daughter risks being exposed in a 'criminal conversation' trial. Exposing the 'lurid details of family secrets' in public represents the ultimate disgrace, as the plotting Mrs Marwood gleefully threatens. First she describes the atmosphere of the imagined court room, where the elderly judge gloats pruriently over the salacious details. Then, she warns, the scandal will ripple out and out, first to the junior lawyers discussing the case in the taverns, after which 'it must be consigned by the Short-Hand Writers to the public Press; and from thence be transferr'd to the Hands, nay, the Throats and Lungs of Hawkers with voices more Licentious than the loud Flounder-Man's or the Woman that crys Gray-Pease.'

The threat is physical, visceral. Mrs Fainall's reputation as a 'person of quality' will be absorbed deep into the bodies of the lowest street-dwellers of London, it will be pawed at by their unwashed hands, gobbled down and vomited up as obscenity – 'flounder' and 'pease' are slang words for sex and urine, while 'Gray' seems a direct reference to the Berkeley case. As property, the physical body of a woman in a 'crim-con' suit has abdicated its right to its owner's protection and may be brutally violated, invaded by then broadcast on the filthy airs which emanate from London's foul belly.

Lady Berkeley confessed in court that she had been aware of the relationship between Harriet and Lord Grey, but that initially she had kept the secret from her husband, afraid that he would 'let it break out into the world'. Once discretion had ceased to be an option, the Berkeleys could have gambled that if it could be proved that Harriet had been abducted against her will, it was the only chance of saving her reputation as a 'person of quality'. Taking the step of advertising for her in the *London Gazette* was galling enough, but the suit at the King's Bench could only have one out-come for Harriet herself. Whatever transpired in court, Harriet's honour would be lost forever once she was exposed to a voracious and 'Licentious' public. Why then would her parents be prepared to take such a calamitous risk?

The answer lies in part with the political events of the early 1680s, which directly impacted the career of Aphra Behn and prompted her to turn from play-writing to the creation of *Love Letters*.

In November 1677, another Mary Stuart was mar-ried to another William of Orange. The wedding of the King's fifteen-year-old niece, Princess Mary, daughter to the Duke of York, to her cousin William took place in her bedroom at St James's Palace. With its reluctant bride bestowed by the King on a military leader, the match bore more than a resemblance to Aphra's earlier play *The Forc'd Marriage*. Mary had burst out sobbing when she was told about the wedding, but she knew her duty. For the English, the match renewed the alliance with the Dutch and promised to shore up the Protest-ant succession to the crown: pageants, processions and bonfires expressed the public joy even as Mary was put to bed with her short, rotten-toothed and equally unwilling twenty-seven-year-old bridegroom. Uncle Charles poked his long Stuart nose through the bed curtains to encourage William with a rousing 'Now nephew, to your work, eh? St George for England!'

Not Gold, nor Gemms can purchase the fair
    Prize,
Which Thou thy self must now Monopolize;
A VIRGIN Princess 'tis, in whom alone,
More than the Gain of many Camps is won.
Hence forward Thou securely may'st disdain
Those who small Towns with great Expences
    gain
Their Conquests (tho' they Nations should
    subdue)
Seem poor, when once compared unto you:
For Thou hast got what well may termed be
EUROPA, Kingdoms in Epitome.

Thus the rather less rousing congratulatory poem to the Prince of Orange on his marriage printed in January 1678. Aphra chose not to bother with churning out similar drivel, though she could have profited from it. As Mary embarked glumly for her new home in Holland, Aphra was at work on her most political play yet, *Sir Patient Fancy*. The background to the play was the growing disagreement on the safe direction of the nation between two groups which were coalescing into 'Whigs' and 'Tories'. It is far too simplistic to define their members in the manner of contemporary political parties; nonetheless, this moment was the first in which the term came into use.

*

When the Duke of York had failed to take Anglican communion at court at Easter 1673, the diarist John Evelyn had written of the 'exceeding grief and scandal' this had provoked 'to the whole nation, that the heir of it, and the son of a martyr for the Protestant religion should apostasize. What the consequences of this will be God only knows and wise men dread.' Ever since the Duke's conversion to Catholicism, fears of a return to Rome had been swelling and by the end of the 1670s many shared Evelyn's dread that the nation would once again find itself embroiled in civil war. It was against this background that the ideologies of the 'court party' (the Tories) and their opponents 'the country party' (or Whigs) began gravely to divide.

The aims of the emergent Whig party were wide-ranging and disparate. Some, most prominently the Earl of Shaftesbury, began to campaign with increasing vigour for 'Exclusion', that is that the Duke of York be disbarred from inheriting the throne. Others went further, positing that the crown in the next generation should be offered to the Duke of Monmouth, the eldest of Charles II's illegitimate sons, whilst others went still further in anticipating a potential return of republicanism. Some Whigs were conservatives who wished to retain a strong Protestant monarchy, even suggesting that Charles divorce his Queen in order to beget a legitimate Protestant heir, whilst others advocated thorough constitutional reform. Though the Whig interest thus included a wide range of political beliefs and had no formal leader, the 'country party' was in the eyes of the court nonetheless 'disturbingly well organized'. Certain figureheads for the faction emerged within the peerage, amongst them Shaftesbury, the Duke of Buckingham and Lord Grey.

Sir Patient Fancy was first performed on 17 January 1678. Its reception prompted Aphra to some very specific observations on her status as a woman in the theatre after nearly a decade as a professional writer. Based on the French playwright Molière's *Le Malade Imaginaire*, its themes are sexual hypocrisy and the threat posed to the social order by the Whigs. Sir Patient himself would have been recognized by audiences as Sir Patience Ward, a merchant who served as a sheriff of London and an outspoken supporter of the ultra-Protestant Dissent associated with the country party. It was by far the sauciest play Aphra had written so far and also the most overtly political. Characters run riot in disguised bed-swappings and the heroine, Isabella, bemoans the lack of choice imposed on women in a hypocritical world where money, rather than love, decides marriage. The transactional nature of emotional exchange is equated in the play with the avarice and deceit of Protestant Dissenters, who cloak their inferior values beneath displays of virtue. As the enthusiastic adulterer Lady Fancy puts it in the play, 'a psalm is not sung so much out of Devotion as 'tis to give notice of our Zeal and Pious intentions, 'tis a kind of Proclamation to the Neighbourhood.'

The Puritans who overthrew the social order in the Civil Wars remain a political threat as they act not from spiritual conviction but a desire for power, wealth and the destruction of the status quo. Dissent, the play suggests, is as subversive as Catholicism, if not more so.

Aphra was by no means the first to make this connection; anti-Puritan satire had existed as long as there had been Puritans. Thus the 1641 ditty *The Character of a Roundhead*, where Dissenting meetings serve as a cover for illicit sex:

> What's he that met a holy-sister
> And in the haycock gently kissed her,
> Oh! Then his zeal abounded,
> Close beneath a shady willow,
> Her Bible served her for a pillow,
> And there they got a Roundhead.

What is different about the portrayal of Dissent in *Sir Patient Fancy* is the explicit correlation between its religious and political form in the rising force of Whiggism. The country was careering once again towards civil war, with the Exclusion crisis encouraging the exploitation of faith. 'Sedition, Mutiny and Rebellion' could be evoked with the authority of Scripture.

In the epilogue to the play, spoken by the actress Ann Quin, Aphra returned to the theme of the prejudice she experienced as a woman writer. Anticipating *Sir Patient*'s critics (who duly abused the play for plagiarism and bawdiness), Aphra flagged up the sexism with which her work was often dismissed:

> I hear and there o'erheard a Coxcomb Cry,
> Ah Rot! It is a Woman's Comedy.

The assumption of men's innate intellectual superiority was not one Aphra allowed to go unquestioned:

> What has poor woman done, that she must be,
> Debarr'd from Sense and Sacred Poesie?
> Why in this Age has heaven allowed you more
> And Women less, of Sense than heretofore?

In fact, on the first night, the audience were more interested in the scandal unfolding in the boxes than the antics of old Sir Patient and his spirited young wife. The King had recently taken yet another mistress, Hortense Mancini, Duchess of Mazarin, to the despair of his current *inamorata*, Louise de Kérouaille. Learning that Hortense was attending the premiere, with Charles, Louise 'got up, had herself dressed and dragged herself to her Sedan chair, to be carried to the play, where she heard the King was to be with Mme Mazarin.' The triumph of Hortense and the public wretchedness of Louise proved more grippingly entertaining than Aphra's drama. When the play was published by Tonson shortly afterwards, Aphra defended its poor reception on the grounds that:

The play had no other Misfortune but that of coming out for a Woman's: had it been owned by a Man, though the Most Dull Unthinking Rascally Scribbler in Town, it had been a most admirable Play.

A rather mournful piece of defiance, but as it transpired, Aphra was exactly right in identifying Sir Patient with a scheming faction planning to meddle with the succession to the crown. This play and the three that followed, *The Feign'd Curtizans* (1678), *The Roundheads* (1681) and *The City Heiress* (1682) cemented Aphra's political stance as an avowedly Tory writer. She despised the intellectual limitations her age imposed on women, but her pro-Royalist stance did not admit of any radical changes to the system which oppressed them. Aphra was rebellious but not disobedient; insofar as she was a 'feminist' writer she advocated change for women within the system, but women's rights outside it were not an ideal she envisaged.

Concern over the alliance between the Whigs and Protestant Dissent was overshadowed that year by the pernicious self-promotion of a thoroughly disreputable fantasist named Titus Oates. In the summer of 1678, Oates achieved an extraordinary degree of power and influence by revealing a European threat to the sovereignty of the British nation. That anyone at all was prepared to believe Oates, a disgraced pries whose sexual tastes ran to young boys, says a good deal about the febrile political climate of the time, bu

the 'Popish Plot' of which he claimed to have knowledge provoked a crisis the consequences of which
would reach into the following century.

That August, Oates had given a sworn testimony
before the Westminster magistrate, Sir Edmund Bury
Godfrey. He claimed to have proof that the Jesuit
order were planning to send agents into Scotland and
Ireland to co-ordinate a Catholic uprising. Charles II
would be murdered, London razed and Protestants all
over the country put to the stake if they did not return
to the Catholic faith. Charles himself was sceptical of
Oates and keen to keep the matter quiet, but true to
perennial self-sabotaging form, the Duke of York
insisted on a thorough investigation. Oates duly
appeared before a royal council and despite the evident inaccuracy of much of his account, he was
sufficiently convincing for arrests to be made.

On 17th October, Sir Edmund's body was found
run through with his own sword on Primrose Hill and
the Popish Plot ignited. It was immediately assumed
that Sir Edmund had been murdered by the conspirators Oates had warned the government against.
Anti-Catholic hysteria gripped the country: over
200,000 people attended pope-burning processions in
London in November and similar demonstrations
took place throughout England and Wales. Public
protest was fuelled by an avalanche of pamphlets and
periodicals, according to some estimates as many as
five million, with titles such as the *Imperial Protestant*

Mercury or the *Protestant Intelligence*, aimed at informing readers of the latest machinations of the plot and in true tabloid style stoking the flames of anger and paranoia ever higher.

It was in this febrile atmosphere that Aphra dedicated her play *The Feign'd Curtizans* to the woman who, in the eyes of posterity at least, was the most famous of the Restoration, Nell Gwynn, the 'Protestant whore'. Their relationship may well have stretched back to the early 1660s, as Nelly (she was always Nelly) had begun her spectacular climb into Charles II's bed working as an orange girl at Killigrew's theatre in 1663, the year before Aphra arrived in London. By 1665 she had made her stage debut and returned to the theatre when it reopened after the Great Plague to star as Florimell in Dryden's *Secret Love*. Samuel Pepys gave her a five-star review, claiming hers was the best comic performance he had ever seen. With her male lead Charles Hart, Nelly launched the 'gay couple', the sparky sparring lovers who came to define the Restoration stage. Nelly made no secret of her lower-class origins; indeed, she positively revelled in discomfiting people of 'quality' with the tale she told to Pepys, that she had been 'brought up in a bawdy house to fill strong waters for the guests'. Cheerfully illiterate, she managed to learn her lines to perfection nonetheless and by 1669 her comic talent, vivacity and pocket sexiness had captivated the King. She was pregnant by Charles that year, but her return to the stage in 1670 was designed as a slight, to embarrass him for the stingy provision he had made for her. The King produced a grand house which may still be seen today at 79 Pall Mall, Nelly retired and produced another baby and managed the truly extraordinary feat of being liked by almost everyone apart from the odd sanctimonious bishop and Charles's other mistresses.

One such rival was Moll Davis, a mediocre actress with a beautiful singing voice with whom Charles dallied long enough to produce a child. The story of Nelly presenting Moll with a box of laxative-laced sweets, the consequences of which were enough to put the King off her, became a Restoration urban myth. Some versions credit Aphra with the scatological scheme, though there's no proof of it. Aphra's dedication of her play is much stronger evidence of their friendship, though it is so flattering as to be positively emetic in itself. Indeed, some interpretations claim that in dedicating a play set in Rome featuring a pair of heroines who disguise themselves as (Catholic) prostitutes at the height of the Popish Plot panic, Aphra was taking swipe at Nelly. The dedication addresses her with compliments fit for a duchess, praising her divine beauty and Apollonian wit. It's certainly excessive, but to waste a potentially lucrative dedication on spite seems untypical of Aphra's professional pragmatism. The play was given at court the next year, suggesting that Nelly herself didn't object to the compliments. Nonetheless, she didn't go so far as to introduce the humble poetess herself at court.

Whilst Titus Oates had not initially named the Duke of York as being party to the conspiracy, the make-up of the House of Commons after the general election of February 1679 indicated that resistance to Catholic tyranny had become a political objective. In the new Parliament the 'country party' outnumbered that of the court two to one. On 27th April a motion was proposed on the 'Duke of York's being a Papist', which fact had given 'the greatest Countenance and Encouragement to the present Conspiracy and Designes of the Papists against the King and [the] Protestant Religion'. The first of three Exclusion Bills was then introduced, which would be heard in May 1679, October 1680 and March 1681. Their object was to remove York from the succession. All were ultimately defeated, but it is possible that the Exclusion crisis may have had a bearing on the Earl of Berkeley's decision to drag his son-in-law Lord Grey into court.

14

Willmore, the hero of Aphra Behn's most celebrated play, *The Rover*, is a drunken, cheating, unreliable ne'er-do-well whose roguish Cavalier charms nonetheless get him the girl. Compared with the 'consummate scoundrel' Ford, Lord Grey though, Willmore can only ever be a stage villain. Grey was a privileged mediocrity whose ruthless lack of principle and disregard for the values ostensibly most treasured by his time and class saw him betray not only his wife and his lover but his monarch and still come out on top.

The eldest son of Ralph, 2nd Baron Grey of Werke and his wife Catherine Ford, Grey was born in Sussex in 1655 and baptised in the small village of Harting, folded into the high downs near the Grey estate of Uppark. He had come into his fortune, which included the impressive estate of Chillingham Castle in Northumberland, at the age of twenty and married Harriet Berkeley's sister Lady Mary three years later. Unlike the majority of his peers, Grey never experienced military action in the field. In 1679 he had withdrawn from the command of a regiment on grounds of conscience, not that this prevented him from swaggering about at court in the role of gallant Cavalier. As Grey was to prove to disastrous effect when tested in battle in 1685, he had unquestioningly absorbed his age's belief in the innate superiority of his class. His impenetrable self-esteem convinced him that he was quite capable of commanding an army in the field, even though he had no practical experience of doing so.

Grey was a Whig and a strong advocate of Exclusion. His personal ambitions were centred on his great friend the Duke of Monmouth, the first illegitimate son born to Charles II in exile in Rotterdam 1649. Monmouth was the product of a brief affair between the exiled royal heir and an eighteen-year-old girl from a Welsh gentry family named Lucy Walter. Lucy's personal story was a sad one, which demonstrated the powerlessness of women in the face of male authority. Her mother, Elizabeth, had endured a miserable marriage to a violent adulterer, who had fathered two children on a maid whilst beating and abusing his wife. Elizabeth tried to leave him and took the bold step of fleeing to London and bringing suit against him for the support of his family. In 1641, she had been rewarded with a meagre settlement of £60 per year. On that she brought Lucy up as best she could amidst the threatening turmoil of the Civil Wars, but in 1647 the House of Lords responded to a countersuit from Lucy's father and reversed their original ruling. Lucy and her siblings were ordered back to their father in Wales, but Elizabeth would not submit and instead escaped with her daughter to Holland, where Lucy met Charles at The Hague in 1648. Even according to the accounts of her enemies, Lucy was a stunningly attractive girl and had already had at least one sexual affair. By July that year, she was carrying Charles's child. By the time Lucy's son was born, Charles I had been executed and her lover was King, in name if not in fact.

Lucy always maintained that she had evidence that Charles had married her in secret, though she never produced it. Throughout the 1650s, she pursued him through France and Holland, demanding her rights and creating scandal wherever she went, even threatening to paste up his letters to her for the public to read. Charles succeeded in having his son forcibly kidnapped from his mother, to be brought up by a guardian, Lord Crofts, but Lucy refused to go quietly. She kept up a determined and courageous campaign to recover little James, who she maintained to the end of her short, sorry life, was Charles's legitimate son. Lucy died in 1657 in Paris of venereal disease, lonely and impoverished. She didn't live to see Charles restored, or her son given the title of Duke of Monmouth in 1662. Charles may have treated Lucy with cruel neglect, but he absolutely doted on her boy, showering him with money, arranging a marriage to a wealthy heiress and indulging even the most scandalous of his transgressions.

At the time of the Exclusion crisis, Monmouth was in his early thirties. His education had been patchy, but after a period in which he indulged in all the wild excess of court life he had matured and become an exceptionally brave and talented soldier. He was also widely acknowledged as the handsomest man in a famously handsome family. What he wasn't was terribly bright. His principles were strong but simple and he was easily led by more sophisticated men like Grey and the Earl of Shaftesbury, who saw in him the chance to realize their own political and personal ambitions. Monmouth was uncomplicatedly loyal to the Church of England, of which his father was head, his marriage had produced healthy children, he was young, attractive and extremely popular with the people. To many Whigs, he represented a logical solution to the problem of York's Catholicism. Though Monmouth himself had never shown anything but absolute loyalty to the crown, he favoured Exclusion as far as setting aside his uncle's claim in favour of that of his daughters Mary and Anne.

Grey was playing a dangerous game in his private as well as political life. His wife Lady Mary Berkeley had given birth to her first daughter in 1678 and when she briefly returned to court had a short, infatuated affair with Monmouth. In the winter of 1679 Grey sent his wife to his seat at Chillingham in Northumberland, publicly agreeing with the court gossip about the affair. The lampoons were vicious and apparently Mary had been wildly in love with the handsome-but-dim Duke, yet Grey appeared to mount no objection to the affair between his friend and his wife beyond her banishment. This was out of character – Grey was a pugnacious type and given to duelling – but the reasons for his equanimity were twofold: first, in alliance with Shaftesbury, he was determined to promote Exclusion and could not therefore break with Monmouth, and second, he was already having a secret affair with his wife's younger sister Harriet.

In early 1681, Grey had received Monmouth at his Sussex house, Uppark, where Grey had organized a reception at nearby Chichester cathedral with the two local Members of Parliament. In a flamboyant display of support for the Whig cause, Monmouth was led in a procession of 400 men carrying flaming torches to receive the compliments of the county dignitaries. *The Lady Grey Vindicated*, a Tory pamphlet released at the time of the Chichester gathering, raked up Monmouth's affair with Mary Grey, envisioning her being visited in her bedroom by a spectral 'apparition' adorned with a glistening Garter star. Monmouth (for it was he) predicted the forthcoming doom of the nation to his 'sweetheart'. Grey himself appeared untroubled by the slander, but for the Earl of Berkeley, it was clear that Grey had no scruple about dragging his family into the dirt if it served his ends.

The second Exclusion Bill had been heard and rejected by the House of Lords on 15 November 1680, during a day-long debate in which the Duke of Monmouth addressed the House in its favour. It was defeated by sixty-five votes to thirty, with all the lords spiritual, the bishops, voting against. Beyond this, there is no accurate extant record for the division of the vote, but it had been noted that of the forty-nine lords temporal who rejected Exclusion, twenty-seven owed their titles directly to Charles II, as opposed to eight of the thirty who voted in favour. Harriet's father, the first Earl of Berkeley, numbered amongst the first group, Ford, Lord Grey of Werke amongst the second. Grey was a significant player within the group of Whig magnates who favoured Exclusion; Berkeley was a staunch defender of the status quo. His support for the succession of the Duke of York was to be rewarded three years after the trial when he was made Privy Councillor to King James II in July 1685.

Looking forward to 1682, Berkeley obviously had strong personal motives to loathe Grey, who by then had disgraced two of his daughters. But it is possible that his decision to prosecute him was also politically motivated. Exposing Grey as a wicked seducer would naturally discredit one of the crown's most influential political enemies; moreover, a successful prosecution would put him out of action as a player in the ongoing crisis. Grey's actions after the case more than fulfilled Berkeley's apprehensions of the threat he presented, so in taking the unprecedented step of besmirching his daughter's reputation in public, the case might represent more than a matter of paternal choler. When the Attorney General described the background of the case during the trial, he emphasized both the possibility that Harriet's flight might have been kept private and the enormity of its having been revealed:

> there were some hope of retrieving the matter, that this scandal on so noble a family might not be made public; for certainly an offence of this nature was not fit to be so, nor indeed was ever heard of in any Christian society.

In ultimately bringing his daughter's lover to court then, the Earl of Berkeley actively chose to ruin her. As her father's property, Harriet was being used for his political ends.

November 1681 saw the publication of *Absalom and Achitophel*, a satire by Aphra's friend Dryden which discussed the controversies of the Exclusion crisis figured through a story from the Old Testament in which Absalom, the beautiful, popular son of King David, rebels against his father. The timing of the poem's release was pointed, as just a week after it was printed the Earl of Shaftesbury was to stand trial for high treason. Alongside Charles II as David, the Duke of Monmouth as Absalom and Shaftesbury as Achitophel, the poem featured 'a great many characters of all the great men on both sides', including Ford, Lord Grey, as the plotter 'cold Caleb'. London was fascinated with both poem and trial, with hundreds of onlookers crowding against the coaches of the witnesses as they rumbled towards the hearing at the Old Bailey. Dryden's heavy-handed propaganda might have made the consequences of defying royal authority clear, but the trial proved a humiliating defeat for the crown. Shaftesbury was acquitted for lack of evidence, with his bail put up by Monmouth himself. It was a triumph for the Whigs, whose supporters rioted their way through the City, some with swords drawn, crying blessings on Shaftesbury and death to popery.

Royal efforts to calm the crisis centred for the next year on gaining control of London for the Tories. The City had been the power base for the Whig cause, but in the July elections of 1682 the mayor and sheriffs were now replaced by Tories, which provoked some Whigs to contemplate stronger measures for wresting control of the country away from the court. The meddling of the ageing Shaftesbury was taking a frantic turn; he was frustrated by the moderate position of Monmouth, who was in favour of seeking a compromise. The position of another prominent Whig, Lord Grey, was unclear at this crucial juncture. In August 1682 he had another matter on his hands.

On the night of the 20th of that month, Harriet went to bed at Durdans with her maid, Mrs Doney, who had laid out her clothes ready for the morning, two petticoats, one striped and one quilted, to be worn over her multicoloured striped nightgown. (As formal dressing was a lengthy business of stays and sleeves, hooks and buttons, gowns and fichus which required at least one maid to fasten on, ladies wore more simple attire first thing in the morning, while they prayed and breakfasted.) Harriet crept from the house and entered a waiting coach, driven by Grey's personal servant Robert Charnock, who drove her as fast as he could through the sleeping countryside towards London.

In the early hours of the morning, Mrs Doney awakened to find her mistress gone. Before long, the household at Durdans was in uproar. A thorough search for Harriet was conducted along the galleries, into the attics and around the gardens and stableyard, but the family knew in their hearts that it was futile. As they had long feared might happen, Harriet had eloped with her own brother-in-law. All that could be done now was to gain time, to try, desperately, to prevent the scandal from leaking out.

Harriet was not the only one taking risks in the summer of 1682. Aphra's four political plays had brought her as much respect from fellow Tories as opprobrium from their Whig opponents and she was becoming increasingly confident in expressing her political views in the prologues and epilogues for the theatre where she was now being asked to write. As well as being a satisfactory indication of her heightened status, such work brought in funds, and Aphra had earned £10 for a prologue to a play called *Romulus and Hersilia* for the Duke's Company. Aphra's introduction referenced the dismissal of the charges against the Earl of Shaftesbury the previous year. The Whigs were figured as vermin preying upon a royal lion, 'Conscientious Knaves' whose 'Lawless tongues' committed perjury. Her epilogue, spoken by the actress Mary Lee, made an obvious reference to the Duke of Monmouth:

> Love! Like Ambition, makes us rebels too;
> And of all treasons mine was most Accurst:
> Rebelling 'gainst a King and Father first.
> A Sin which Heav'n nor Man can e'er forgive
> Nor could I Act it with the face to live.

To hint at treason within the royal family was too much. Four days before Harriet Berkeley ran away Aphra was once again threatened with prison. *The Protestant Mercury* printed an announcement:

> Thursday last being acted a Play called the Tragedy of Romulus ... and the Epilogue spoken by the Lady Slingsby [Lee's married name] and written by Mrs Behn which reflected on the Duke of Monmouth the Lord Chamberlain has ordered them both into custody to answer that affront to the same.

Mary Lee had married into a Royalist family who had remained loyal to Charles II during the Interregnum, so perhaps she called on her contacts to have the custody warrant withdrawn. Or perhaps Aphra called in a favour from the Lord Chamberlain himself, Lord Arlington, who had been head of the intelligence service at the time of her Antwerp mission. However it was handled, neither lady went to jail. It was a warning to Aphra, and she didn't forgive Monmouth, characterizing him in *Love Letters* as an 'ungovernable fool, nothing more obstinate, wilful, conceited and cunning; and for his gratitude, let the world judge what he must prove to his servant, who has dealt so ill with his lord and master.' In Aphra's frustrated view, it was Monmouth who was the true threat to the national stability, rather than a pair of hard-working women.

While Aphra was trying to dodge prison, the Berkeley family pursued Harriet and Grey for the next month, without coming closer to recovering her or even discovering her whereabouts. In September the Earl of Berkeley took the desperate step of placing the notorious advertisement in the *London Gazette*. Perhaps his intention was to prevail on Harriet's sense of family honour to persuade her to return home, but equally once the appeal ran it may have made her feel she had nothing to lose. She remained obdurately hidden. Incensed, the Earl took the case to the King's Prosecutor, and Grey was sensationally arrested and committed to the Tower of London to await trial at the King's Bench.

Harriet's flight had taken place at a moment when the disagreements between Whigs and Tories had literally exploded. On 5 November 1682, while she was in hiding in London, the traditional 'Pope burnings' in celebration of the failure of Guy Fawkes's

Gunpowder Plot had descended into a City-wide riot, with brawling apprentices screaming 'No York!' and 'Monmouth!' as they reeled between the bonfires. A good number of them were arrested and set in the pillory as an example, but to the consternation of the government, instead of pelting them with rubbish, passers-by cheered the culprits and kept up their spirits with presents of wine, chocolate and oranges. Aphra's hatred for Whiggism and her belief that its much-vaunted principles concealed nothing more than a seditious craving for republican power was further stoked by the chaos she now saw in the streets.

Even within the rarefied circle of the court, whose lifeblood was the most scurrilous gossip, the news of Grey's arrest came as a delicious shock. ''Tis certain he has deluded her and enticed her from her father,' crowed one lady correspondent, 'but where she is is not yet known – he must soon produce her or his Lordship must remain a prisoner.' As a professional writer and contributor to the lampoons, Aphra had been following the scandal closely. It is not impossible that she now joined the crowd in Westminster Hall on 21 November 1682 to observe every detail of this outrageous quarrel amongst the 'quality'.

15

The *Trial of Ford, Lord Grey of Werke for a Misdemeanor in debauching the Lady Henrietta Berkeley* might in itself have come straight from the pen of Aphra Behn, complete with secret correspondence, contriving servants, a silver-tongued seducer and even a duel. The proceedings opened on a note of pure comedy, with some of the twelve jurors challenged and rejected by the defence and others inadvertently excluding themselves. Once the court had settled down, the Attorney General Sir Robert Sawyer read the charges. Alongside Grey, five other people were indicted for Harriet's abduction: Robert Charnock, Anne Charnock, David Jones, Frances Jones and Rebecca Jones. All the defendants including Grey had entered a plea of Not Guilty. The first shocking revelation of Sir Robert's speech was that Grey and Harriet had been conducting their liaison for four years, that is, since Harriet was just fourteen years old.

In Westminster Hall, the charges continued, detailing that on 20 August 1682 the defendants had 'seduced' Harriet to 'desert her father's house', emphasizing that she was still a minor and 'under the custody and governance of her father'. Sir Robert explained that

Harriet had left Durdans in the company of Robert Charnock and travelled with him to London, where she was 'hurried from one lodging to another' to avoid detection.

As the charges were announced, the background of the affair began to emerge. Harriet's mother had originally discovered the relationship in July, while the family were still in London. When she had found Harriet writing a letter to Grey, Lady Berkeley confronted her son-in-law, who begged her to keep it a secret from Lord Berkeley 'for if this should once come to be known to him, he and the young lady would not only be ruined, but it would occasion an irreparable breach between the two families'. Lady Berkeley immediately banned Grey from her home, but he persuaded her that since he had been so frequent a visitor, his sudden absence might give rise to gossip. Surely it would be better 'that his departure might be by degrees, and so the less taken notice of'?

Foolishly, Lady Berkeley had consented. Harriet had thrown herself in tears at her mother's feet, begging forgiveness for her indiscretion and claiming that Grey had exploited her youth and inexperience. She had promised that if Grey were permitted one last visit to Durdans for the sake of appearances, she would have no more to do with him. Grey arrived in Surrey, giving out that he was breaking his journey down to Sussex, but he stayed so long that Lady Berkeley began to suspect a scheme was in train. He did eventually leave, claiming he planned to spend the night at Guildford before continuing on to Uppark, but that same night Harriet vanished.

At this point, just as the witnesses were about to be called, Harriet herself was escorted into the court room and seated below the table of Chief Justice Sir Francis Pemberton, Sir Thomas Jones, Sir William Dolben and Sir Thomas Raymond, the four judges in the case. It was the first time she had seen her parents for three months. Her father attempted to interrupt the proceedings, demanding that his daughter be restored to him, whilst Lady Berkeley, who was just about to be sworn in as the first witness for the prosecution, was visibly overcome and unable to speak. Lady Berkeley's natural emotion at the appearance of her lost daughter was compounded by the all too obvious fact that Harriet was pregnant.

Lady Arabella Berkeley was hastily sworn in in her mother's place and gave further details of the discovery of the letter which had given Harriet away. She had, it seemed, attempted to play for time to protect her sister from the blow that was about to fall, implying that she already had knowledge of the affair. Arabella explained that Lady Berkeley had discovered Harriet with a freshly inked pen, which Harriet had claimed she had been using to write up her accounts. Unsatisfied, Lady Berkeley demanded her room be searched, but Arabella stalled her by saying it was time for family prayers. Harriet then gave up her keys to her private closet and cabinet, passing a letter to Arabella at the same time. 'My sister Bell did not suspect our being together last night', Harriet had written to Grey, 'for she did not hear the noise. I pray come again Sunday or Monday, if the last I shall be very impatient.'

Arabella recounted that a servant of Grey's had then joined the sisters with a message from his master saying that he intended to wait upon the ladies. Harriet fainted on Grey's appearance, whilst Grey threatened Arabella that he would take revenge on the whole Berkeley family if Arabella spoke out. Horrified by what she had learned, Arabella stoutly told Grey he might go to the Devil and berated him for his shocking infidelity to their sister Mary. Suspecting that her own maid had been involved in the correspondence, Arabella reported that she had questioned the woman and subsequently discovered that she had passed letters from Harriet to Grey via Grey's coachman, Robert Charnock. The maid justified herself by saying, 'How could I think there was any ill between a brother-in-law and a sister?'

Mortifyingly, Arabella was then obliged to repeat her testimony whilst Grey got to his feet and attempted to stare her down, which provoked another interruption from Lord Berkeley on his 'barbarous impudence' in looking thus at his daughter. Lady Berkeley meanwhile covered her face with her hood and attempted to continue her own testimony. She had believed Harriet to be truly penitent, she explained, had forgiven her and promised that she should not be sent away. Weeping, she spoke of 'my wretched unkind daughter, I have been so kind a mother to her and would have died rather, upon the oath I have taken, than have done this, if there had been any other way to reclaim her and would have done anything to have hid her faults and died ten times over rather than this dishonour should have come upon my family.' At this point Lady Berkeley broke down and fainted. Proceedings paused while she was revived.

Lady Berkeley's fragmented testimony suggests that Harriet and Grey may have manipulated the situation so as to arrive in the country together. Lady Berkeley had found the letter in London, Arabella attempted to conceal it, the truth came out and the supposedly repentant Harriet specified that Grey should visit Durdans for the sake of appearances. The removal to Surrey may well have been long planned, as it was customary for upper-class families to leave the city for the summer, but Lady Berkeley seems to have been led to Durdans by the nose.

With Lord Berkeley still unaware of what was going on, the household duly went down to the country, where they were joined by Mary, Grey's wife. In turn, Grey expressed his intention of removing to Sussex and summoned his wife back to London. Mary pointed out the impracticality of this and suggested he came to dine at Durdans instead, after which they could go on to Guildford and continue to Uppark. Having Grey in the house overnight was obviously the last thing poor Lady Berkeley wanted, but she was so afraid of arousing her husband's suspicions that she consented to the arrangement. Grey swore that he would only remain overnight and talked of going on a long visit to France with Mary.

The situation became even more theatrical when Lady Berkeley visited Harriet in her bedroom after dinner and attempted to comfort her by saying that she was only pretending to be angry with her in public in front of Grey so as to deter him from further contact: 'I will seem to whisper with you, and look frowningly on you, and that if he hath any tenderness for you, he may . . . do the more to leave you quiet.'

As Lady Berkeley told it, it was a touching scene in the candlelit bedroom, she reassuring the weeping Harriet that all would be forgiven, even that 'good-natured and religious' Mary would be sure to pardon her and the whole dreadful matter forgotten. Harriet was told to be cheerful and that her mother would settle everything down, but her contrition was a heartbreaking sham. Lady Berkeley fainted a second time when she came to her next words – 'yet that very night when I was in my sleep she ran away'. Her love and her shame and her humanity spring from the dry words of the trial records with an immediacy that spans centuries.

Grey left Durdans at four o'clock in the afternoon, after having a long private conference with Robert

Charnock, who had mysteriously been recently promoted from coachman to personal attendant.

Lady Lucy Berkeley then described how once Harriet's flight had been determined she had pursued Grey by coach to Guildford to charge him with her sister's abduction. Grey denied any knowledge of Harriet's whereabouts and disingenuously promised Lucy that he would do all that he could to discover her and restore the family's tranquillity. Meanwhile, Robert Charnock had called at the house of a London landlady, Eleanor Hilton, to enquire whether she had a spare room to let. Eleanor testified that a 'young lady' had then appeared alone, at about ten in the morning, oddly dressed in a coloured nightgown and a red and white petticoat. She looked exhausted and red-eyed and could not be persuaded to eat anything. The young lady said she was tired and lay down to rest in Mrs Hilton's room, before Mrs Charnock appeared. Eleanor Hilton said she was unable to confirm that the lady standing before her in court was the same who had come to her house, even when Harriet was obliged to stand and remove her hood. Confirming the strength of the period's codes of behaviour, Mrs Hilton was then asked if Mrs Charnock had behaved towards the young lady 'as to a lady of quality', as this might confirm her identity. Mrs Hilton thought she had. Robert Charnock had given Mrs Hilton a letter for his wife, which was handed over, but the young lady was then disturbed by the noise of people gathering outside. She told Mrs Hilton she was afraid that it might be her father's servants.

In fact, the crowds in the street were trying to catch a glimpse of the 'blazing star', one of two comets which appeared in 1682 in June and August. A correspondent in New England reported that the latter had been seen there in the morning and that letters from London had reported sightings in the evening. In London, the comet was seen as a fantastical portent which would inaugurate the conversion of the Turks and the fall of Rome. The American astrologer disapproved of such improbabilities but conceded that Saturnine Comets were a sign of 'a cold and tedious Winter, much snow and consequently great floods, Malignant and Epidemical diseases and fires'. One wonders if Aphra Behn too stepped outside her lodgings to watch for this wonder, but the fugitives were more alarmed than delighted. Mrs Hilton's house had no back door through which to escape, so the three women 'whipped out' and made off together for another house close by in Wild Street, belonging to a Mr Patten.

Mr Patten's evidence suggested that Harriet's elopement had been planned for some time and been hastily brought forward by the discovery of her letter to Grey. Equally, Harriet's determination to meet Grey at Durdans might signify that the discovery was intentional, as time was running out before her pregnancy began to show. The Charnocks had visited Mr Patten at the end of July to reserve lodgings for 'a person of quality' which they said would be needed in mid-September. When Mrs Charnock, Eleanor Hilton and the young lady turned up on 20th August, Mr Patten was dismayed as he had no suitable accommodation to offer a gentlewoman, there being no hangings on his only spare bed. The young lady was still in her nightgown, by now 'very much sullied' and retired to the inadequate bedroom. Mrs Charnock told Mr Patten that he was to deny their presence in the house if anyone came to ask, and not to show a light in the dining room lest it be seen in the street. The young lady was clearly in a state of panic, and after discussing what to do, Mrs Charnock went back out into the street, where she found a hackney coach and they set off once more into the night.

Mr Patten was more confident than Mrs Hilton in confirming Harriet's identity, though she had attempted to keep her face concealed under her hood. The stop at the Patten house was to be further explained by the fact that Mrs Patten was a midwife, who had previously attended Mrs Charnock. Mrs Patten was given to understand that Mrs Charnock was expecting a baby in mid-September when the Berkeley family would be in London and did not want to inconvenience her employers by giving birth at their home. Mrs Charnock was not asked whether she had indeed given birth before the trial, whilst Harriet was obviously pregnant.

At this juncture it was noted that the court could

now confirm the involvement of Robert and Anne Charnock and a new witness, Mary Fletcher, was deposed. Mrs Fletcher (whom the court addressed encouragingly as 'sweetheart') was a maid in yet another lodging house, this one belonging to David Jones at Charing Cross. Grey had visited the house the day after Harriet's flight to request a room from Jones, which Mary was ordered to prepare. He returned on the Tuesday, trying to disguise his appearance by leaving aside his periwig and keeping his cloak over his face. Such disguises might have passed on the stage, but the sharp-eyed Mary Fletcher identified the wigless Grey and observed the warming pan and candlesticks being taken up to the room, which led her to think that 'Some great intrigue or other' was in train. Peering round the door the next day, Mary saw a lady lying in the bed. Her mistress denied that the gentleman who visited the lady was Grey, pretending he was a gentleman from the country, but Mary was sure of herself. The lady stayed nine days in the room, during which time Mary washed her shift for her. In her opinion, the garment did not belong to 'a person of quality' as 'the body was finer than the sleeves and ladies use to make the sleeves finer than the body', a statement which produced much amusement in the court. Harriet's maid was called back to confirm that the shift belonged to her mistress.

The emphasis placed upon Harriet's petticoat focused the attention of the court pruriently on her body. Her dirty linen was literally being washed in public, 'sullied' like her character as a consequence of her transgression. The sweat and grime of her journey were the focus of a sort of proto-forensic examination, physically and intrusively intimate. Clothes were a vital signifier of status in the seventeenth century, a trope which was repeatedly exploited in Aphra's plays. Actresses could dress as men or courtesans and pass unquestioned by their fellows on the stage in a manner which seems implausibly forced to modern eyes but made immediate sense in a world where garments indicated 'quality'. Harriet's bedraggled nightgown thus becomes the objective correlative of her descent in status, soiled and bedraggled, a legitimate target for prying eyes.

Once the laughter over Harriet's shift had died down, another lodger in the house, a Captain Fitz-Gerrard, was questioned. He had heard from Mary Fletcher that the mysterious guest in the upper room was Lord Grey's mistress, so when he heard of the disappearance of Lady Harriet Berkeley from some companions in a Covent Garden tavern, he made the connection and spoke that night to Jones, the lodging house owner. Jones told the Captain to keep out of his business, the Captain insisted on seeing the lady and when Jones refused he drew his sword. Jones promised that the Captain could satisfy himself as to the lady's identity at a more 'civil' hour the next day, but unsurprisingly she was gone the following morning before the Captain could confirm his suspicions.

The Berkeley family were growing increasingly frantic – 'in such a confusion and trouble they are all mad almost'. A friend of the family reported that Lord Berkeley was so deeply affected 'it will go near to break his heart'. Every hour that passed made it more likely that the scandal would come out. It seems possible that they had an idea that Harriet could be pregnant, as the Earl now proposed that if a willing bridegroom could be found, he would give him £6,000 to make an honest woman of his daughter. This was an astronomical amount of money. Comparative values for the period are notoriously unreliable, but a survey of incomes for 1688 shows that just 5 per cent of English families had an income of more than £100 annually. A family of 'middling station' was estimated to need £315 per year to maintain two adults and four children plus a maid, whilst a gentleman needed £500 per year to live up to his status. Six thousand pounds was the equivalent annual income of the wealthiest aristocrats in the country. The Berkeleys even considered paying off Grey himself in order to get Harriet back, proposing that he take £2,000 to deliver her to a safe place and cease to visit her. When approached by Mr Smith, another Berkeley son-in-law, as a representative of the family, Grey cruelly continued to claim that Harriet was not 'in his power', suggesting indeed that she had left for France, whilst nonetheless hinting that he did know where she was since he could write to her.

Grey had been in London with Harriet on the

Tuesday after her disappearance, but by the end of the week he had returned to Uppark. He continued to pretend that he wished to make amends to the Berkeleys for his indiscretion and agreed that a nominated friend of Lady Berkeley, a Mr Craven, might accompany him. Mr Craven testified that in Sussex he had tried to persuade Grey that for the sake of the reputations of all involved, the crisis needed to be discreetly resolved. Another solution was now proposed – Harriet could be sent to a convent at Calais or Dieppe and from there could write to her mother with the story that she had fled to avoid being forced into marriage with a man not of her choosing. Lady Berkeley could show this letter to her friends and once the story had spread might go to France to recover her daughter, who could return to her family as though nothing had happened. Once again, the device might have come from the stage. Grey continued to protest that while this was indeed an ingenious plan he was unable to help since Harriet herself 'did not think fit to let him know where she was'. Until this point then, Grey was not denying the affair, or that he was in contact with Harriet, whilst simultaneously claiming she had run away of her own accord. But now he changed his story.

As Grey and Craven walked out with their guns on the downs near Uppark, Grey confessed all. He had taken 'great delight' in Harriet since she was a child and had written to her to tell her of his 'passion'. At first, Harriet warned him that if he did not stop writing to her, she would tell her parents, and he claimed he had then resolved to stay in Sussex and not see her until she was safely married off. The Berkeley parents, however, were pressing him to join them in London and Harriet agreed. Grey said he had warned Harriet that if they were together in London, 'I shall not be able to contain myself', but Harriet took no notice. One day as the ladies were out on horseback, being led by the gentlemen, she took Grey's hand and squeezed it against her breast. After that, they took every opportunity to be together, sleeping together every night for almost a year. Harriet always shared her room with a maid, but slipped out of the room once she was sleeping. On one occasion, which might have seemed unbelievable even in a whirlwind comedy, Grey was concealed in her room for two whole days, hiding in a cupboard with nothing to eat except the 'sweetmeats' Harriet smuggled from the family table.

Serjeant Jefferies interrupted Craven's account of Grey's confession to ask him if it was true he had made love to other women in an attempt to distract himself from Harriet. Grey had casually admitted to seducing two other ladies, both of whom he had 'enjoyed', but he was unable to break from Harriet. Finally, he had admitted to Craven that he did know where she was, that he 'had her in his power' and did not intend to give her up.

In his version of the story, Grey plays the romantic

hero, gripped by uncontrollable love which he nonetheless tries to suppress. It is Harriet who leads him on, Harriet who entices him to London and keeps him in her room like a lapdog. He is hopelessly enchanted, almost to be pitied. What was going on in Harriet's mind? Viewed through a modern lens, she might be seen as a victim, an abused child who comes to love her abuser, relishing the special secrecy of their relationship. Was she excited by her power over Grey, did she relish being the object of his love as a rival to her older sister? Or was she a bored teenage girl desperate for romance, who believed that she and her brother-in-law were star-crossed, meant to be?

Or was there something darker going on? According to Harriet's sister Arabella, she had no reason to run away, since her parents treated her very kindly. Nonetheless, Harriet had tried to escape from her family on more than one previous occasion. Grey claimed she had told him she was 'ill-used' at home and Lady Berkeley conceded that she had been so concerned for her daughter's safety that she had forbidden her to go out or write letters after she had first tried to run away. According to Grey, Harriet had told him that she was treated like a dog or a 'slave', that her life at home was unendurable and that if he would not help her get away she would harm herself. Was there then something truly desperate about Harriet's flight, something that made her choose Grey's perverse protection over her parents' roof? Or was she, in fact, manipulating Grey, exploiting his love for her with an invented story of suffering to push him into freeing her into a new and more independent life?

Mr Williams, counsel for the defence, was now called to make his case. His argument was clever. Since all parties in the trial were 'persons of honour and quality', it followed naturally that they would all prefer to part with their lives than that honour. If the jury acquitted Grey, they would therefore be acquitting the Berkeleys of the scandal. It was essentially the argument used for duelling – if one gentleman perceived he had been insulted by another he would challenge him to fight, through which process the insult, or dishonour, would be erased as though it had never been. The consideration of the jury, Mr Williams proposed, would be to arbitrate the duel; they could 'lay a stain on both of them, or acquit them both'. Grey had been very much in love, which was most reprehensible, but 'there are degrees in love' and some degree of guilt did not necessarily mean that a crime had taken place. Using the language of the duel, Mr Williams claimed that his proofs would provide 'satisfaction' for both parties.

Mr Williams now took the highly unusual step of asking that Harriet be sworn as a witness. The Attorney General objected, saying that this would be contrary to the law. Since Harriet was a woman, a minor and hence in the 'tuition and custody' of her father, allowing her to be questioned could be seen as excusing the crime that Grey had committed against Lord Berkeley. The legal language obfuscates the bare truth behind their dispute, that two of the most powerful men in England were each contesting the other's right to possession of the body of an eighteen-year-old woman. Harriet was not so much objectified as entirely reduced to an object, a stolen bundle of flesh.

Nevertheless, Mr Williams adroitly observed that since Harriet was indeed not party to the cause, there could be no legal objection to her being a witness. Finally, Lady Henrietta Berkeley was permitted to take the stand.

Harriet proceeded to perjure herself thoroughly and shamelessly. No, Grey had nothing to do with her escape. It was 'all my own design'. No, she had not left Durdans with Robert Charnock, nor gone to Mrs Hilton's house, nor to Mr Patten's with Mrs Charnock, nor to Mr Jones's. 'Upon my oath', she repeated again and again, as she lied to the highest legal officers in the land.

Then Harriet demanded that she be allowed to tell the court why she had left her father's house. Both prosecution and defence insisted there was no need for this. Harriet insisted: 'I desire to tell it myself.' She pointed out that the court had spent much time discussing her and that her reputation had suffered as a consequence and that therefore— but the Chief Justice would not stand for such audacity:

You have injured your own reputation and prostituted both your body and your honour and are not to be believed.

Taking no more notice of Harriet, the Chief Justice, Sir Francis Pemberton, began his summing up to the jury. The essence of the charges, he explained, was that Grey had 'unlawfully' begun a legally incestuous relationship with Harriet, that he had taken her from her father's house and 'did live in fornication with her'. He explained that the testimonies of the accused and Grey's series of feints, false trails and disguises had been rehearsed, whilst Harriet's claim that she had been ill-treated at home was 'not fit to be believed'.

As the jury withdrew to reflect upon their verdict, the Earl of Berkeley insisted that his daughter be delivered to him. Uninvited, Harriet defiantly spoke up. She would not go with her father. There was no coercion behind this refusal, she claimed. She would not go because she was already married.

The crowd in Westminster Hall pressed forward, astonished and delighted by this latest twist in an already outrageous story. Harriet's husband, she said, was a Mr Turner, and he was already in court. Turner pushed his way through the disorderly onlookers and came to stand beside Harriet and the judges. He confirmed that they were married. As the Earl of Berkeley spluttered his objections, Serjeant Jefferies identified Turner as the son of a Somerset lawyer who had previously been questioned in a fornication suit. Turner had apparently been living with a woman at Bromley by whom he had 'divers' children, claiming that they were legally married. Turner replied that this was untrue and repeated that he was married to Harriet.

Lord Berkeley once again demanded that Harriet go with him, but an abashed Sir William Dolben pointed out from the judges' table that the court had no power to separate man and wife. Harriet insisted that she would go with her husband.

'Hussey!' thundered Berkeley. 'You shall go with me home.'

Harriet repeated that she would go with her husband.

The bench was now in a state of confusion, with Mr Williams arguing that Lord Grey should be freed, Serjeant Jefferies and the Attorney General that he remain in custody, Lord Berkeley that *he* should take his daughter and the Chief Justice that the suit was void. Judge Dolben announced that it was now Harriet who was the plaintiff in the original suit of *Homine Replegiando* and that she could bail Lord Grey if she chose.

(As Harriet had known it would, this astonishing announcement entirely altered her legal status. When and where her marriage to Turner had taken place is not recorded, since until the Marriage Act of 1753, couples could marry anywhere so long as the ceremony was conducted by a Church of England priest. As a married woman, Harriet was now subject to her husband's authority, rather than her father's. Therefore, Lord Grey's detention was no longer legally valid. Without a date for the wedding, it is impossible to know whether Grey had included it in his original plan to run away with Harriet, or whether he had pushed her into marriage with Turner to protect himself when the Earl of Berkeley brought the case against him.)

Lord Berkeley called out to all his friends in the hall that they should immediately 'seize' Harriet. While the Chief Justice shouted that the peace must be kept there was 'a great scuffle about the lady', with swords drawn on both sides. Beating about with their clubs, the tipstaffs (armed court officials), surrounded Harriet and Turner and on the Chief Justice's order escorted them to custody at the house of the Marshal of the King's Bench.

The next morning, they were released from custody on the order of the court. Harriet had done it. She was free.

16

Pleasing though it is to imagine Aphra Behn attending the scandalous proceedings of the Berkeley trial, the genesis of *Love Letters* is uncertain. The opportunity, though, was delicious. Harriet's escape and secret marriage had been widely publicized in London's newsletters and pamphlets so Aphra would not have to look far for the details on which she based her plot. The use of letters to tell the story was partly inspired by *Five Love-Letters from a Nun to a Cavalier*, a translation of a French work entitled *Lettres Portugaises*, but Aphra has not been given enough credit for her own originality. She had, after all, successfully deceived the secret service for some time with letters of her own invention as a means of prolonging her spying income during her 1666 stay in Antwerp. Epistolary fiction was already a familiar genre to her, and she used it to create the first novel of its kind in English.

Aphra reset her plot slightly, placing the action in France, where Cesario/the Duke of Monmouth has an affair with Myrtilla/Lady Mary Grey. Myrtilla is married to Philander/Lord Grey who, disappointed by her continued affection for Cesario, begins to pursue Myrtilla's younger sister Silvia/Harriet 'whose early bloom promised wonders when it came to perfection'. Silvia is in love with Philander and when their affair is discovered, they run away together. Philander is set to be arrested for this incestuous elopement, so Silvia is persuaded to marry his servant Brilliard. Philander has been involved in a plot with Cesario to overthrow the King of France; he is imprisoned, escapes and summons Silvia. Eluding all attempts at capture, the lovers escape together. This 'Argument', placed at the beginning of the novel, teasingly recapitulates the already familiar Berkeley trial and the politics behind the Exclusion crisis, adding another apparent layer of verisimilitude with the claim that:

> After their flight these letters were found in their cabinets, at their house ... where they both lived together for the space of a year; and they are as exactly as possible placed in the order they were sent and were those supposed to be written at the latter end of their amours.

Aphra's novel was written in under a year following the trial, keeping pace with the events of Grey's subsequent arrest for treason and escape. Allowing for this, the latter part was written in just a few months, since the book was licensed for publication by October 1683.

Love Letters maps the political tensions which threatened to destroy the increasingly fragile consensus between the King and his subjects and, terrifyingly, to bring about another civil war. Whilst effectively being a true story, the novel is profoundly political, engrained with debate between loyalty and rebellion. Philander's flight to Holland with Silvia thus represents the abandonment of Tory/Royalist values for those of the pro-Dutch Whigs. Exposed to air which 'naturally breeds Spirits avaricious', within the framework of its melodramatic eroticism, *Love Letters* examines the fate, as Aphra Behn saw it, of the system she lived under and supported.

Contemporary readers of the novel would have recognized its political dimension immediately. Philander's seduction of Silvia is founded in his attempts to persuade her of the correctness of a libertine philosophy, that is, to cast off the artificial constraints imposed by convention and religion and adhere to the more 'natural' law of desire. In Philander's reasoning, neither extramarital sex nor even incest can be sins. In his arguments there is a direct echo of the opening of Dryden's satire on the Exclusion crisis, *Absalom and Achitophel*, published the year before the trial:

> In pious times, ere priest-craft did begin
> Before polygamy was made a sin,
> When man on many, multiplied his kind,
> Ere one to one was cursedly confin'd

Aphra's readers would hear the poem in Philander's voice, locating it precisely in the debate about the succession which was menacing the security of the realm.

Those in the know could make the connection even more explicitly, since both Aphra's Philander and Dryden's Caleb are portraits of Grey.

Aphra's transposition of the details of the trial to *Love Letters* summarized Harriet's position before and afterwards concisely:

> he pursues it, she permits it and at last yields, when being discovered in the criminal intrigue, she flies with him, he absolutely quits [his wife], lives some time near [London] with this betrayed unfortunate, till being found out and likely to be apprehended [one for the rape the other for the flight] she is forced to marry a cadet, a creature of [Grey's], to bear the name of husband only to her, while [Grey] had the entire possession of her soul and body.

Harriet, Grey and Turner remained in London after the case. Harriet's baby was due and she was found lodgings in the parish of St Martin-in-the-Fields, while Grey continued with his political scheming. In the novel, as Silvia and Philander, Aphra has them discuss the situation, with Silvia taking the lead. She warns her lover of the danger and dishonour of plotting against the King in language which echoes Aphra's audacious prologue. Such contriving represents 'a sacrifice to the private revenge of a few ambitious knaves and rebels whose pretence is the public good'. As Silvia, Harriet is shown to be thoughtful, well-informed and intelligent, to the extent that her lover describes the male opinion of women's intellectual inferior capacities as a 'vulgar error'. If Aphra had indeed attended the trial, she had been impressed by how brave and articulate Harriet was. Recalling the thoroughly unpleasant John Hoyle, perhaps she even sympathized with her for falling in love with a man who was so clearly a bad lot.

Grey appeared entirely unashamed of the havoc he had wrought on the Berkeley family. The servants who had assisted him, the Charnocks and the Joneses, had been embroiled in a criminal investigation through his fault, but he was equally unconcerned with the consequences for them.

(NOTE: The parish registers of London give some slight indications of what became of the other protagonists in the trial. Robert and Anne Charnock were living to the west of the City in 1682, but had moved to the other end by 1692. The Joneses appear also to have moved after the trial, from Charing Cross to Saffron Hill, a far less salubrious address. The Pattens of Wild Street, which lay appropriately enough in 'theatreland' between Drury Lane and Lincoln's Inn, could not be traced, but Eleanor Hilton died in the Holborn workhouse in 1734, elderly and obviously very poor. This is very scant evidence indeed, but it does suggest that none of Grey's helpers gained much profit from their involvement in Harriet's escape.)

Grey had got what he wanted in Harriet; now he was set to pursue his dreams of political power. Following his acquittal on the treason charge, the Earl of Shaftesbury had been living quietly at his home at

Thanet, but while ill health imposed an irreproachably domestic existence, his brain was churning out ever more frantic plots to assure a Protestant succession. He attempted to persuade Monmouth to join a plan to capture the royal guards and declare London for the Exclusionists, but rumours of the plan soon rustled through London and Shaftesbury realized he had been fatally indiscreet. He left Thanet and went into hiding in the warrens and alleyways of the East End. By now seriously concerned that Shaftesbury was planning an uprising in which they would be implicated, Monmouth and his friends made another attempt to dissuade him, arranging a meeting at Shepherd's, a wine shop on the edge of the City. Grey attended, along with Lord Russell and Sir Thomas Armstrong, but Shaftesbury failed to appear, sending two deputies in his stead. Monmouth again spoke out firmly against the absurd and treacherous plan; Grey kept his views to himself. Shaftesbury could hardly hope that his scheme would not reach the ears of the King and rather than facing another arrest, he left for Amsterdam, where he died two months later.

During the Earl's final days, the ever-busy pens of the secret world had reported from Holland that Shaftesbury had been seen walking in the streets on the arm of Robert Ferguson, one of the two men he had sent as substitutes to the wine shop meeting. Ferguson had now returned to London, where Monmouth called in person at his lodgings to confirm that Shaftesbury had died. Ferguson and Grey had been in contact for some years by this point. A Presbyterian minister and active anti-Catholic propagandist, Ferguson was one of the slipperiest and, as he would prove, most dangerously persuasive men amongst the Exclusionist faction. He boasted of his connections with the exiled dissidents on the Continent, declaring that 'I shall never be out of a plot so long as I live.' Ferguson devoted much of his time to producing muck-raking pamphlets against the Duke of York and in 1680 had authored a masterpiece of fake news, *A Letter to a Person of Honour concerning the King's Disavowing* [. . .] *Having been married to the Duke of Monmouth's mother*. The tract raked through all the details of the long-ago affair between Charles II and Lucy Barlow, but rather than overtly disagreeing with the King's statement that he had never married her, it ingeniously appeared to support him, whilst leaving such glaring ambiguities that it was obvious Charles was lying. An infuriated Charles had been forced to publish a denial in the *London Gazette* the week after the pamphlet's release. Ferguson made no secret of his belief that the only hope for a Protestant succession was Monmouth, and now that Shaftesbury was gone, he insinuated himself further with Lord Grey.

The news of Shaftesbury's death left Monmouth and his supporters in a quandary. Whilst Monmouth continued to refute any suggestion of rebellion, it could be possible to at least compel the King to listen to the grievances of the Exclusionists. Organizing any show of force would be impossible without first learning if the Whig magnates could count on Scottish support, and after another meeting at Shepherd's an agent was despatched to Scotland, for which each member of Monmouth's inner circle, including Grey, provided £15. Several further meetings took place at Uppark, where Grey and Monmouth had repaired to go hunting. Presumably Harriet and her husband William Turner were of the party, possibly with Harriet's newborn baby. Did Harriet imagine that if Monmouth became heir to the throne she would regain a position in society as the consort of one of his closest friends? Could she have dreamed of becoming a duchess, assuming the new King was grateful and her sister Mary put aside? According to Aphra's novel, this was precisely what Grey had been offered. When the suggestion was made is uncertain, but *Love Letters* mentions a dukedom and 'honours' having been promised him.

As the plan took shape, there was of course no mention aloud that such a thing might come to pass. All the conspirators knew that to even mention the idea of deposing the anointed King was a crime. Monmouth was to command the 'protest', which in absolutely no way resembled a coup, the aim of which was to achieve 'an accommodation between the king and a Parliament'. By May, the group were back in London, where Grey visited Monmouth at his house in Soho Square. Walking round the garden until dawn, the two men went over and over the implications of the monumental step they planned to take, with Monmouth assuring Grey, or perhaps himself, that there was no need for bloodshed, since a show of force would be sufficient to bring his father round. Grey, it seemed, had already had other ideas.

In February, while Grey and Monmouth were galloping across the Sussex uplands, two gentlemen had got into conversation with a London man named Josiah Keeling at the Sun Tavern. After listening sympathetically to Keeling's views on the oppressive policy of Charles II's government, and no doubt buying him a few drinks, the gentlemen outlined a plan which they claimed would dispose of the King and his Catholic brother and secure the realm against popery. It wasn't a very convincing scheme – the conspirators were to disguise themselves as farmworkers and intercept the royal coach at Rye House in Hertfordshire, which lay on the Newmarket road. The King would be caught unaware on his return from the races, the road would be blocked with a cart and the servants and royal passengers shot. Set for March, the scheme was never attempted, as following an outbreak of fire at Newmarket the King and his party returned to London earlier than planned, but Keeling, motivated by genuine guilt or fear of arrest, nonetheless decided to confess.

On 12th June he revealed the assassination plan to

one of Charles's Privy Councillors, Lord Dartmouth. He was then questioned by the King himself at Hampton Court and an investigation put in train. Keeling's comrades claimed they had never met the Duke of Monmouth, who was ignorant of the plan, but further enquiry revealed that one of the plotters was John Rumsey, one of the men sent by Shaftesbury in his place to the assembly at Shepherd's wine shop. Monmouth's plan of a measured military statement had bled into a conspiracy to murder the King and the Duke of York, and as the names of senior Whigs began to drop faster and faster from the mouths of the Rye House conspirators, Grey's was amongst them.

Disastrously for Monmouth, he was also named, though there was never any serious suggestion that he was directly behind the plot. Grey, however, seems to have been playing a double game. He later admitted that he had been stockpiling weapons openly for two years and his connection with the Rye House scheme linked him to a more extreme solution to Exclusion than that posited by Monmouth. While maintaining plausible deniability, Grey was dabbling seriously with the possibility of regicide.

John Evelyn summarized the Rye House Plot in his diary:

After the Popish plot there was a new . . . Protestant plot discovered, that certain lords and others should design the assassination of the King and the Duke as they were to come from Newmarket, with a general rising of the nation, and especially of the city of London, disaffected to the present government, upon which were committed to the Tower the Lord Russell . . . the Earl of Essex, Mr Algernon Sidney . . . and others. A proclamation was issued against my Lord Grey, the Duke of Monmouth, Sir Thomas Armstrong and one Ferguson, who had escaped beyond the sea.

Less than a year after his trial for the abduction of Harriet, Grey once more found himself under arrest. Along with Lord Russell, Algernon Sidney and the Earl of Essex, he was taken to the Tower on the 5th June. According to Grey's own memoir, he had once again been staying at Uppark, having left London after the all-night stroll with Monmouth in May. He had found time to fit in a duel with the Duke of Albemarle before his departure, though neither man was hurt. Grey later claimed that he was only returning to London for (yet another) appearance at the King's Bench, this time to be fined for his involvement in an Exclusionist riot in the city. Grey was (yet again) planning to plead not guilty, but as he made his way to Westminster he was stopped by a messenger who presented him with a warrant for a far graver charge: high treason.

Keen to appear in the best light, Grey noted that the messenger was alone whilst he was travelling as

was customary for a man of his rank with a group o
stoutly armed servants. He could easily have escape
but consented to proceed to the Tower. Fleeing woul
have been a tacit admission of guilt and once he ha
put himself beyond the law he also risked his estate
becoming forfeit to the crown. Yet, as he put it, Go
was to grant him a second chance. Grey implied h
had actually escaped from the Tower itself, which wa
certainly a better story, but he didn't quite get there
Still, the account is incredible enough.

Accompanied by the messenger, Grey went b
carriage to Whitehall, where he was questioned per
sonally by King Charles. He denied all knowledge o
any conspiracy but mentioned his awareness that 'I ha
nothing but death to expect unless I would discove
my friends.' What appears at first as loyalty, that Gre
would have given his life rather than condemn his fel
lows, thus confirms that there was indeed somethin
to betray. His subsequent escape he put down to hi
own ingenuity, claiming that he certainly had no
bribed the messenger who then conveyed him to th
Tower gate. 'None can imagine I foresaw' the oppor
tunity presented by a drunken coachman who fe
asleep at his post, allowing Grey to take advantage an
disappear into the City. He found a ferryman to tak
him across the river and hid at the Pickled Herring in
before making his way back to Sussex, where Harrie
was waiting for him.

Grey spent a week lurking in the woods aroun

Uppark before taking a boat, the *Hare Pink*, from Chichester harbour, accompanied by Harriet, her legal husband Turner and a couple of servants. Harriet was dressed as a man, the better to avoid detection. The boat's captain had a wooden leg, but his piratical skills were otherwise lacking, as he mistook the tide and the party were obliged to wait six hours, bobbing about off Dell Quay and concealing themselves once more in the trees before they could cross safely to Holland. They were gone by 28th June when the Privy Council officially ordered Grey's detention for 'treasonable consultations to levy men and make an Insurrection in this Kingdom'. A bounty of £500 was placed on his head.

The Earl of Essex committed suicide in the Tower a fortnight later, slitting his throat with a razor. Eight days after his death, Lord Russell was publicly beheaded after being found guilty of high treason at the Old Bailey. Had he remained in London, Grey would likely have suffered a similar fate. If Harriet had indulged in imagining a glamorous future, her reality now was horribly altered. The man for whom she had 'sacrificed her good name and the affections of her doting parents' was a fugitive, on the run for his life. If Grey was captured, what would become of her?

Harriet's home for the next two years was to be Cleves, the ancient duchy on the Lower Rhine on the very edge of modern-day Germany. It was a famously beautiful city, flanked by the great river, rising up to the white-walled Schwanenburg Castle. In the 1680s, Cleves was controlled by the Elector of Brandenburg and a series of paintings of the gubernatorial residence, the Prinsenhof, were purchased by James II before 1688. They show the Prinsenhof as a brick palace in the latest style next to the Stiftskirche, surrounded by landscaped Baroque 'prospects' including the Tiergarten, a hill lined with avenues of trees. Arriving there in July, Grey professed himself 'so well pleased with the place and the kind reception we met with that we resolved to continue there till God's providence should otherwise dispose of us'.

The account Grey subsequently gave of this period in his memoir never once mentions Harriet, his lover and the mother of his child. This may well have been to protect her, but she is utterly erased from his version of events. Nevertheless, in noting the welcome he received in Cleves there is a hint that the stress and secrecy surrounding his relationship with Harriet had eased. William Turner was also in Holland, but there Harriet and Grey could live more openly as a couple. As Aphra had been nearly two decades earlier, Harriet now found herself part of the secret world. Grey maintained he had no correspondence with England other than dealing with his finances and estates, but he had not ceased working closely with Robert Ferguson for Monmouth's cause. He received intelligence from Utrecht and Amsterdam, assisted by a merchant, Herman de Bressau, and developed a close friendship with the Elector's ambassador Monsieur Fuchs. Cleves was hardly a buzzing metropolis but Harriet and Grey were safe and being received in diplomatic company, thrilling political news swirled through the small town and Harriet could ride or walk in its elegant gardens without fear of opprobrium. One hopes it was a happy time for her.

Or perhaps not. Spies and agents clustered in the taverns of Cleves as they had done in Antwerp and Harriet and her lover were obviously of interest. One agent reported Harriet to have been about four months pregnant in July 1683: 'she looked very thin and is a perfect trollop, in a plain scarf and black hood.' Harriet had been heavily pregnant during the trial the preceding year and the arrangements made by the Charnocks suggest that she was soon to give birth, which event may have been the catalyst for her flight. What became of her child is unknown, but it cannot be the one referred to by the agent, so she must have conceived again in the spring of 1683, when she was at Uppark with Grey. A satire written in 1684 claims this baby was born at Cleves and that Harriet 'escaped great danger' in childbed, having suffered throughout the pregnancy. Harriet's children are not heard of again – quite possibly they died, as so many infants did.

Monmouth had been pardoned for his part in the planned uprising, but it was a short-lived reprieve and he had consented to go into exile. Grey had attempted to find him a general's post in the army of the Elector of Brandenburg, but the Elector was unable to oblige, explaining that he wasn't engaged in any wars at the present moment, though he should be glad if Monmouth might visit him in Berlin. Instead, after a meeting with his first cousin William of Orange at The Hague, Monmouth went to Brussels, where he was formally received on 7 May 1684 at the residence of the Governor General, the Marquis of Grana. Monmouth was to command a cavalry force in the ongoing wars against France, but before he could take up his post the French offered a truce. Grey attempted to contact Monmouth, who made only a short formal reply, preferring to spend the summer with his royal relations rather than his discredited cronies. Kicking their heels in Cleves while Monmouth hunted with William and danced with his cousin Princess Mary, Monmouth's 'friends on that side of the water were very sensible of [his] ingratitude'.

Shunned by the Duke, Grey and Harriet looked set to remain in increasingly impoverished exile for some time. As the months dragged on, their relationship began to deteriorate. Harriet was unwell and possibly grieving; according to a cruel rumour she had completely lost her bouncing looks. Grey, who had perhaps loved defiance and transgression more than he had ever loved Harriet, was frustrated by Monmouth's lack of interest in further plotting. So charming in July, Cleves was dull and freezing in winter. There were also money troubles. According to the satires

Grey was now exceedingly poor and neither he nor Harriet was accustomed to economizing. Again keeping her ear to the ground for the gossip that filtered incessantly from the Continent, Aphra imagined the lovers' discontent in Part Two of her novel.

As Philander in the novel, Grey steals, seduces and corrupts Silvia (the real-life Harriet Berkeley), in a manner which suggestively mirrors the Whigs' attempts to control the occupation of the throne; the obedient Royalist daughter kidnapped and ruined stands in for the usurped crown of England. Who owns Silvia/Harriet as a piece of property is the question of the novel as it was of the trial, and Aphra's answer was politically at least a surprisingly conservative one.

Aphra's connection with Holland stretched back to the earliest period of her life. She had learned Dutch and her husband (if he ever existed) may have been Dutch, but *Love Letters* displays the 'Hollandophobia' which was associated with Aphra's Tory politics. The Dutch Republic was seen as rapacious, obsessed with gain and devoid of any values beyond the getting of wealth, hence untrustworthy, slippery, undependable. Back at the Rosa Noble inn in Antwerp in 1666 Aphra had experienced for herself the tricksy world of deceit and mistrust of the spies who clustered at Holland's border, and in her contempt for Dutch money-grubbing we might hear the echoes of her nagging landlord.

As a contemporary observed, Dutch values were mutable and false, evident even in the appearance of their homes:

> When you are entered the house, the first thing you encounter is a Looking Glass. No question but a true Emblem of politic hospitality, for though it reflect yourself in your own figure, 'tis yet no longer than while you are there before it. When you are once gone, it flatters the next comer without the least remembrance that you ere were there.*

In the English section of the story, the Grey character seduces Harriet by explaining that theirs is a pure form of love, untainted by the materialism of the upper-class marriage market. Once in Holland though, the Grey character is revealed as a hypocrite who cares far more for 'Dutch' values than he pretends. As the novel proceeds, Harriet's character comes to recognize that her lover's world is as false as a Dutch looking-glass and decides to beat him at his own corrupt game.

Love Letters is a political allegory, but it's also an unashamedly sexy read. Aphra had been more explicit on the stage than even the raciest of her contemporaries, but the novel form offered a more expansive medium for erotic, even graphic writing. Harriet's character continues in her male dress, which Aphra notes, gives

* Feltham, Owen, *A Brief Character of the Low Countries* (1659)

her considerably more freedom in her daily life, 'a thousand little privileges which otherwise would have been denied to women', but cross-dressing is more than a practical choice. She is 'pleased with the Cavalier in herself' and delights in flirting as a man with other men. The Grey character too is drawn as being as alluring to men as he is to women and there are several daringly ambiguous love scenes. William Turner is portrayed as a voyeur, sleeping in the same room as Harriet and Grey, where he becomes 'a witness to all their sighs of love'. Everyone is disguised and the seductions come thick and fast. Turner observes with satisfaction that now Grey has secured Harriet, he is growing cold 'as possessing lovers do' and plots to make her his wife in more than name. Aphra's imagining of Harriet's life with Grey showed a remarkable prescience; the ending she wrote for Harriet did indeed come true, several years after its creator had died.

17

On 16th February 1685, shocking news arrived at The Hague. Charles II had died at the age of just fifty-four. The King had seldom been ill and his rapid decline had taken the court completely by surprise. He had collapsed after prayers on the morning of 2nd February and was dead by noon on the 6th. The King had succumbed to kidney disease, possibly caused by his amateur chemistry experiments with mercury. History has inaccurately though not unfairly blamed his doctors, who prescribed fifty-eight drugs as well as bleeding him and attempting to draw out the illness with red-hot irons held against the shaven royal head. With a last effort at wit, Charles apologized to his attendants, 'Forgive me, gentlemen, for being so long a-dying.'

Evelyn's description of Charles's last night at his court is worth quoting at length:

I am never to forget the unexpressable luxury and profaneness, gaming and all dissolution and as it were total forgetfulness of God (it being Sunday evening) which this day sennight I was witness of; the King, sitting and toying with his concubines . . .

a French boy singing love songs in that glorious gallery whilst about twenty of the great courtiers and other dissolute persons were at basset round a large table, a bank of at least £2,000 in gold before them, upon which two gentlemen that were with me made reflexions with astonishment, it being a scene of utmost vanity and surely as they thought it would never have an end. Six days after, all was dust.

From Evelyn's framing of the scene, the gallery, the singing boy, the choreographed extras, it might be a description of a play. Charles had famously sent his coronation robes to Thomas Killigrew's theatre in 1660, as good a sign as any of how this secretive, mercurial man viewed the throne he had so improbably reclaimed. He was the second Stuart King to die in his bed, and the last. Naturally it was instantly rumoured that the Duke of York had poisoned his brother, a rumour hardly less shocking than that the King had at the last been received into the Catholic church, with the rite administered by Father John Huddleston, the priest who had helped him escape from the battle of Worcester. The number of people who knew initially that the last slander was in fact true was small, but in York, now His Majesty King James II, England had its first officially Catholic King for the first time in over a hundred years.

Aphra's response to the King's death was professional and astonishingly comprehensive. She ground out three poems, an elegy on Charles, a consolatory ode to his widowed Queen, Catherine of Braganza, and eight hundred lines for the coronation of King James. They are predictable, workmanlike pieces, grandiose and sententious, though as a long-time supporter of York Aphra did include a rather brash hint that it was about time she was rewarded for her literary services. The coronation poem contains an unsubtle grumble about the humble author's 'silent dull obscurity', which of course she only minds as it 'Set me at a distance, much too far / The Deity to view or Divine Oracle to hear'. It would be just like James II to believe Aphra meant such tosh and still not pay her for it, which he didn't.

The only surviving member of Monmouth's circle of senior Whig plotters was Grey, who had no doubt that his hour had finally come. He made for Amsterdam on the news of Charles's death, where he joined forces with Robert Ferguson. Immediately they began pressuring Monmouth (close by in The Hague), to raise his standard in rebellion. In another convergence of Harriet's present and Aphra's past, Colonel Bampfield was wheeled on for a brief guest appearance. The man of whom Aphra's long-ago mark William Scot had been so afraid re-emerged, slippery as ever, trying to sell information on the English exiles gathering at Rotterdam. No one took much notice of Bampfield or his wares; they hardly needed to as the Monmouth party were no longer bothering to keep their activities undercover. Aphra, certainly, seemed to know every move they made.

Monmouth himself was still coy. Six days after Charles's death he made for Brussels, proclaiming his intention to leave to fight the Turks on the edge of Europe. But the new English king made it clear he did not wish Monmouth to remain in Flanders and the Duke agreed to return to Holland, passing through Rotterdam to meet his hopeful supporters. He was there during his uncle's coronation on 23rd April.

Grey now saw himself as a kingmaker. In *Love Letters,* he is described at this moment as 'every evening caballing there, where all the malcontents of the Reformed Religion had taken sanctuary'. The precise situation the Whigs had campaigned so long to prevent – a Catholic King – had now arrived, but Monmouth remained uncertain as to if and how he should act. Frustrated, Robert Ferguson complained of the Duke's 'numbness of spirit and slothfulness'. He would have to be persuaded into rebellion, so Grey and Ferguson set about a campaign of pressure and outright lies to bring him round.

When Monmouth had left England, he too had been accompanied by his mistress, Lady Henrietta Wentworth. Born in 1660, Henrietta, like Harriet, was born into the centre of the aristocratic Royalist establishment. Her father had been an Interregnum Cavalier and unusually she had inherited her title of Baroness and her country estate at Toddington in Bedfordshire from him in her own right. Aphra knew of Henrietta first through the theatre. In 1676, Etherege's play *The Man of Mode* had opened at the Duke's at Dorset Garden. The clever, virtuous heroine 'Harriet Woodvill' was acknowledged to be a portrait of the sixteen-year-old Henrietta, freshly arrived at court. Harriet had met Henrietta during her own first court season in 1680, though what friendship they might have developed was short-lived, for to the delight of the lampoonists, Henrietta's mother had whisked her back to the country when it emerged that she had begun an affair with Monmouth. Both Henrietta and Harriet had been adamant that they would not give up their lovers, but Henrietta's relationship, whilst adulterous, was not actually criminal. She and Monmouth were deeply in love and believed that they were married in spirit, if not in law. Once he met Henrietta, the Duke had abandoned his womanizing and gradually their relationship was accepted as an established fact, to the extent that when Henrietta joined him in Holland she had been formally received by William of Orange and Mary.

Love Letters presents a rather pathetic picture of Harriet's attempt to rekindle a relationship with Henrietta when they were both living in exile with the married men with whom they had cast their lots. Though they had so much in common, Henrietta refused to have anything to do with Harriet. Harriet apparently sent a servant every day to the house where Henrietta was living with Monmouth, paying her a formal compliment and apologizing that she was unable to call in person because she was 'ill' (or heavily pregnant). Henrietta returned the courtesy, but only in the form that she would receive from a person with whom she was not acquainted. In the novel, 'Hermione' (Henrietta) is appalled when Silvia (Harriet) suggests that they meet in person, since she 'looked on you as a lost creature and one of such reputation she would not receive a visit from for all the world'. Eventually, Harriet gave up and the two did not meet.

The hypocrisy of Henrietta's stance was not lost on Aphra. However, it may also have been that Grey was using Harriet to try to get close to Henrietta, as the rebels perceived her influence over Monmouth as a block to their plans. When Harriet was rejected, they turned to magic. In the novel, Robert Ferguson is portrayed as 'Fergusano' who preys upon the gullible Monmouth character with sorcery. Monmouth was known to be highly superstitious – in happier days he had lost a huge amount of money at the Newmarket races on a tip from a 'conjurer' and now Ferguson showed him a horoscope which proved that he was born to be a king. In the novel, his fictional counterpart stages a surreal scene to persuade Monmouth to take up his magical destiny. Aphra's description comes straight from the special effects she would have known at the Dorset Garden Theatre: the Monmouth character is taken to a cavern, where with a 'noise like rushing of wind' the rocks divide 'to discover a most magnificent apartment'. Various changes of scenery are specified, and a cast of extras who perform a pageant revealing that unless Monmouth's character renounces his lover he will never succeed. Whether any such theatrics really took place is unknown, but given Monmouth's credulousness it would not be altogether implausible. The Duke, however, refused to abandon Henrietta, so Ferguson changed tack. As Fergusano, he presents 'Hermione' with a fabulously bathetic gift, a magical toothpick case, which will render her lover invincible if he fights for his true cause.

Grey meanwhile was concentrating on more practical arrangements. He had found a source of funds in a rich Englishwoman, a widow named Ann Smith living in Amsterdam, and had also been in contact with a disaffected Scottish peer, the Earl of Argyll, who boasted that he had already acquired three ships, 500 barrels of gunpowder and sufficient arms to equip 10,000 men. Argyll was reluctant to collaborate with Monmouth but was persuaded that together, by launching attacks in Scotland and England simultaneously, they could succeed in taking the kingdom. All that remained was for Grey to convince Monmouth to act.

Together with Robert Ferguson, Grey set about deceiving Monmouth into believing that there was widespread support for the deposition of the newly crowned King James. Delving into his contacts in the secret world, Ferguson produced a series of agents who confirmed that the people of England were eager to be rescued from the Catholic threat. Monmouth didn't need to know that they were being paid by Ferguson to spread the news he wanted to hear. Grey was similarly active, successfully preventing a warning to Monmouth from reaching its destination. Aphra treats this fakery with wry humour in the novel, as after all she herself had experience of concocting evidence. William Disney, a Whig bookseller, wrote that Monmouth should not think of coming to England, but Grey destroyed the letter. Pressured from all sides, Monmouth eventually consented and gave his word that the invasion would go ahead.

By May, the preparations were advancing. Argyll sailed for Scotland while Monmouth set about pawning the contents of his luxurious house in Brussels to raise funds. Three ships were acquired and docked near Amsterdam and stocked with cannon, gunpowder and arms. Harriet's location during the spring is unknown, but William Turner was at Grey's side, recruiting eighty soldiers to the cause.

The actions of William of Orange are worth scrutinizing at this point. King James had made it clear that he didn't want Monmouth at The Hague any more than in Brussels, but William brushed him aside with vague promises. One explanation for William's willingness to displease his father-in-law might be that he had taken Monmouth at his word when the latter promised him solemnly that he would never rebel. The two men were close friends and William was aware that Monmouth had grieved acutely for his father and may have had no wish to add to his distress. However, the activities of the rebels, who had bribed the officials at the port of Texel, where their little fleet was mustering, to turn a blind eye to the barrels and weapons being carried up the gangplanks could not have passed unobserved. Moreover, the intelligence on which Monmouth had based his decision to invade was false, but from the double and triple dealings of the secret world, William's own agents may have brought him a different version. It would not be inconvenient for William if Monmouth's rebellion failed, as it would bring him one step closer to the English throne at no trouble to himself. It is quite possible that he was allowing Monmouth to proceed as part of his own long-term strategy.

As Monmouth's ship the *Rising Sun* finally reached the English coast off Lyme Regis in Dorset on 11 June 1685, the reality of Grey's deception became abruptly and painfully clear. The promised army was dismally small, only eighty-three men, and the soldiers of the local militia, whose support he had been promised, had failed to materialize in any number. Grey marched at Monmouth's side through Lyme, where they waited for three nights for supporters to trickle in. Monmouth issued a 'Declaration', written by Grey and Ferguson, which denounced the 'absolute tyranny' of James's rule and even repeated the rumour that he had been responsible for the late King's sudden death.

A regiment of cavalry had been promised from London, but no horsemen arrived. Volunteers were joining the rebels in small bands, but the overall numbers were hopeless. Grey and Ferguson explained the pathetic lack of support by arguing that men loyal to the monarchy, if not the occupant of the throne, had misunderstood Monmouth's intentions. They feared he had come to abolish kingship altogether, but if Monmouth were now to declare himself the rightful King, all would become clear. Furthermore, if Monmouth subsequently proclaimed himself and the rebellion failed, then his supporters would be spared execution, as taking up arms for one they acknowledged as King offered them legal protection. Whether Monmouth believed this or just wanted to believe it, he agreed and Charles II's bastard son claimed the crown at Taunton on 21st June.

In Scotland, the Earl of Argyll had spectacularly failed to execute his half of the plan. What few supporters he had raised rapidly fell away when they saw how ill-prepared and incompetent he was, and he had ended by quarrelling with an elderly drunk on the bank of the River Clyde. The man had bashed the Earl on the head with a sword as old as he was and Argyll was arrested. Monmouth had little choice but to continue, but he already knew there was no promise of success. He proposed retreating, but Grey once again persuaded him, appealing to his sense of aristocratic honour. Flight, Grey argued, 'was a thing so base that it could never be forgiven by the people to be so deserted'. Grey himself preferred death to the prospect of a shameful exile, or so he said.

The royal army was closing in. Cornered, Monmouth determined on a surprise night attack at Sedgemoor in Somerset. He was to command the foot, Grey the 600-strong cavalry. Monmouth himself was a highly experienced soldier, whose skill and bravery had won the respect of his men and commanders over a lengthy military career. His decision to give the cavalry to Grey, who had no qualifications beyond being born a lord, cost Monmouth the battle and ultimately his life. Grey made a decent show of charging the royal line, but while Monmouth brought up the foot Grey then found himself trapped by a deep ditch and retreated. Monmouth drove his men forward, fighting so bravely that even his opponents praised him, but with the cavalry routed Sedgemoor was lost almost before the battle had begun. By dawn many of the rebels had been slaughtered and Monmouth retreated eastwards, where Grey caught up with him.

In a poignant echo of Charles II's legendary escape after the battle of Worcester, Grey convinced Monmouth that if they escaped cross-country to Sussex, they would be able to embark for the Continent as he had done with Harriet two years earlier. With a cluster of companions, the two made a sixty-mile ride in two days, before Grey separated from Monmouth as they neared the coast. His party was rounded up by a royal

295

patrol, to whom Grey promptly betrayed the man h
had accepted as his King. Monmouth was capture
near the village of Horton at dawn on 8th July an
taken under guard to Whitehall.

Aphra's novel *Love Letters*, which had begun b
charting Harriet's escape to join Grey and continue
in their imagined life on the Continent, ends in Pa
III with the execution of Monmouth. Much of th
excitement for Aphra's readers came from the sens
that the story was happening in real time, a serial whic
kept up with the true-life adventures of its thinly di
guised protagonists. Aphra continues the tantalizin
conceit established in Part I, that she has access to th
actual documentation of her story. Describing Mor
mouth's dismal progress towards London after h
capture, she reports what little good sense he had eve
possessed as having declined with his fortunes:

> His style was altered, and debased to that of a
> common man, or rather a schoolboy, filled with tau-
> tologies and stuff of no coherence; in which he
> showed neither the majesty of a prince, nor sense of
> a gentleman; as I could make appear by exposing
> those copies, which I leave to history.

After three nights in prison at the Tower of Londo
Monmouth was executed on Tower Hill on 15th Jul
The penalty for traitors was to be hanged, drawn an
quartered, but James II mercifully commuted h
nephew's sentence to beheading. Since Monmout

was to die in public, rather than within the precincts of the Tower, his fellow prisoner Lord Grey could not have watched his final moments, but both men would have heard the hammering of the carpenters as they constructed the black-draped scaffold. Monmouth died bravely but horribly. As he lay stretched out, his head on the block, the executioner took three swings of the axe and then, crying 'God damn me, I can do no more!', recoiled in horror from the twitching, still-living body, slipping in the blood which foamed over the boards from the gouges in Monmouth's neck. The onlookers erupted in horrified yells and he staggered forward to swing again, but the head refused to be severed. Even a fifth blow was resisted and the executioner was reduced to sawing away at the last fragments of sinew before holding up the head to the crowd.

From his room in the Tower, Grey could have heard the screaming and weeping as the man he had sworn to serve as King was butchered. He too had been condemned for high treason, yet did he already know that he was not doomed to the block? Grey had given up Monmouth without a moment's hesitation and was busily pouring out his confession. He saved his life with a combination of bribery and betrayal, ransoming himself with a payment rumoured to be as huge as £40,000 and spilling all the details of the rebellion at the trials of his co-conspirators. (His creditors were also rumoured to have had a hand in his preservation, since he had run up such monstrous debts that they needed him alive to honour them.)

Whilst Grey was wriggling off the hook, Aphra was preparing the third instalment of her novel. The rebellion itself had of course been the only news for months in the newsletters and gazettes, and the letters written by Monmouth to his uncle and his father's widow Queen Catherine were widely discussed. Yet in Part III of *Love Letters*, Aphra reported with intriguingly uncanny accuracy on the real-time movements of Monmouth and Grey in Holland at the inception of the rebellion. The most probable source for Aphra's knowledge was Grey himself, and she worked out what many others had not, that his support for Monmouth had concealed an even greater duplicity than the betrayal of the King.

18

Lord Grey wrote out his confession to his part in the rebellion in 1685, but it was not published until 1757 when it was released as *The Secret History of the Rye House Plot* (price two shillings). How then did Aphra come by her source material? She was not listed amongst the official recipients of the circulars which reported foreign news, but her knowledge is far too detailed to have been picked up from the lampoons. The rustle of gossip had leaped upon Grey's delivery from the axe, with poems such as *Monmouth Routed and Taken Prisoner with His Pimp the Lord Grey*, appearing almost before the unfortunate Duke's head was finally hacked off, but they contained no new information about the pair's activities in the United Provinces. Aphra must have had an inside source.

It has been suggested that Aphra herself travelled to the Netherlands and may even have met with Monmouth's mistress Henrietta Wentworth, but there is no evidence as yet that she did so. Aphra's treatment of Henrietta in the novel is less than kind but it too is based upon details not widely known to the public. Monmouth and Henrietta had been genuinely, deeply in love. Whilst staying with her in the English country-side, the Duke had even been moved to poetry:

> This is a better fate than kings,
> Hence gentle peace and love doth flow
> . . . for a heart that is nobly true
> All the world's arts can ne'er subdue.

Would that he had taken his own advice, but the sentiment at least was sincere. In the short period between his imprisonment and execution, Monmouth had been pressured to denounce his adulterous relationship with Henrietta as a sin, but his commitment to her never wavered. Even on the scaffold he tried to protect her reputation, declaring that:

> I have had a scandal raised about me about a woman, a lady of virtue and honour. I will name her, the Lady Henrietta Wentworth. I declare that she is a very virtuous and Godly woman. I have committed no sin with her, and that which has passed betwixt us was very Honest and Innocent in the sight of God.

In a sense, Monmouth's words supported the theme of so many of Aphra's plays, that true love was innately possessed of its own justification, yet this could not, it seemed, be resolved against the greater claim of duty, the contradictory challenge at the heart of *Love Letters*. Aphra has her Monmouth character going bravely to die clutching the enchanted toothpick case presented to him by Henrietta. Aphra meanly observed that

Henrietta was already well past her best at the age of thirty (in fact she was twenty-five) and that with Monmouth gone there was nothing better for her to do but die of grief, which is what poor Henrietta did. She returned to England the autumn after the rebellion and died a few months later. A lampoon gave out that 'My Lady Henrietta Wentworth is dead, having sacrificed her life to her beauty by painting so beyond measure that the mercury got into her veins and killed her.' Aphra's novel claims that she deliberately starved herself to death, but she also mentions another 'charm' sent by the superstitious Monmouth to protect his beloved. Henrietta had indeed received a visit on her deathbed from the Bishop of Ely, who had given her a note with a spell or incantation written out in Monmouth's hand. How could Aphra have known of this?

Aphra is rather cruel to Henrietta in *Love Letters*, portraying her as an absurd, hysterical character, given to melodramatic swoonings. Perhaps she felt the injustice of the different ways in which Henrietta and Harriet had been treated, and of that cold rejection of Harriet's overtures when she was alone and friendless in Holland.

The most likely source for Aphra's precise account of Harriet and Grey's movements in the months before the rebellion is Robert Spencer, the Earl of Sunderland. Sunderland had been a friend of Aphra's dear Rochester; they had made the Grand Tour in Europe together many years before, and he was also connected with the theatre, being the patron of several (male) writers including Dryden. His political mentor was Lord Arlington, Aphra's former employer. Sunderland had briefly flirted with the Exclusion cause, which had led to a temporary loss of his position as Secretary of State, but he had been reinstated after the Rye House Plot in 1683. It was to Sunderland that Grey made his confession.

In *Love Letters*, Aphra has the Grey character declare himself 'weary' of the plot before Monmouth's ship has even hauled anchor. He asserts that he has been coerced into the uprising, which he intends to abandon at the first opportunity:

> since self-preservation was the first principle of nature, he had resolved to make that his aim and rather prove false to a party who had no justice and honour on their side than to a King whom all the laws of heaven and earth obliged him to serve, however he was so far in the power of these people that he could not disengage himself without utter ruin.

How could Aphra have known that Grey intended to betray Monmouth, which is precisely the position his counterpart Philander takes in *Love Letters*? Grey himself had known what the hapless Monmouth had not, that the promised military support for the rebellion was a concoction brewed up by his own and Ferguson's imaginations. Given that he knew the rebellion would surely fail, why would he have joined it had he not been sure he would survive? William of Orange, it should be recalled, had also seemed remarkably serene about the insurrectionary preparations which were taking place under his nose. Sunderland was no ideologue – his momentary support for Exclusion had been predicated on the likelihood of its success rather than the justice of the cause – and he had long maintained a relationship with William of Orange. In 1685 the new Queen, Mary of Modena, had as yet to produce a living child, so William and his wife Mary were next in line to the throne. Were Monmouth to have succeeded, another civil war would have been inevitable, and Sunderland, whether from self-interest or sheer love of the game of power, stood to gain considerably if he could manipulate Monmouth off the political chessboard and assure the crown for William. Sunderland had been present at Whitehall on the day when Grey was questioned after the Rye House Plot imploded. Had it been he rather than a drunken coachman who had been responsible for Grey's escape to Holland with Harriet?

Sunderland has been posited as the commissioner of the entire *Love Letters* series, but the only strong connection between him and Aphra is in Part III, which she dedicated to his son, Robert Spencer. The first part of the novel had been dedicated to Robert Condon, an otherwise obscure young military captain who seemed to have caught Aphra's eye. Writing of the handsome Philander, her preface suggests 'give me leave to fancy him such a person as yourself, and then I cannot fail of fancying him too'. Perhaps they had a fling? The personal compliments in the dedication 'you are as young as new desire, as beautiful as light, as amorous as a God' might just have been written with another kind of inside knowledge, but sadly no more is known of this potentially erotic relationship. *Love Letters* Part II is dedicated to Lemuel Kingdon, another military man who served as paymaster general of the forces in Ireland. Its tone is jolly rather than gushing, but it is interesting that the dedicatees of the first two sections of the novel were soldiers. Was there a (very) veiled warning of what might be to come were Philander/Grey to return triumphant? For Part III, the Spencer dedication is fairly generic; Aphra compliments him on his noble birth and the possibilities of a splendid future if he will resist the temptation to unlawful ambition. Spencer was a ne'er-do-well in the roistering Rochester tradition but without the brains; he drank himself to death the following year. Aside from the compliment to his son, what did Sunderland have to gain by possibly giving Aphra access to the top-secret information which enabled her to complete her book?

If Sunderland had positioned Grey to bring down Monmouth, it would cement both their relationships with the present King and the King to come. Part III of *Love Letters* can be read as an attempt to restore Grey's public reputation. By 1686, Grey was in full enjoyment of his title and fortune, though not of Harriet, who had been left behind in Holland. If Aphra had taken the commission from Sunderland though, it does not mean that she wrote a propaganda tract. Aside from being very funny, Part III might equally be read as an indictment of the supple self-interest of men like Grey and Sunderland himself, and a more general disenchantment with the obdurate foolishness of James II. His lover forgotten, his sins redeemed, Philander/Grey 'kissed the King's hand and came to court in as much splendour as ever'. Readers of the full novel could see that Philander is an utterly false non-character, who, by his own confession, has nothing but his own preservation at heart. Aphra couldn't afford to express it anywhere else, but the King who receives this viper is the greatest booby in the story.

Aphra seemed to have had a crystal ball concealed somewhere in her Whitefriars lodgings. Or perhaps her contacts within the royal court were closer than we know? Her performance as a spy in Antwerp might have been just that, but since then she had certainly improved her sleuthing skills. When she had parodied Sir Patience Ward, the sheriff of London, in her 1677 play, she had positioned his hypocrisy as a cover for insurrectionary tendencies. As it turned out, when the list of subscribers to Monmouth's cause was published years later, Ward's name was on it. The return of the Grey character in *Love Letters* III is ominous. Leniency is no solution to treachery, since the

Philanders of the world will always manipulate the gullible to their own advantage. Aphra's hints at the threat to come were to prove entirely accurate.

Aphra's writing life between 1685 and 1689 was startlingly productive. She released at least twenty-seven poems, five plays, four stories, including *Oroonoko*, and six essays and prologues as well as translations from the French. Many more stories and poems were published after her death, leaving the dates of their composition more uncertain. This phenomenal output reflects both Aphra's mastery of her craft and also the continued exigencies of earning her living. It continued to grate that she did not have the access to court circles her male contemporaries enjoyed, despite her unwavering loyalty to James II.

In 1688 she published a translation of Jean-Baptiste de Brilhac's *Agnes de Castro*, an exotic story of a love quadrangle set in Portugal. Its two heroines, Constantina and Agnes, struggle to preserve their intense friendship in the case of sexual demands from all the wrong men, but Constantina (like Henrietta Wentworth), eventually dies of grief. In her dedication to the story, Aphra wrote bitterly that:

> It would be a happy world for us Traders in Parnassus if . . . we could Barter, pay Debts and obligations with Poems and Dedications: But this is a World not generous enough for such noble Traffic . . . In our Age the Noble Roman Poets would have starved.

Her complaint is as true today as it was then – as every writer who has contributed free content in return for publicity knows, exposure pays no bills.

Huddled over a stingy fire in Whitefriars, squinting in inadequate candlelight, scratching away at yet another manuscript, Aphra's legacy might have offered cold comfort even had she known of it. *Love Letters* is undoubtedly a contender for the title of first English novel, and though the question of which book exactly inaugurated the genre isn't a particularly important one, the fact that the credit is usually given to a man, Daniel Defoe, for *Robinson Crusoe*, published nearly forty years later, deserves to be challenged. The epistolary form first used for long-length fiction by Aphra in the seventeenth century dominated until well into the eighteenth, including Samuel Richardson's *Clarissa* (another story of the seduction of a well-born girl by a ruthless rake). Aphra reshaped the model in which men wrote about women: from Defoe's Moll Flanders to Fielding's Shamela, Cleland's Fanny Hill to Thackeray's Becky Sharpe, she is the literary godmother to a canon of tough, sexy, intelligent heroines as independent-minded as they are witty. The debt owed to Aphra by women writers, as Virginia Woolf observed, is even greater. For twenty years she had been the only woman writing for the stage, but in the theatrical season of 1695–6, one third of all the new plays performed were by women. Five notable women playwrights emerged after Aphra, including Delarivier

Manley and Susanna Centlivre. The foremost women playwrights of the following century owed their careers in part to her. It's hardly an accident that one of Centlivre's early publications was a short story told in epistolary form recounted by a pair of lovers named 'Astrea' and 'Celadon'.

Virtuosity would have to be its own reward for Aphra, but her own time denied her even virtue. A woman who exhibited herself on the stage, as actress or writer, was assumed to be a whore. *The Poetess, A Satire*, by Robert Gould put it bluntly:

> Hackney writers when their verse did fail,
> To get 'em brandy, bread and cheese and ale,
> Their Wants by prostitution were supplied,
> Show but a tester you might up and ride,
> For Punk [whore] and Poetess agree so pat
> You cannot well be this and not be that.

Aphra may have been praised by some as 'the wonder of her sex', but the fact that she wrote for the public meant that for the majority she represented 'a monster of immorality'. When Anne Wharton, a young relative of the Earl of Rochester, had written a shy verse fan-letter to Aphra commending her for his elegy, her spiritual counsellor Bishop Gilbert Burnet, had admonished her:

> she is so abominably vile a woman and rallies not only Religion but all virtue in so odious and obscene

a manner that I am heartily sorry she had writ anything in your commendation . . . the praises of such
as she are great reproaches.

It would be nice to think that women in any form
of public position are no longer subjected to the personal attacks Aphra endured for the whole of her
professional life. 'Whore' and 'slut' have, however,
stayed a distance of over three centuries as the scared
misogynist's insult of choice.

19

Monmouth's rebellion had been an abject failure, but many people in England now feared that the Catholic 'tyranny' it had aimed to prevent was coming to pass. In the autumn of 1685, King James's cousin, Louis XIV of France, had repealed the Edict of Nantes, the legislation which permitted freedom of worship to Protestants. London was suddenly flooded with 'Huguenots', religious asylum seekers fleeing Catholic persecution. (They were not welcomed by the King, but they made an important contribution to London's economy, as many of them were silk weavers who brought their expertise with them, and whose houses can still be seen today in Spitalfields.) Their arrival spread anxiety – might King James follow Louis's example? He had already permitted Catholic officers to join the army and by the end of the year five members of his Privy Council were Catholics. When the Parliament he had summoned on 9th November raised their objections, the King responded by dissolving it after just eleven days.

William of Orange had commissioned a special fast boat service to bring news and agents back and forth to Holland. While Aphra worked at her book, discreet meetings were being arranged with leading men who were disquieted by the King's actions.

The announcement in the spring of 1688 that Queen Mary was expecting a child was not met with the customary rejoicing. King James of course already had two legitimate daughters, Mary of Orange and Princess Anne, but there was now the prospect of that longed-for legitimate son which had always eluded Charles II. On 10th June, the Queen was delivered of a boy, James Francis Edward Stuart.

Just five days after the birth of the new Prince of Wales, a deputation of seven statesmen sent a letter to William of Orange, claiming that they along with 'much of the nobility and gentry' of England were 'dissatisfied with the present conduct of the government'. Four years after the Monmouth rebellion, it looked as though the country was once again at risk of civil war. The mood in London was not yet volatile, but subdued and tense, the streets almost as eerily silent as they had been in the year of the plague. John Evelyn confirmed in his diary that there was 'some great thing to be discovered. This was the Prince of Orange intending to come over.'

Gradually the news began to arrive that the Prince of Orange had declared an invasion and was preparing his fleet. His stated intention was not the overthrow of James but the summoning of a free and lawful Parliament, yet many, including Lord Grey, believed he would not stop there. The King began to prepare fo war, summoning the county militias and adding thirty-three warships and sixteen fireships to the Navy. The standoff continued until November, when William landed at Brixham in Devon on the 5th. He had chosen the most symbolically appropriate day, the anniversary of the failure of the Gunpowder Plot. By 9th November William's forces were at Exeter and the country was in an uproar. Rioters stormed through Nottingham and York, Leicester, Carlisle and Gloucester crying for 'the Protestant religion and liberty'. One witness described the situation on the streets, 'the drums beat, the bells rang backwards, the women shrieked and such doleful consternation seized upon all persons.'* The houses of known Catholics were attacked, the Spanish and Florentine embassies were burned down. At this moment of crisis King James began to suffer from a series of debilitating nosebleeds which left him exhausted and sleepless. He had never been as astute or as slippery as his brother Charles and the strain affected what little judgement he had ever possessed.

And now the coats began to turn. Princess Anne fled her father's court and escaped to Nottingham in a hired carriage. Several noblemen, including Harriet's father the Earl of Berkeley, declared for William. As the invaders closed in on London, the Queen took flight, escaping to Calais disguised as a washerwoman.

* Thoresby, Ralph, *Diary 1677–1724* (thoresby.org.uk)

Two days later, James himself left his capital, crossing the river at Vauxhall and riding hard for the coast. Mortifyingly, he was apprehended on the Isle of Sheppey disguised under an unflattering black wig and escorted sheepishly back to Whitehall. He was then informed that he would have to leave his palace as the Prince of Orange would shortly be arriving in London. James retreated to Rochester, but the nature of this imperious order had made it clear; effectively he was a prisoner in his own realm.

(NOTE: After the King's failed attempt at escape, a group of senior noblemen assembled at the Guildhall to declare a provisional government whose mandate would last until William's arrival in the capital. Amongst them was the Earl of Berkeley. An intriguing unpublished letter in the Berkeley family archive throws light on the involvement of the Berkeley women, and potentially Harriet herself, in the change of regime.

On 8th September, as William was preparing his coup, Elizabeth, Viscountess Dursley, the wife of Harriet's oldest brother Charles, wrote to her father-in-law the Earl of Berkeley from The Hague, where she had been staying since 29th August. The aim of her letter was to give 'an account of your 4th grandchild', who 'looks (or I hope he is) as well as ever I knew him'. Elizabeth then goes on to say that she has been unable to find any 'tea' at The Hague, but will attempt to procure some in Amsterdam, 'where I will not hesitate to obey yours and my lady's commands'.

There are two ways of interpreting this letter. Possibly, Elizabeth was discreetly giving news of her sister-in-law Harriet, which suggests that she was still in the Netherlands and had had further children by Grey. Could the 'commands' of 'the lady' Elizabeth refers to be Harriet's? Perhaps Harriet and her father had become sufficiently reconciled to be making provision for her living child or children?

Sadly for Harriet, it seems more probable that Elizabeth was herself acting as some sort of agent or go-between for the soon-to-be King of England. The Earl of Berkeley had not been one of the 'Immortal Seven' who had invited William to England in June that year, but we know that he had officially declared his support by November. Was Elizabeth acting covertly on the Earl's behalf in a situation which closely resembled the secret negotiations preceding the Restoration of Charles II, just possibly with Harriet's help? William of Orange would be the fourth King to reign since the accession of the Stuart dynasty, so '4th grandchild' might be a plausible codename. As for the 'tea', mysteriously unobtainable at The Hague, it could refer to other commodities, money or even gunpowder. Elizabeth's letter could be read as evidence that she, like so many other women of the period, including Aphra herself, was momentarily part of that secret world, as crucial as it was clandestine, which had the power to move nations from its shadows.)

William rode into London on 18th December, greeted by bonfires and bellringing. It had been a bloodless coup, but his entry marked the last battle of the Civil Wars. There was no need this time for regicide. England's last Stuart King was simply allowed to escape, slipping through the back door of his host's home on 22nd December to a waiting boat on the Medway. In 1660, James had sailed to England on the *Royal Charles*, exulting in his brother's triumph. Just seven years later, the Dutch had stolen this emblem of the Restoration and now the last Stuart King followed its course into exile. Soon after, Parliament announced his abdication.

When the crown was offered to Mary Stuart and William III of Orange on 6 February 1689 Aphra was confronted with the same test she had scorned Lord Grey for failing. Grandiose conceptions of Royalist honour had long since become meaningless, even if she still believed in them, and there was, as ever, the rent to pay. Aphra speedily turned out a dutiful *Congratulatory Poem to Her Sacred Majesty Queen Mary*, but her heart wasn't in it, not least because it was selling for tuppence.

Besides, she was by now growing very ill. The picture of Aphra's health painted in the lampoon *The Epistle to Julian* was not a pretty one:

> Doth that lewd Harlot that Poetick Quean,
> Fam'd through Whitefriars, you know who
>   I mean,
> Mend for reproof, others set up in Spight
> To flux, take glysters, Vomit, purge and write,
> Long with a Sciatica she's beside lame
> Her limbs distorted, Nerves shrunk up with pain,
> And therefore I'll all harsh reflections shun,
> Poverty, Poetry and Pox are Plagues enough
>   for one.

The nasty lampoonist Robert Gould added gout to Aphra's afflictions, and her colleague Wycherley also claimed that she had the 'clap'. In the next century, Lady Mary Wortley Montagu recorded a conversation with a friend who told her that a 'Mrs Been' who had once been famous had, like several other 'remarkable poetesses and scribblers', left her lovers with some unfortunate tokens of her affection. But then almost everybody who was anybody had the pox – William Davenant had lost his nose to it, Rochester his life and the King had probably killed himself with his self-medications against it. If it was venereal disease that killed her, she was finally in the very best of company.

In her lampooning verses Aphra had written of the sweating cure for venereal disease, but she doesn't appear to have taken any such measures herself. The punishing workload she had maintained for the past fifteen years may have had more to do with whatever illness now afflicted her. Thomas Tryon's abstemious regime (see p. 180) could only have gone so far to mitigate the endless strain of producing, day after day after day, the words upon which her livelihood depended. In *Oroonoko* Aphra had made reference to her nervous disposition as a young woman, and constant uncertainty can be tremendously draining. She had achieved so much, yet at the end there was very little evidence that she had been rewarded. The *Memoirs* blamed her death on an 'unskilful Physician', but whether or not that was the case, it's hard not to believe that Aphra was exhausted and overwhelmed with disappointment.

Aphra and the Restoration died together, in the week that William of Orange was crowned King. As with so much of her life, there is very little information about her death on 16 April 1689. She might never have achieved a position at court, or the security of a pension, but in death she was given the greatest accolade the country could offer to a writer, a grave in Westminster Abbey.

Her black marble gravestone was inscribed not with any of the many spellings of her elusive name but the pseudonym under which she had published for so many years, the codename Thomas Killigrew had given her, 'Astrea'. The epitaph (attributed by some to her former lover John Hoyle) was disappointingly banal:

> Here lies a Proof that Wit can never be
> Defence enough against Mortality.

I don't think that Aphra would have approved of the verse, but perhaps she would have been pleased to have gone down to the ages as 'Astrea'. It had been her choice to retain the name long after it had served its professional purposes. 'Astrea' was, after all, the classical figure chosen by Dryden in his ascension poem on Charles II's Restoration as the symbol of a new age. Astrea's imagery had been potently employed in the cult that grew up around Elizabeth I, another notably intelligent, defiantly single woman. Astrea was famously a virgin, like the Queen. St Afra, Aphra's other namesake, was a converted whore. Whoever Aphra Behn really was, in using both she showed in her name, her writing and her life that a woman did not need to be a queen, a saint or even a goddess to become extraordinary.

20

What became of Harriet? Somehow, Aphra knew. She knew that Grey had grown tired of Harriet and abandoned her. She knew that Harriet and William Turner, shackled together as man and wife, had formed a partnership which, if not loving, was certainly collaborative. She knew that Harriet, disgraced and destitute, had survived, and in the persona of Silvia in *Love Letters*, she gives her the revenge on the masculine world whose hypocrisies pardoned her seducer while leaving her as an outcast.

Harriet had sacrificed everything in her love for Grey, including her entitlement to a share of her family's wealth. At Easter 1683, while Harriet was in Sussex with Grey and the Rye House Plot was brewing, the Earl of Berkeley had filed a bill with the Exchequer against his daughter and her lawful husband William Turner. Lord Berkeley had given allowances to his children and as a major shareholder in the East India Company he had purchased considerable stockholdings in their names, though he had reserved the dividends for himself in order to recoup the capital. His Exchequer suit was aimed at preventing Harriet from ever claiming the profits from the financial investments supposedly made on her behalf. On 9 May 1683, Harriet and William Turner brought suit in turn against Berkeley in Chancery, claiming the right to her dividends as well as 'diamonds and jewels' to which she claimed to be entitled. The claim gave her parish of residence as St Martin-in-the-Fields, where Aphra was believed to have lived on her return from Surinam.

At that moment, the spring of 1683, Grey had not yet been arrested for the Rye House conspiracy. Was Harriet attempting to raise funds to pay for arms and men in the event of an uprising? Or was she prudently hedging her bets in the hope of having something to live on if her lover was arrested on a treason charge and his estates sequestered? Either way, the timing of the suit suggests that Harriet knew a good deal about what was being planned, that she was more than a passive witness to Grey's activities.

When the Monmouth rebellion collapsed, both William Turner and Robert Ferguson managed to escape the battlefield of Sedgemoor and return to the United Provinces. Ferguson resumed his former career as a subversive pamphleteer whilst Turner returned to his wife. In Aphra's novel, Turner has long been infatuated with Harriet and longs for Grey to leave her so that he can have her as his own. Aphra's description of Harriet's character at this stage of her life reads as though she really had met her. Her wit and beauty are praised, but she is also said to be vain, proud and conceited, stubborn, censorious and opinionated. That is, she sounds like a human being rather than a one-dimensional stage heroine. Harriet's feelings at Grey's betrayal are also vividly captured:

> we must allow her to have loved [Grey] with a passion that nothing but his ingratitude could have decayed in her heart, nor was it lessened but by a force that gave her a thousand tortures, racks and pangs, which had almost cost her her less-valued life . . . she suffered a world of violence and extremity of rage and grief by turns at his affront and inconstancy.

Like so much of Aphra's writing, this passage startles in its vividness and conviction. Harriet's pain, her sense of helplessness in the face of her loss and the hapless fury this provokes are feelings recognizable to anyone who has ever experienced a failed love affair. Unlike Henrietta Wentworth though, Harriet does not die of grief and remorse. Exposed to the Dutch air which 'naturally breeds Spirits avaricious', Harriet becomes more and more grasping, transforming from a lovestruck romantic heroine to a shamelessly avaricious prostitute. What has seemed a glorious adventure – risking all for love – is exposed as so much self-serving rhetoric which disguises but does not wholly conceal a rapacious lust for power. *Love Letters* is most obviously a brilliant combination of the political and the erotic, yet Aphra was fascinated by power and the limitations imposed on women who exercised it, and here a straightforwardly political reading of *Love Letters* becomes more complicated.

Perhaps we are meant to feel disgust at 'Silvia's' departure from honourable values, but 'Silvia' doesn't seem to. She is rather gloriously unrepentant. The novel has been described as ' a protracted portrait of untamed female insubordination', and as with the hyperbolic violence featured in *The Fair Jilt* and *Oroonoko* there is a comically exaggerated quality to 'Silvia's' career as a whore, which suggests Aphra was using the novel to challenge the limits of the patriarchal prerogative which governed her world. Aided by 'Brilliard', her heroine embarks on a career of ruination, running through fortunes and reputations in a whirlwind of revenge. She becomes as unscrupulous and grasping as, well, a man. The shift in her values is also expressed in her attitude to sex. From dressing as a 'Cavalier' she progresses to thinking like one:

> fond of catching at every trifling conquest and loving the triumph, though she hated the slave.

Whatever Harriet has become, she is not a victim. In real life, too, she continued to fight back. In 1691, Harriet and William Turner launched another lawsuit, this time against the almighty East India Company itself. In excluding the Earl of Berkeley personally, Harriet dropped her claim to her jewellery, but she persisted in demanding her share of the stocks. The

Company responded that the bill against Lord Berkeley filed eight years earlier was still pending and that, according to their accounts, the monies had been correctly paid in trust to Harriet's father. The decree ruled in favour of the Company, and Harriet as the plaintiff was obliged to pay the costs. Aphra was lying in Westminster Abbey by 1691, but one wonders what she would have made of this – a scathing poem, or even a play? Harriet had been cast off by her family and cheated of her rights for privileging true love over self-interest, while her lover, treacherous in every sense, was permitted to flourish.

It is not certain when Harriet returned to England, though the fact that she did so with William Turner suggests he was confident that he would not be arraigned for his part in the Monmouth rebellion, which indicates that it was after 1689. Grey did do something for the woman whose life he had so comprehensively ruined; he paid her a pension of £200 per year, exactly the price that her father had once set upon her body. It was a modest sum for someone of Harriet's status and she and Turner would have been obliged to live very quietly. They settled in Tonbridge in Kent, the county where Eaffrey Johnson, the woman who probably wasn't Aphra Behn, was born.

In her late story *The History of the Nun*, Aphra wrote of women as being 'by nature more constant and just than men, and did not their first lovers teach them the trick of change they would be doves that would never quit their mate.' At the conclusion of *Love Letters* though, she had struck a different note, when 'Silvia' discovers 'that vulgar error, the impossibility of loving more than once'. There is something in 'Silvia's' sexual cynicism and her determination to outwit her circumstances, which is reminiscent of the greatest Cavalier of them all, King Charles himself. After his death, the Marquis of Halifax had written of him that 'he lived with his ministers as he did with his mistresses; he used them but he did not love them.' Honour and love, for women as well as men, are no more than pretty dreams, baubles for poets to juggle. This is the contradiction at the heart of Aphra's writing, as it was her friend the Earl of Rochester's. The proof that the world now belonged to Philander could be seen at Grey's house at Uppark.

It would be interesting to know how Lord Grey and the Earl of Berkeley first greeted one another at the court of their new master, William III. Grey had outplayed even the Earl of Sunderland in the long game of Protestant politics. Sunderland had for once miscalculated when the Prince of Wales was born, immediately announcing his conversion to Catholicism, but with William's triumph he had been forced to escape (disguised, of course, as a woman). Sunderland took his own turn as an exile in Holland until 1690, while Grey was ingratiating himself with the new regime. He was made Privy Counsellor to William in May 1695 and created Earl of Tankerville a month later. Harriet's sister Mary had endured him long enough to become his Countess. The Tankervilles' new home at Uppark was finished the same year, described as 'new built' by the diarist Celia Fiennes. It's the epitome of a swagger house, fit for a Restoration rock star, dominating the Downs with its bright, bold Dutch brick. The old Tudor mansion which Harriet had known, to which she had perhaps brought her first, lost baby, had been ripped down, part of a past which Grey no longer cared to acknowledge. The new Uppark was a party pad, with huge stables, ornamental gardens and terraces giving vast views of the countryside. It's a house built for a man in every aspect of his prime and it might have been some consolation to the many enemies of the 'cowardly, perfidious Grey' that he only lived until 1701 to enjoy it. There is no evidence that Harriet Berkeley ever went there.

Perhaps Harriet and William did grow to love one another, or perhaps they merely made shift as best they could. Possibly they lived separately, as they had lodgings in Holborn in London, where three possible burials for a William Turner are listed at St Andrew's church in November 1692, June 1694 and February 1703. The second lawsuit against the East India Company was filed from Aphra's old stamping ground, Lincoln's Inn in Holborn, where Harriet herself was buried on 10 August 1706. Her place of residence is given as Tonbridge, but given the timing of her death, she might have been in London for the end of the Trinity legal term at the close of July, perhaps in a further attempt to improve her finances. She was only forty-two years old. Harriet had outlasted Lord Grey and the husband he had forced upon her, but both her parents were still living. It is not known whether they or anyone else mourned at her grave.

Note on Sources

This book is in no manner intended as a comprehensive account of Aphra Behn's life. Janet Todd's magisterial *Aphra Behn: A Secret Life* is presently the most detailed and thorough imagining of Aphra as Eaffrey Johnson, drawing in turn on Maureen Duffy's important *The Passionate Shepherdess*. Professor Todd's work is quoted here on pages 18, 72, 82 and 142. In positing an alternative theory of Aphra's biography, I have found the work of many scholars extremely useful, notably Karen Britland's article 'Aphra Behn's First Marriage?', Nadine Akkerman's brilliant *Invisible Agents: Women and Espionage in Seventeenth Century Britain*, which informed many of the suppositions in Chapter 8, and Emily Cockayne's joyfully riotous *Hubbub: Filth, Noise and Stench in England 1600–1770*. Readers wishing to explore Aphra's plays and poems further cannot do better than *The Cambridge Companion to Aphra Behn*, edited by Derek Hughes and Janet Todd.

Bibliography

Volumes

Akkerman, Nadine, *Invisible Agents: Women and Espionage in Seventeenth Century Britain* (Oxford: 2018)

Barber, Sarah, 'Power in the English Caribbean: The Proprietorship of Lord Willoughby of Parham' in Roper, Louis and Van Ruymbeke, Bertrand (eds), *Constructing Early Modern Empires* (Leiden: 2007)

Beckles, Hilary, *White Servitude and Black Slavery in Barbados 1627–1715* (Knoxville: 1989)

Blome, Richard, *A Description of the Island of Jamaica; With the Other Isles and Territories in America, to which the English are Related* (London: 1678)

Cameron, W. J. (ed.), *New Light on Aphra Behn: An Investigation into the Facts and Fictions Surrounding Her Journey to Surinam in 1663 and Her Activities as a Spy in Flanders in 1666* (Auckland: 1961)

Carey, Daniel, 'Sugar, Colonialism and the Critique of Slavery: Thomas Tryon in Barbados' in Wells, Byron R. and Stewart, Philip (eds), *Interpreting Colonialism*, vol. 2004:09 (Oxford: 2004)

Carey, H. (ed.), *Memorials of the Great Civil War in England from 1646–1651* (London: 1842)

Chalmers, Hero, *Royalist Women Writers 1650–1689* (Oxford: 2004)

Cobbett's Complete Collection of State Trials and Proceedings for High Treason and Other Crimes and Misdemeanours from the Earliest Period to the Present Time (London: 1811)

Cockayne, Emily, *Hubbub: Filth, Noise and Stench in England 1600–1770* (New Haven: 2021)

Cools, Hans, Keblusek, Marika and Noldus, Badeloch (eds), *Your Humble Servant: Agents in Early Modern Europe* (Hilversum: 2006)

Daybell, James, *The Material Letter in Early Modern England: Manuscript Letters and the Culture and Practice of Letter-Writing, 1512–1635* (Basingstoke, 2012)

Du Tertre, Jean Baptiste, *Histoire générale des Antilles habitées par les Français* (Paris: 1671)

Duffy, Maureen, *The Passionate Shepherdess: Aphra Behn 1640–89* (London: 1977)

Evelyn, John, *The Diary of John Evelyn* (Oxford: 1955)

Fraser, Antonia, *The Weaker Vessel: Woman's Lot in Seventeenth-Century England* (London: 1984)

Feltham, Owen, *A Brief Character of the Low Countries* (London: 1659)

Fitzmaurice, James, 'Writing, Acting and the Notion of Truth in Biofiction About Early Modern European Women Authors' in *Authorizing Early Modern European Women* (Ch. 14) (Amsterdam: 2022)

Gowing, Laura, *Domestic Dangers: Women, Words and Sex in Early Modern London* (Oxford: 1996)

Graunt, John, *Great News from the Barbadoes* (London: 1676)

Grey, Ford, Lord, *The Secret History of the Rye-House Plot and of Monmouth's Rebellion* (London: 1754)

Harris, Tim, *Restoration: Charles II and His Kingdoms* (London: 2005)

Hendricks, Margo, *Race and Romance: Coloring the Past* (Arizona: 2022)

Hughes, Derek, and Todd, Janet (eds), *The Cambridge Companion to Aphra Behn* (Cambridge: 2004)

Keay, Anna, *The Restless Republic: Britain Without a Crown* (London: 2022)

Larman, Alexander, *Blazing Star: The Life and Times of John Wilmot, Earl of Rochester* (London: 2014)

Linebaugh, Peter, *The London Hanged: Crime and Civil Society in the Eighteenth Century* (London: 2006)

The Manuscripts of Rye and Hereford Corporations, Etc.13 Report Appendix Part IV (The Manuscripts of Capt. F. C. Loder-Symonds) (London: 1892)

Marshall, Alan, *Intelligence and Espionage in the Reign of Charles II 1660–1685* (Cambridge: 1994)

Miyoshi, Riki, *Thomas Killigrew and Carolean Stage Rivalry in London 1660–1682* (Oxford: 2016)

Motten Vander, J. P., 'Recycling the Exile: "Thomaso", "The Rover" and the Critics' in Major, Philip (ed.), *Thomas Killigrew and the Seventeenth-Century English Stage* (Farnham: 2013)

Neill, Edward D., *The Founders of Maryland as Portrayed in Manuscripts, Provincial Records and Early Documents* (Albany: 1876)

Newman, Simon, *Freedom Seekers: Escaping from Slavery in Restoration London* (London: 2022)

Parker, Matthew, *Willoughbyland: England's Lost Colony* (London: 2015)

Pepys, Samuel, *The Diary of Samuel Pepys* (Project Gutenberg)

Pollak, Ellen, *Incest and the English Novel 1684–1814* (Baltimore: 2003)

Porter, Linda, *Mistresses: Sex and Scandal at the Court of Charles II* (London: 2020)

Pritchard, R. E., *Scandalous Liaisons: Charles II and His Court* (London: 2015)

Reynolds, George William MacArthur, *Reynold's Miscellany of Romance* (London: 1850)

Sackville-West, V., *Aphra Behn* (London: 1927)

Slaughter, Thomas P. (ed.), *Ideology and Politics on the Eve of Restoration: Newcastle's Advice to Charles II* (Philadelphia: 1984)

Speckhart, Amy, *The Colonial History of Wye Plantation: The Lloyd Family and Their Slaves on Maryland's Eastern Shore: Family, Property and Power* (Berkeley: 2011)

Stubbs, John, *Reprobates: The Cavaliers of the English Civil War* (London: 2011)

Todd, Janet, *Aphra Behn: A Secret Life* (London: 1996 and 2017)

Todd, Janet (ed.), *The Works of Aphra Behn* (London: 1996)

Tryon, Thomas, *Friendly Advice to the Gentlemen-Planters of the East and West Indies* (London: 1684)

Underdown, David, *Royalist Conspiracy in England 1649–1660* (New Haven: 1960)

Van Horn Melton, James, *The Rise of the Public in Enlightenment Europe* (Cambridge: 2001)

Wiseman, Susan, *Conspiracy and Virtue: Women, Writing and Politics in Seventeenth-Century England* (Oxford: 2006)

White, C., *The Dutch Pictures in the Collection of H.M. the Queen* (Cambridge: 1982)

Zook, Melinda, *Protestantism, Politics, and Women in Britain 1660–1714* (London: 2013)

Journals

A Discourse Concerning Comets, Evans Early American Imprint Collection quod.lib.umich.edu

Bernbaum, Ernest, 'Mrs Behn's Biography: A Fiction' in *PMLA*, vol. 28, no. 3 (1913)

Britland, Karen, 'Aphra Behn's First Marriage?' in *The Seventeenth Century*, vol. 36, issue 1 (2021)

Campbell, Elaine, 'Aphra Behn's Surinam Interlude' in *Kunapipi*, vol. 7. (1985)

Chan Smith, David, 'Useful Knowledge, Improvement and the Logic of Capital in Richard Ligon's "True and Exact History of Barbados"' in *Journal of the History of Ideas*, vol. 78, no. 4 (2017)

Chibka, Robert L., '"Oh! Do Not Fear a Woman's Invention": Truth, Falsehood and Fiction in Aphra Behn's *Oroonoko*' in *Texas Studies in Literature and Language*, vol. 30, no. 4 (1988)

Duchovnay, G. 'Aphra Behn's Religion' in *Notes and Queries* 221 (1976)

Fatah-Black, Karwan, *Surinam and the Atlantic World, 1650–1800* (2013)

Ferguson, Margaret, 'Juggling the Categories of Race, Class and Gender: Aphra Behn's *Oroonoko*' in *Women's Studies*, 19 (1991)

Fitzmaurice, James, 'Aphra Behn and the Abraham's Sacrifice Case' in *Huntington Library Quarterly*, 56, no. 3 (1993)

Games, Alison, 'Cohabitation, Suriname-Style: English Inhabitants in Dutch Suriname after 1667' in *The William and Mary Quarterly*, vol. 72, no. 2 (2015)

Green Carr, Lois and Welch, Lorena S., 'The Planter's Wife: The Experience of White Women in Seventeenth Century Maryland' in *The William and Mary Quarterly*, vol. 34, no. 4 (1977)

Greenfield, Susan, 'Aborting the Mother Plot: Politics and Generation in *Absalom and Achitophel*' in *ELH*, vol. 62, no. 2 (1995)

Howlett, Kathy, 'Trials, Tabloids and Texts: The Debauching of Lady Henrietta Berkeley and Aphra Behn's *Love Letters*', *Southeastern American Society for Eighteenth-Century Studies AGM* (1993)

Hume, Robert D., 'The Economics of Culture in London 1660–1740' in *The Huntingdon Library Quarterly*, vol. 69, no. 4 (2006)

Kegan Gardner, Judith, 'The First English Novel: Aphra Behn's *Love Letters*, the Canon and Women's Tastes' in *Tulsa Studies in Women's Literature*, vol. 8, no. 2 (1989)

Loftus, John E., 'Congreve's *Way of the World* and Popular Criminal Literature' in *Studies in English Literature 1500–1900*, vol. 36, no. 3 (1996)

Marshall, Alan, '"Memorialls for Mrs Affora": Aphra Behn and the Restoration Intelligence World' in *Women's Writing* 22, no. 1 (2015)

Noldus, Badeloch, 'Dealing in Politics and Art: Agents between Amsterdam, Stockholm and Copenhagen' in *Scandinavian Journal of History*, no. 28 (2003)

Roberts, Justin, 'Surrendering Surinam: The Barbadian Diaspora and the Expansion of the English Sugar Frontier, 1650–75' in *The William and Mary Quarterly*, vol. 73, no. 2 (2016)

Roper, Alan, 'Aeneas and Agathocles in the Exclusion Crisis' in *The Review of English Studies, New Series*, vol. 56, no. 226 (2005)

Sheffey, Ruthe T., 'Some Evidence of a New Source for Aphra Behn's *Oroonoko*' in *Studies in Philology*, vol. 59, no. 1 (1962)

Sheppard, Jill, 'A Historical Sketch of the Poor Whites of Barbados: from Indentured Servants to "Redlegs"' in *Caribbean Studies*, vol. 14, no. 3 (1974)

Van Hensbergen, Claudine, 'Aphra Behn: Portraiture and the Biographical Account' in *The Review of English Studies*, vol. 72, issue 305 (2021)

Wehrs, Donald R., 'Eros, Ethics, Identity: Royalist Feminism and the Politics of Desire in Aphra Behn's *Love Letters*' in *Studies in English Literature 1500–1900*, vol. 32, no. 3 (1992)

Wolsk, Rebecca S., 'Muddy Allegiance and Shiny Booty: Aphra Behn's Anglo-Dutch Politics' in *Eighteenth-Century Fiction*, vol. 17 no. 1 (Toronto: 2004)

Zijlstra, Suze, *Anglo-Dutch Surinam: Ethnic Interaction and Colonial Transition in the Caribbean 1651–1682* (Amsterdam: 2015)

Acknowledgements

One of the great pleasures of writing this book has been the opportunity to work with Kristina Bedford, whose archival knowledge and professional insight proved invaluable. Many thanks also to Angela Aldam for her help in identifying several of the defendants in the Berkeley trial. Rebecca Wallis, Cultural Heritage Curator for the National Trust South East, very kindly advised on research at Uppark. At Berkeley Castle, Karen Davidson, Estate Archivist, and Joshua Nash, Castle Custodian, went to great trouble to unearth family letters which it has been a fascinating privilege to reference. Giles Ramsay's lecture on seventeenth-century theatre was a delight and an inspiration. My thanks to the staff of the Chichester Records Office, the London Library, the British Library and the Royal Library of the Netherlands.